International Commercial Policy

SERIES ON INTERNATIONAL BUSINESS AND TRADE

SERIES EDITOR-IN-CHIEF
Khosrow Fatemi

Fatemi   Selected Readings in International Trade

Robinson   The International Communication of Technology

Vaghefi, Paulson, and Tomlinson   International Business: Theory and Practice

Root and Visudtibhan   International Strategic Management: Challenges and Opportunities

Fatemi and Salvatore   Foreign Exchange Issues, Capital Markets, and International Banking in the 1990s

Kreinin   International Commercial Policy: Issues for the 1990s

International Commercial Policy:
Issues for the 1990s

Edited by
Mordechai E. Kreinin

Taylor & Francis

USA	Publishing Office:	Taylor & Francis
		1101 Vermont Avenue, N.W., Suite 200
		Washington, DC 20005-3521
		Tel: (202) 289-2174, Fax: (202) 289-3665
	Distribution Center:	Taylor & Francis Inc.
		1900 Frost Road, Suite 101
		Bristol, PA 19007-1598
		Tel: (215) 785-5800, Fax: (215) 785-5515
UK		Taylor & Francis Ltd.
		4 John St., London WC1N 2ET
		Tel: 071 405 2237, Fax: 071 831 2035

INTERNATIONAL COMMERCIAL POLICY: Issues for the 1990s

1 2 3 4 5 6 7 8 9 0   B R B R   9 8 7 6 5 4 3

This book was set in Times Roman by Taylor & Francis. The editors were Radhika Rao Gupta and Merrie Kaye; the production supervisor was Peggy M. Rote; and the typesetter was Phoebe Carter. Cover design by Michelle Fleitz. Printing and binding by Braun-Brumfield, Inc.

A CIP catalog record for this book is available from the British Library.

⊕ The paper in this publication meets the requirements of the ANSI Standard Z39.48-1984 (Permanence of paper).

Library of Congress Cataloging-in-Publication Data

International Commercial Policy: Issues for the 1990s / edited by
    Mordechai E. Kreinin.
      p. cm.

    1. Commercial policy.   2. European Economic Community countries—
Commercial policy. I. Kreinin, Mordechai Elihau, date.
HF1411.I5166   1993
382'.3—dc20
                                        92-43631
                                          CIP

ISBN 0-8448-1732-5 (case)
ISBN 0-8448-1733-3 (paper)

ISSN 1052-9160

Contents

Contributors

Hamdi F. Ali—Visiting Associate Professor, Department of Accountancy, Faculty of Commerce and Administration, Concordia University, 1455 de Maissoneuve Boulevard West, Montreal, Quebec, CANADA H3G 1M8

Indudeep Chhachhi—Assistant Professor, Department of Finance & MIS, Western Kentucky University, 1526 Russellville Road, Bowling Green, KY 42101-3576

Alfred E. Eckes—Ohio Eminent Research Professor, Ohio University, Brown House, Athens, OH 45701

H. Peter Gray—Professor Emeritus, Graduate School of Management, Rutgers University, Newark, NJ 07104

Paolo Guerrieri—Professor of Economics, University of Naples 'Federico II,' Via dei Coronari 47, 00186 Rome, ITALY

Kristin Hallberg—The World Bank, 1818 H Street, NW, Washington, DC 20433

Masoud Kavoossi—Associate Professor of International Business, School of Business, Howard University, 2400 Sixth Street, NW, Washington, DC 20059-0001

Mordechai E. Kreinin—University Distinguished Professor of Economics, Michigan State University, East Lansing, MI 44824

James O. Luke—Assistant Professor, School of Business, Madonna University, 36600 Schoolcraft Road, Livonia, MI 48150

Sarianna Lundan—Graduate Student, Graduate School of Management, Rutgers University, Newark, NJ 07104

Ike Mathur—Southern Illinois University, Carbondale, IL 62901

Hormoz Movassaghi—Department of Marketing, School of Business, 953 Danby Road, Ithaca College, Ithaca, NY 14850

Anton P. Mueller—Institut f. Staatswissenschaft, der Friedrich-Alexander Universitat, Erlangen-Nurnberg, Kochstr. 4/V, D-8520 Erlangen, GERMANY

John Nash—Trade Policy Division, The World Bank, N 10-037, 1818 H Street, NW, Washington, DC 20433

C. W. Neale—Lecturer in Accounting and Finance, Management Center, University of Bradford, Emm Lane, Bradford, West Yorkshire BD9 4JL, ENGLAND

Julio Nogués—Economic Advisor to the Ministry of Economy of Argentina, 307 Great Falls Road, Rockville, MD 20950

Lois S. Peters—Center for Science and Technology Policy, Rensselaer Polytechnic Institute, Troy, NY, 12180-3590

Nanda Rangan—Southern Illinois University, Carbondale, IL 62901

David Robertson—National Centre for Development Studies, Research School of Pacific Studies, Australian National University, GPO Box 4, Canberra ACT 2601, AUSTRALIA

Dominick Salvatore—Professor, Department of Economics, Fordham University, Bronx, NY 10458

Anthony Scaperlanda—Professor, Department of Economics, Northern Illinois University, DeKalb, IL 60115

P. Sercu—Katholieke Universiteit, Leuven, BELGIUM

Paul Steidlmeier—School of Management, State University of New York at Binghamton, P.O. Box 6000, Binghamton, NY, 13902-6000

Sridhar Sundaram—Assistant Professor, Division of MMFE, 410 Creme Hall, Box 58, School of Business, Emporia State University, Emporia, KA 66801

Wendy E. Takacs—The World Bank, N10-001, International Bank for Reconstruction and Development International Development Association, 1818 H Street, NW, Washington, DC 20433

Pochara Theerathorn—Assistant Professor of Finance, Department of Finance, Insurance, and Real Estate, the Fogelman College of Business and Economics, Memphis State University, Memphis, TN 38152

Alfred Tovias—Senior Lecturer, Department of International Relations, The Hebrew University, 91905 Jerusalem, ISRAEL

Fahri Unsal—Department of Marketing, School of Business, 953 Danby Road, Ithaca College, Ithaca, NY 14850

Dominique Vacheron—Ph.D., Candidate in Finance, Department of Finance, Insurance and Real Estate, The Fogelman College of Business and Economics, Memphis State University, Memphis, TN 38152

Burhan F. Yavas—Professor, California State University-Dominguez Hills, School of Management, 1000 E. Victoria Street, Carson, CA 90747

Preface

As the 1990's decade opens, the international economy finds itself in a state of transition. It faces many issues, the outcome of which will determine the shape of the global economy in the next century.

Several east-European countries have gained military and political independence from the former Soviet Union and are presently engaged in a restructuring process that would lead them away from central planning and towards a market economy. They will certainly aspire to become integrated in the global economic system. The Soviet Union itself has disintegrated into its 15 constituent Republics, and the major ones have begun a process of conversion to market economies. Central planning remains the rule only in China, North Korea and Vietnam.

Profound changes are also taking place in relations among industrial nations. The Uruguay Round of GATT trade negotiations is now in its second phase, after having reached an impasse in 1990. Although the negotiations have resumed, the outcome is far from certain at the time of writing. Should the Round fail, trade disputes between nations may intensify and become more widespread, and the trend towards regionalism may be accelerated. The EC of twelve west-European countries is going through the steps of forming a Unified Market (EC-1992) and is contemplating the possibility of monetary union before the year 2000. In the process, special relations have been forced with the EFTA countries, including free trade throughout western Europe (in the so-called European Economic Area), and special association treaties *may* be concluded with some east-European countries. In North America, the U.S. and Canada negotiated a free trade area, and are currently holding talks with Mexico to form a North American Free Trade Agreement (NAFTA) consisting of the three countries. It is too early to determine whether the existence of two regional groupings would stimulate the formulation of a third one in Asia, thereby creating a tri-polar trading world.

Many changes are also taking place in the developing world. Several Latin American countries, notably Mexico, are lifting government controls of the economy so as to permit markets to function in an unfettered way. As a result, growth in their real GNP and exports has accelerated and foreign investments have resumed their inward flow. Likewise, the economies around the Pacific rim have integrated themselves into the global economy and are growing rapidly. Thailand, Malaysia and even Indonesia are now referred to as "second-tier" NICs, and may join the ranks of the NICs (Korea, Taiwan, etc.) in the next decade. And all the while, there are winds of regional integration blowing in Asia and Latin America, designed to expand the size of their domestic market. The ASEAN group of six Asian countries, for example, decided to proceed towards the formation of a free trade area, as did a group of four South American countries.

Against this background, the International Trade and Finance Association (ITFA) held its annual professional convention in Marseilles, France on May 30–June 2, 1991. Over one hundred papers were presented and discussed; they were distributed to all participants in a five-volume conference proceedings. Yet not all the issues mentioned above could be covered by even such a comprehensive convention. This book is even more selective, containing 23 chapters, revised and updated from the proceeding volumes. Of the topics in international trade and finance, covered at the Conference, this book concentrates on various aspects of *international commercial policy*. Thus, the selection criteria for inclusion in the volume were as follows:

   a. Topic: The paper addresses some aspect of commercial policy.
   b. Quality of the paper.
   c. Accessibility of the paper to wide readership (extremely technical or mathematical papers are not included).

The 23 selected papers are grouped into four themes: General commercial policy, regional integration, direct foreign investment and the multinational corporation, and country studies. Each paper opens with an abstract that should enable the reader to determine whether he/she wishes to read the entire paper. The following introduction to the volume offers the global framework for the 23 selections, the context within which each chapter is to be interpreted. The reader is strongly urged to read the introduction before tackling the individual chapters.

Mordechai E. Kreinin
E. Lansing, Michigan

Introduction

At the core of the world trading system is an organization called the General Agreement on Tariffs and Trade, or GATT. Located in Geneva, Switzerland, GATT has a membership of 108 countries. It sponsors periodic multinational conferences, known as "rounds," designed to reduce tariffs and otherwise liberalize trade. Each round lasts several years, and any agreement reached is then implemented gradually over several years. The session being negotiated in the early 1990s is known as the Uruguay Round (UR). In the 1970s the Tokyo Round was negotiated, and in the 1960s the Kennedy Round was negotiated. In addition to providing the institutional framework for multilateral trade negotiations, GATT lays down ground rules for the conduct of international trade. For example, it outlaws import quotas and export subsidies, although the subsidies code is difficult to articulate and implement. A second example is the principle of nondiscrimination in international trade, known as: the Most Favored Nation principle, or MFN. It states that a country must assess the same tariff rate (and other restrictions) on an imported product regardless of its country of origin. Another function of GATT is to investigate and adjudicate trade disputes between nations.

Part I of the book, which contains seven chapters on contemporary issues in commercial policy, opens with a chapter on the Uruguay Round (UR) of GATT, authored by Professor Kreinin. The UR is the eighth general session of trade negotiations under GATT in the postwar period. It is through these successive "rounds" that tariff rates in the industrial countries were brought down from an average of 60% after WW II to 6% today. The UR began in 1986, reached an impasse in 1990, and was resuscitated in 1991, only to be deadlocked again in 1992. Eventually the round may be fully successful, fail completely, or emerge as something in between. Fears are being voiced that failure of the UR would spell collapse of the GATT system, precipitate a host of hostile bilateral trade measures, and bring about the division of the world into three trading blocs (a tri-polar world). Even if one does not share all these apprehensions, it is clear that much is at stake in the outcome of these trade negotiations.

This is underscored in the opening chapter. The essay begins by describing the *new* areas that the 108 negotiating countries expect to tackle (service transactions, trade-related investment, patent protection, agricultural protection, and subsidies), in addition to the traditional matters addressed by all previous rounds of GATT, such as tariff reduction. This is an ambitious agenda, and the chapter reviews the difficulties in the various segments of the negotiations that may have contributed to the impasse. But the most immediate cause of the deadlock was a dispute over the Common Agricultural Policy of the European Community (EC), which contains farm price support, import protection, and export subsidies, with the United States and the EC being the major (though not the sole) protagonists. Although agriculture was a major stumbling block in previous rounds of trade negotiations, it did not cause the collapse of the negotiations. This chapter addresses the question of what has changed since the 1970s, and why agriculture caused a deadlock this time around. Finally, the chapter discusses the consequences of a possible (partial or complete) collapse in the UR for the international trading system.

From a general discussion of the UR, Chapter 2 (authored by Professor Alfred Eckes, of Ohio University) deals with one aspect of the Round—antidumping policies. Article VI of GATT defines dumping as the introduction of products of one country into the commerce of another at less than their normal value in the exporting country. If such dumping causes or threatens injury to a competing domestic industry, the importing country may impose an *antidumping duty,* which equals the price differential (charged by the exporter) between the two countries. The duty lasts until the dumping margin is eliminated, with exporters undertaking to raise export prices to the level that they charge domestically. This is to be distinguished from *countervailing* duty, which is imposed to counteract a foreign *government export subsidy.* Hundred of antidumping complaints *against foreign companies* are filed every year in the United States, EC, Canada, and Australia[1] (in Japan they are rarely used), and more recently in certain developing countries (Mexico, Korea, and Brazil). For example, the 1992 collapse of the steel accord between the United States and a dozen countries that export steel to it is likely to usher in numerous dumping complaints by American steel companies. Also in 1992 the U.S. government determined that two Japanese auto companies dumped minivans in the United States.

How complex such cases can become is illustrated by a dispute between two typewriter manufacturers: Smith Corona (U.S.) and Brother (Japan). For years Smith Corona (S-C) had been accusing Brother (B) of dumping, but B had been able to "dodge the bullets." After the U.S. Commerce Department imposed a 48.7% antidumping duty on B in 1980, the company added a computer memory to its typewriter and claimed, successfully, that the "new" product was not subject to the duty. In 1991 the Commerce Department again found in favor of a new petition by S-C and imposed a 60% antidumping duty on B. But again the triumph proved hollow, because by then B was assembling its word processors in Tennessee and the duty applied only to equipment made in Japan. Smith Corona countered by invoking a provision in the 1988 Trade Act that prohibits circumvention of antidumping orders by importing parts and assembling them in the United States. But B argued successfully that the law applies only to cases in which the parts are shipped from the home country (Japan), whereas its parts were shipped from third countries. Then in 1992 B turned the entire battle on its face by taking the offensive and filing an antidumping suit against S-C. Brother noted that it now supplied the U.S. market out of its Tennessee plant, while S-C (now 47% British owned) had a plant in Singapore. So the Japanese company claimed to be the real U.S. producer. Both companies are incorporated in the United States and conduct their manufacturing operations in several countries (including the United States), the main difference being that S-C does most of its research in the United States and B does its in Japan. The Commerce Department would have the unenviable task of determining which company is more "American."

Although sanctioned by GATT, many economists view antidumping duties as a protectionist device. The very filing of a complaint can easily discourage imports and antidumping action reduces imports further.[2] The entire policy is formulated with the interest of domestic producers in mind, while the interest of consumers, who benefit from lower prices, is ignored. If the import in question is an intermediate product, such as computer chips or steel, the industries using these goods would be adversely affected by an antidumping duty that raises their price. Only predatory dumping, in which foreign exporters are intent on driving local competitors out of business and then raising their price, is demonstrably harmful.

But the author of Chapter 2 is no ordinary economist. Professor Eckes was a commissioner on the U.S. International Trade Commission (ITC) from 1981 to 1990 and served as chairman from 1982 to 1984. Among other things the ITC is responsible for the administration of the antidumping laws in the United States. The author brings a perspective to the issue that is different from the one found in ordinary textbooks. Having been involved in 435 dumping investigations, he defends antidumping protection on the grounds that dumping often tends to be predatory, and it is almost always highly disruptive to the importing country. He also calls for strengthening the antidumping code of GATT. His argument is as compelling as it is lucid; yet it is made from a very special vantage point.

Antidumping measures are a prime example of what has become known as administrative protection, or policies applied against unfair trade practices. These policies, and the way they are administered in various countries, are currently a subject of intense study by economists. Unlike the tariff, such measures are not transparent, and can be applied on an arbitrary basis. They are certainly difficult to police by an international agency. As tariff protection in industrial countries has declined over the postwar period from an average of 60% to around 6%, other protective measures have mushroomed. Protection seems to have a "fungible" quality; as one measure declines in importance through international liberalization, others seem to take its place. These "others" include "voluntary export restraints" (VER) and antidumping measures.

In both cases, the consumers in the importing countries are hurt by having to pay a higher price for the product. But in the political calculus of protection the consumer does not receive much weight. After all, the cost of protection (in terms of higher prices) is diffused over many millions of consumers, where each pays only a little more, and very few can identify protection as the source of increased prices. On the other hand, the benefits from protection are heavily concentrated in the hands of producers of the domestic substitute for the imported commodity and their workers. They are willing to expend money and efforts to lobby for protection. Hence, even though import protection is harmful, it is a common phenomenon. And as tariff rates have declined, new instruments appear to take their place.

Although the foregoing discussion centers on the effect of administrative protection on consumers and producers in the importing country, this is only half the story from a global perspective. Chapter 3, authored by Julio Nogués of the World Bank, is concerned with the effect on the exporting countries. Many antidumping complaints in the United States and Europe are lodged against corporations in industrial countries, such as Japan. But increasingly such complaints are filed against companies in developing countries. And since LDC[3] economies are heavily dependent on exports, administrative protection directed against them can be particularly harmful. Dr. Nogués' chapter concentrates on antidumping actions against companies in Latin American countries, the incidence of which has risen in recent years. He demonstrates that the average antidumping duty applied by the United States against Latin American exports averaged 32%—ten times higher than the average duty paid on all U.S. imports. The United States is the heaviest user of countervailing duty, and again Latin American countries are increasingly affected. The average duty in this case is 15%. Chapter 3 assesses the effects of these measures. It then turns to consideration of a reverse phenomenon: the adoption, and increasing use, of antidumping and countervailing policies by the Latin American countries themselves. The author argues that these policies are being captured by interest groups, and that in future years the cost to these countries from unfair measures initiated by them will exceed the cost of such measures initiated against them by other countries. He suggests that the best measures to protect domestic industries are a stable macro-economy and a realistic exchange rate. Indeed, several Latin American countries, notably Mexico, adopted such policies in recent years and to good advantage.

Macro-economic reforms are often accompanied by trade liberalization. Many developing countries that were heavily protectionistic in the period up to the early 1980s, relying on an import substitution development strategy, introduced reforms and/or moved towards an export promotion strategy during the 1980s. Under the policy of import substitution, a country imposes high tariffs and nontariff barriers to imports, and behind this shelter it expands domestic production to replace imports. Over time this policy causes gross inefficiencies, and countries are led to switch to an export promotion strategy. This involves changes in the system of incentives in favor of exports, minimizing or eliminating the discrimination against them.[4] Rather than shelter itself behind a protective wall, the country tries to integrate itself into the global economy. Studies have been shown that countries pursuing export promotion fared far better in terms of growth rate and employment than countries following an import substitution strategy.

As often as not, macro-economic reforms and trade liberalization were introduced at the behest of the World Bank (and the IMF), as part of a loan package provided for structural adjustment. Located in Washington, D.C., the World Bank makes loans to developing countries out of subscription capital of its member countries and capital raised on the world financial markets. The Bank's experience with trade liberalization is the topic of Chapter 4, authored by John Nash of the World Bank's Trade Policy Division. It discusses the recently completed study by the Bank, designed to assess the experience of countries in liberalizing their trade regimes. Much of the study is conducted by comparing the policies and performance of 40 countries that received loans from the World Bank with 47 nonrecipients. Reforms tended to be strongest in reducing nontariff barriers and correcting overvalued exchange rates, although some of this progress could be reversed if certain LDCs moved towards the adoption of active antidumping and countervailing policies. Often the reforms are intertwined with macro-economic stabilization, designed to lower the rate of inflation. Where reforms were strong and sustained, economic performance (as measured by the growth of GNP and exports, and by the decline in inflation and deficits) improved. Replete with examples from the experience of individual countries, the study highlights the policies that contributed to success. As such, it can be a useful guide to the future.

It was mentioned earlier that the postwar period witnessed a massive reduction in tariff rates that occurred as a result of seven trade liberalization conferences in the GATT. The last completed session was the Tokyo Round; the Uruguay Round (UR) has been in session since 1986. The United States, the leading world economic power during most of the postwar period, has played a leading and critical role in this process. Indeed, it is sometimes suggested that one reason for the difficulties faced by the UR is the decline in the relative position of the United States. In other words, the world needs a *hegemon* to pursue effectively a policy of trade liberalization.

American participation in the various GATT rounds requires prior enabling legislation. Indeed, the United States is the only major negotiator requiring such legislation. Thus the Kennedy Round was negotiated under authority of the 1962 Trade Expansion Act whereas U.S. participation in the Tokyo Round was authorized by the Trade Reform Act of 1974. Typically, every such act specifies the extent to which the administration may go in reducing tariffs and otherwise liberalizing trade. That limit (i.e., tariff reduction of up to 50%) becomes the general target (seldom achieved) of the negotiation. Alongside the "liberalizing" chapters, the legislation usually contains restrictive "safeguard" provisions. These are designed to restrict imports should they threaten injury to a domestic industry. The last major piece of legislation in the trade area is the Omnibus Trade and Competitiveness Act of 1988. Among other things, it authorizes tariff reduction of up to 50%, and the UR is being negotiated under its authority. The outcome of the UR, if there is a positive outcome, will be brought back for Congressional approval on a "fast track" basis (an up or down vote without amendments).

But the 1988 legislation also contains restrictive articles, the most controversial one being the "Super-301" provision. Aimed mainly at Japan, it requires the administration to list publicly countries that "trade unfairly" with the United States, negotiate removal of such practices within 3 years, and take retaliatory action if the negotiations fail. The first such listing was published in May 1989. It designated Japan, for the refusal of its public authorities to purchase American commercial satellites and supercomputers, and for stringent import requirements that keep out American manufactured forest products; India, for barriers against foreign investment and foreign insurance companies; and Brazil, for licensing requirements on most imports. The ensuing negotiations with Japan covered a wide range of "structural impediments" to trade, such as wholesale and retail distribution systems in Japan (that tend to keep out imports), savings and investment patterns, pricing mechanisms, business behavior, bid-rigging, market allocation, group boycotts, industrial organization, and land use. Although these actions are viewed as an incentive for Japan to open up its market to imports, a side effect may be to induce it to import more American products, *at the expense of other supplying countries*. A December 1989 GATT report was highly critical of the Super-301 provision. Japan (as well as Brazil) was dropped from the list of "unfair traders" in May 1990, following an agreement with the United States concerning satellites, supercomputers, and lumber products.

Most (though not all) economists were highly critical of the Super-301 provision, claiming that it set up the United States as both prosecutor and judge in the alleged predatory behavior of other countries. With respect to Japan, an extreme position of those who advocate benign neglect would be that Japanese behavior is no different from that of other countries, and even if it were, we should not react in any aggressive manner, least of all bilaterally. Chapter 5, authored by Professor Kreinin of Michigan State University, develops a contrary view. Discussing Japan's trade practices, the chapter shows that Japan engages in far less intra-industry trade than the United States or Germany,[5] and that its market is "closed" to imports relative to the markets of other industrial countries. It is then shown that Japanese trade practices can be harmful to the United States as well as to the international trading system, and hence "Super-301" is a useful tool in the hands of negotiators trying to induce Japan to open up its market. Its effectiveness is attested to by the fact that, in order to avoid being on the list, countries such as Korea sometimes change their behavior even before the list of unfair traders is published.

While "Super-301" can help remove foreign impediments to U.S. exports, Chapter 6 (contributed by James Luke of Madonna University) argues that such efforts must be reinforced by a positive government policy of exports promotion. After discussing the economic rationale for such a policy and its effectiveness, the paper addresses in detail the *type* of export promotion strategy that is likely to yield the best results.

Shifting away from a U.S. vantage point, Chapter 7 (authored by Paolo Guerrie, of the University of Naples) brings us back to a global perspective. Much has been written in the economic literature about what determines the competitive advantage of nations. This essay addresses the same question but with an emphasis on technology. It classifies products into eight categories (science based, scale intensive, specialized supplier, traditional, fuels, and agricultural raw products, food, and raw materials), and considers the changing competitive position of each major country in these commodity categories. Included in the analysis are the United States, Japan, EC-12 (as a group), Germany, France, the United Kingdom, Italy, and the Asian NICs.

Most international and domestic transactions are financed by exchanging money for a good or a service. But an estimated 5% to 10% of world trade is barter trade, namely, the exchange of a good or a service for another good or service. This phenomenon is often referred to as *countertrade*. And such trade also occurs within the domestic economies of advanced countries. In the United States, for example, there are 400 barter exchanges that assist their 175,000 members to exchange goods and services without the use of money. Although this type of economic activity is usually ignored, it can be important.

An analysis of countertrade is the contribution of Chapter 8, authored by Professors Neale and Sercu of the United Kingdom and Belgium, respectively. They examine the four specific forms of international countertrade and review the reasons for its existence. Exchange control and other imperfections in international markets stand out as major factors. The authors then develop a rationale for domestic countertrade, backed by evidence from surveys in the United Kingdom and Canada. It appears that firms undertake countertrade in the domestic market to hide price cuts and to circumvent credit-financing problems. This suggests that international countertrade would continue even after imperfections in international markets disappear. It would then be motivated by the factors that motivate purely domestic barter.

Part II of the volume contains six essays on regional economic integration. Trade liberalization in the postwar period proceeded along two tracks. First is the multinational track of GATT where trade among 100 nations has been liberalized subject to a principle of nondiscrimination, the Most Favored Nation principle or MFN. Under the MFN rule each importing nation imposes the same tariff (or other restrictions) on a commodity regardless of its country of origin. It means that all measures of trade liberalization, such as tariff reductions, must apply equally to all exporting countries; the country of origin makes no difference. Thus, in the United States the extremely high statutory tariff applies only to the very few nonmembers of GATT. Most imports originate in GATT countries, and are subject to the much lower tariffs (a result of seven rounds of GATT tariff negotiations), known as the MFN rates. Developing countries' export of manufactured products are subject to an even lower preferential duty (often zero).

A second track of trade liberalization, the *regional* approach, is embodied in customs unions (CU) and free trade areas (FTA). A CU is an entity of two or more countries that abolish all or nearly all trade restrictions among themselves and set up a *common* and *uniform* tariff against imports from outside countries, known as the common external tariff. The European Community of 12 countries is a prime example of a CU. An FTA is also a group of countries that abolish all or most trade restrictions among themselves, but allows each member to maintain its own restrictions (such as the tariff level) against imports from outsiders. The United States-Canada FTA and the proposed North American Free Trade Agreement (NAFTA) between the United States, Canada, and Mexico are prime examples. Both a CU and an FTA discriminate against nonmembers, and indeed the MFN clause of GATT, which outlaws discrimination, contains exceptions for these two forms of regional integration.

Because of geographical proximity, the smaller number of countries involved, and other reasons, trade liberalization can proceed further and reach greater depth on a regional than on a multinational level. But since a CU or an FTA is discriminatory in nature (namely, it discriminates against nonmembers) there is a debate among economists whether the regional approach is "good" or "bad" for the global economy. In all probability each CU or FTA needs to be analyzed on its own merit. Such an analysis compares two effects of a regional grouping. First is the favorable *trade creation,* under which inefficient production in one member country is replaced by more efficiently produced imports from other members, now that barriers between them have been removed. This improves resource allocation within the CU. Second is the unfavorable *trade diversion* effect, under which imports from a nonmember country are displaced by less efficiently produced imports from a member country because of the tariff discrimination against outsiders. This pushes global resources towards a less efficient configuration. If trade creation exceeds trade diversion then the CU is judged to be favorable to world welfare. It is judged unfavorable if trade diversion is greater than trade creation.

In any event, CUs and FTAs are proliferating. In Europe, the EC is a CU of 12 members—the most successful case of regional integration. Alongside it there exists an FTA (called EFTA) of six small European countries. There are close ties between the EC and EFTA, and some EFTA members may accede to the EC before the end of the decade. In North America there exists a United States-Canada FTA, while a three-country NAFTA, encompassing the United States, Canada, and Mexico, is under negotiation. Several FTAs exist in South America, such as the one incorporating Brazil, Argentina, Uruguay, and Paraguay. And President Bush has expressed a vision of an FTA encompassing all of the Americas. In Asia there exists a FTA between Australia and New Zealand, and one is proposed for a group of six developing countries known as ASEAN.[6]

Some observers fear that a further push in the direction of regional integration may drive the trading system into a tri-polar world: Europe, the Americas, and an Asian bloc led by Japan. Failure of the UR may provide an impetus to such a development, although to date there is no evidence that Japan, Taiwan, and Korea are interested in forming, or being included in, any regional arrangement. In fact, Japan's trade is about evenly divided between the three regions, and its foreign investments are also directed to all regions. Yet even the remote prospect of a tri-polar world is dreaded by some and welcomed by others, thus producing a heated debate.

Because the EC is the most advanced of all regional groupings, five of the chapters in this section deal with its effects on trade and investment. A short historical background is useful before these chapters are read. In 1957 six European countries—W. Germany, France, Italy, Belgium, Holland, and Luxembourg—signed the Treaty of Rome establishing the European Economic Community or Common Market. Its main features were a customs union for manufactured products; a common agricultural policy that consisted of internal price support, a highly restricted import regime, and, in later years, export subsidies for farm products; and a set of political institutions that were viewed as forerunners of a European government. Its supernational body, the EC Commission, is located in Brussels, Belgium. The EEC set up special and preferential trading arrangements with the former French and Belgian colonies in Africa, and with countries in the Mediterranean basin.

Not all European countries were ready to join the EEC. In particular the United Kingdom preferred to remain outside, maintaining its allegiance to its former empire and avoiding the costly agricultural policy of the continental countries. As a counter to the EEC, the United Kingdom, along with the Scandinavian countries, Portugal, Switzerland, and Austria, formed the European Free Trade Area Association (EFTA). As an FTA it was a loose form of organization, confined to free trade in manufactured goods. But in the 1970s, as the EEC integration process continued apace, the United Kingdom began to view with dismay the prospect of remaining outside. It negotiated an accession treaty to the EEC, and Denmark and Ireland joined at the same time, making for a nine-member CU. The special preferential trading relationship with the former French colonies was extended to the former British colonies in Africa, the Caribbean, and the Pacific (69 countries in all). In 1981 Greece joined the Community, which is now referred to as the European Community or EC, while Spain and Portugal acceded in 1986. As the EC grew to 12 members, EFTA shrunk to six, and now includes Austria, Finland, Iceland, Norway, Sweden, and Switzerland. But some of them, along with certain East European countries, may apply for membership in the EC. And, in any event, EFTA and the EC have free trade between themselves and a close economic relationship.

In the late 1980s the EC announced a plan to complete its integration process by forming a truly integrated market known as the unified market program or EC-1992. It is supposed to go into effect on December 31, 1992 (or January 1, 1993). Although the entire program may not be approved in time, substantial portions are likely to be implemented on schedule. EC-1992 calls for several profound changes designed to convert Europe into one single market. Following are examples of those changes.

All border check points for goods moving between EC countries would be abolished. A truck traveling from the United Kingdom to Italy will no longer be detained at the French and Italian borders, thus increasing the efficiency of the transport system. This step will bring about the elimination of all remaining restrictions on intra-EC trade (trade within the EC). More importantly, national quantitative restrictions against imports from outside countries (such as French, Italian, or British import restrictions on Japanese cars) would either be abandoned or, more likely, replaced by EC-wide quotas. Finally, this step would call for some harmonization of the Value Added Tax (VAT, similar to a national sales tax) rates among member countries.

Next, the EC Commission will issue *technical standards* for products with respect to health, safety, consumer protection, the environment, and other matters, and those will become common throughout the Community. They include, but are not limited to, technical standards relating to chemicals and pharmaceutical products, emission controls on passenger cars and commercial vehicles, food regulations (e.g., rules for food additives and packaging), safety requirements and standards for industrial machines, and liberalization of air and road transport markets. Nonmember countries, such as the United States, have expressed fear that the EC would set technical standards compatible with products manufactured in Europe, and that American and Japanese producers would find it difficult to meet the new standards or comply with the new regulations.

In matters of content and quality of traded goods there will be no uniform standards, and instead the EC adopted the principle of mutual recognition: each EC member would accept the standards prevailing in other member countries. A member state cannot prohibit the import and sale of a product lawfully produced and sold in another member state even if it does not comply with its domestic standards. For example, Germany cannot prohibit the import of French liqueur solely because its alcohol content is too low for it to be deemed a liqueur under German law. In line with this principle, the European court overturned British and French standards for milk, German standards for beer, and Italian standards for pasta.

New products would become eligible for sale in the entire Community after one set of tests and certification, instead of 12 separate sets. This would apply to goods produced in the EC as well as to products coming in from other countries, such as the United States. It would clearly lower the cost of introducing new products.

Public procurement contracts of member governments, which amount to over 10% of the Community's GNP, will be open for bidding by firms in the entire EC. Currently only 2% of such contracts go to companies from other member states. It remains to be seen whether companies from nonmember countries, such as the United States, would also be allowed to bid. This is a matter of contention between the United States and the EC.

There will be mutual recognition of university degrees and professional diplomas acquired in each member states. That would extend intra-EC labor mobility to professional workers. Nonprofessionals already move freely among 10 of the Community members.

A unified capital market will be introduced by the abolition of exchange controls on capital transactions within the EC. This step may require some harmonization of national taxes on capital, to avoid giving advantage to low-tax countries and to countries that do not have withholding taxes, in attracting capital. Without harmonization, countries with lower taxes would be favored in the establishment of new companies.

National insurance regulations will be reduced and unified, and large firms will be able to insure "big risks" with any insurance company throughout the Community. Banks, once they are licensed in an EC country, will be able to open branches and offer banking services in all member states. Apart from capital-adequacy rules, the Commission abandoned attempts to harmonize banking regulations in the 12 countries, and instead adopted the principle of "national treatment": each host country would accord foreign banks treatment no less favorable than that accorded in like situations to its domestic banks.

In regard to non-EC banks, the Commission originally insisted that permission to function in the Community would be subject to a reciprocity clause: before a non-EC bank is granted a license to operate across the Community, the Commission would check to see whether all EC countries have equal access to the home-country market of the bank in question. This clause would not be applicable to financial institutions already established within the EC, which explains the rush of American and Japanese banks to establish subsidiaries inside the EC prior to 1992. Although this principle seems "fair," it is difficult to apply in practice: many countries (e.g., the United States and Japan) have significantly different financial structures and different laws separating banking and securities activities and regional limitations on banking (e.g., United States). Thus, subsidiaries of U.S. banks would have been excluded from investment banking or from branching across EC states, because United States law segregates commercial from investment banking, and interstate banking is not permitted. For these reasons Germany and the United Kingdom expressed reservations about the practice of reciprocity in international banking, and the United States objected vigorously to it. A more acceptable alternative to reciprocity is "national treatment." Reciprocity would require non-EC countries, such as the United States, to treat EC firms in the same manner as the EC treats American firms. National treatment would require the United States to treat EC firms in a manner no less favorable than it treats its own firms. In other words, EC banks functioning in the United States should be subject to the same regulations as American banks in the United States, while American banks in the EC would be subject to the same regulations as European banks in the EC. Under strong American pressure the EC Commission abandoned its insistence on reciprocity in favor of national treatment. But the dispute over reciprocity remains unresolved in the case of other services.

Finally, the EC Commission is increasingly assuming the role of a supranational government in a variety of economic areas, such as antimerger policy, as member governments agree to transfer authority to it.

Table 1 below provides some idea of the size of the EC market by comparing it to the United States and Japan.

The impending unified market has already induced an across-border merger boom and massive business restructuring within the EC, as well as an intensified flow of capital from the United States and Japan, and mergers between EC and non-EC firms. In 1988 there were 383 mergers and 111 joint venture agreements within the Community, a 25% rise over 1987. There exist EC estimates or "guesstimates" of the effect of each of these directives, and it is on the basis of these estimates that EC growth rate and employment are projected to rise considerably. This is a result of the exploitation of economies of scale, enhanced competition, reduced regulations, and greater investment activity induced by the unification of this huge market.

To nonmember countries, EC-1992 presents an opportunity and a danger. They will benefit from faster growth rate inside the community which would increase demand for their exports, a one-step certification of new products, greater efficiency of producing inside the Community (supplying the entire EC from fewer locations), and other advantages. On the other hand, by reason of increased size and efficiency EC firms would become formidable competitors with companies from other countries. Moreover, there is likely to be increased discrimination against nonmember goods and services and in favor of those produced by the Community. (Note, however, that NAFTA may have similar effects.) This can give rise to intergovernmental disputes. An example of such a disagreement is the EC proposed treatment of television programming.

Although the EC expects to have "television without frontiers" within Europe, an October 1989 directive suggests that: "the member states shall insure (where practicable, and by appropriate means) that broadcasters reserve for European works a majority of their transmission time, excluding news, sports, game shows, and advertisements." At the same time the EC and its member states expect to subsidize European TV productions. In the 1980s most European television shows were of American origin, yielding over $2 billion a year in royalties. Not only could the policy curtail such revenue, but it may prevent the U.S. broadcasting industry from taking advantage of a growing market. To the EC claim that the directive merely constitutes protection from American "cultural imperialism," the U.S. trade representative replied: "We don't understand why the Spanish culture is more protected by a film produced in Germany by 'Europeans' than by a Spanish film of Mexican origin, or why the English

Table 1
Comparisons Between the EC, the U.S., and Japan 1987

	EC	US	Japan
Population (millions)	324	244	122
Labor force (in millions)	143	122	60
GNP ($ billions)*	$3782	$4436	$1608
GNP per capita (U.S. dollars)*	$11,690	$18,200	$13,180
Exports ($ billions)	$954[†]	$250	$231
Imports ($ billions)	$955[†]	$424	$151

*Converted to U.S. dollars by purchasing power equivalents.
[†]Includes trade between EC members.

culture is promoted more by film produced in France by 'Europeans' than by a film of New Zealand origin." The United States threatened to take the issue to GATT for arbitration, but the EC claims that GATT has no jurisdiction in this matter. Whatever the outcome, American producers already began seeking European partners in order to ensure access to the EC market.

Monetary unification is *not* part of the EC-92 program. But separately under the Mastericht treaty, the EC hopes to forge a common currency for at least some of its members (those with the strongest economies) by the year 2000. That would call for surrender of national sovereignty in matters of monetary policy and the establishment of a common central bank, to be dubbed, appropriately enough, "Euro-Fed."

In general EC-92 may have profound effects on world trade and the world trading system. This is highlighted in Chapter 9, contributed by Professor D. Salvador of Fordham University. After reviewing briefly the theory of economic integration and the factors likely to influence the relative magnitude of trade creation and diversion, the effects of the EC, the formation of trade blocs, and their effect on the international trading system are discussed. The book then moves from the general to the specific as the next two chapters are devoted to the effect of EC-92 on direct foreign investment.

Chapter 10, authored by Professor Scaperlanda of Northern Illinois university, examines selected directives of EC-92 related to multinational corporations, to determine the degree to which the EC exercises supervision over such enterprises. Chapter 11, contributed by Professors P. Theerathorn and D. Vacheron of Memphis State University, is empirical in nature. It examines major acquisitions of European businesses by U.S.-based multinationals, and finds that the pace of such acquisitions quickened in the late 1980s as companies attempted to establish a European base of operations in anticipation of EC-92. The reactions of stock markets to these moves have been favorable.

Chapters 12 and 13 by D. Robertson of the Australian National University and A. Tovias of the Hebrew University in Jerusalem, respectively, assess the impact of EC-92 on nonmember countries. Robertson's study concerns the rapidly growing economies of East Asia. He argues that the combination of a breakdown of the Uruguay Round, an inward-looking EC-92, and the introduction of NAFTA would reduce access to the markets of the industrial countries, with adverse consequences for the dynamic East Asian economies. Tovias examines the effect on Hungary. He argues that not only are Hungary's exports to the EC likely to suffer from discriminatory practices, but EC firms will become more formidable competitors in third markets with Hungarian producers of similar products. He further predicts that EC-92 will bring about a change in Hungary's industrial structure.

In North America, the U.S.-Canada FTA was signed in 1988. But thus far it has not produced dramatic changes in trade flows. This may be because U.S.-Canada trade had been subject to low duty before 1988 and because trade barriers in certain key sectors, such as textiles and steel, remained largely untouched by the agreement. Or it may be because the agreement is still in its transitional phase. A third possible explanation is the dampening effect of the protracted economic slowdown in both countries on their bilateral trade flows.

The possible conclusion of a NAFTA between the United States, Canada, and Mexico has stimulated a host of studies attempting to forecast its effects on the three countries as well as on the outside world. Combining U.S. technology, Canadian resources, and Mexican labor, NAFTA can generate considerable benefits for all three countries. But the effects would vary from one member to another. For example, Mexico's growth rate is expected to rise considerably, whereas that of the United States would increase only slightly. The net overall effect on U.S. employment is likely to be small, but there would be substantial changes in its industrial composition, as labor-intensive industries move to Mexico while high-technology industries concentrate in the United States and supply the entire North American market.

This volume contains but one industry study: the impact of the U.S.-Canada FTA on the Canadian furniture industry, contributed by Professor Hamdi Ali of Concordia University. It describes the transition that the industry is likely to go through, and the effects on different types of firms. To meet competition in the new market environment Canadian firms will have to introduce modern computerized technology or identify a highly specialized market niche suitable for their operations.

Part III of the book contains five chapters dealing with direct foreign investment (DFI) and multinational corporations (MNC). DFI around the world grew by 25% from 1983 through 1989, compared to a 9.4% growth in world trade. The leading source country for these investments was Japan, which by 1990 accounted for nearly a quarter of global DFI.

Why do firms invest overseas rather than supply foreign markets from home-country locations? The most likely answer is that they expect to increase their profits by such investment. Because profit equals sales revenue minus cost, overseas investments are expected either to raise revenue, lower costs, or both. Producing abroad may raise revenue by being close to customers in the host country, being able to cater to their particular needs, being better able to service the product, being able to meet specific government regulations, and perhaps even satisfying the nationalistic feelings of customers. Certainly the last three factors were important in inducing Japanese automakers to locate production facilities in the United States. Cost reduction may occur if the company moves production to countries where raw materials exist, if labor-intensive products are produced in countries where labor is relatively abundant and therefore cheap (e.g., Mexico in the case of NAFTA and Spain in the case of the EC), or if the foreign investment enables the company to circumvent import restrictions in the host country, such as U.S. and Japanese investment in the EC. When a large company goes abroad it sometimes becomes necessary for the enterprises that supply it in the home country, including banks that provide financial services, to set up overseas branches in order to supply its foreign subsidiaries.

In the immediate postwar period, U.S. direct investment abroad far exceeded foreign direct investment in the United States. But by 1990 the two figures have become roughly equal at about $400 billion. Contrary to common belief, the biggest investors in the United States are not the Japanese but the British. They are followed by the Japanese and the Dutch in that order.

Apart from the general factors that motivate DFI, economists have been hard at work in developing a theory of the MNC. Why would a company set up production facilities overseas, as against exporting from home plants or licensing its technology to host-country firms? Or why would the product not be supplied by firms indigenous to the host country? Although a solid and cohesive explanation has yet to emerge, there are several hypotheses that attempt to explain why production is carried on by the same firm in several countries. The most popular hypothesis suggests that a firm in possession of a unique technology or some other firm-specific advantage (such as low input cost or a better distribution system) finds it best to exploit it within the firm by setting up subsidiaries (as against licensing the technology to other firms).

We can think of the MNC as a huge enclave, an independent economic entity that cuts across national boundaries. It can raise capital or secure the services of highly skilled professional labor anywhere in the word and use it elsewhere. It can locate various stages of production in different countries, and sell the product anywhere. Some special features of MNCs follow from this view. First, many of them are vertically integrated: namely, a subsidiary in host-country I may produce raw materials (e.g., raw wood), the subsidiary in host-country II may process the raw materials into an intermediate product (e.g., rough lumber), the subsidiary in host-country III may further fabricate a more advanced intermediate product (e.g., finished lumber), while the subsidiary in host-country IV may produce the finished product (e.g., furniture), for sale in the host country, the home country, or in third markets. We know that the automobile is a world product in a sense that parts are produced in various countries for assembly elsewhere. As products move from one subsidiary to the next they become part of international trade. In fact, about 25% of all international trade is trade between subsidiaries of the same corporation, or intrafirm trade. And the items entering such trade will not be valued at "arm's length" prices, a term that describes market-determined prices for transactions between firms that are independent of each other.

For in its intrafirm trade the corporation is interested in maximizing its overall after-tax profit, rather than the profit of individual subsidiaries. The prices charged by one subsidiary on sales to another (located in a different country), known as *transfer prices*, may differ significantly from world prices. In particular, they are designed to minimize overall corporate income taxes and tariff payments. If tax rates differ among the countries in which the corporation's subsidiaries are located, the corporation will shift profits from the high- to the low-tax country. Thus, if the country into which components are imported has higher tax rates than the components-exporting country, the corporation will artificially raise the price of the components; it will underprice them when the opposite is the case. In this fashion it tries to maximize the profit of the subsidiaries in the low-tax country and minimize the profit of the subsidiaries in the high-tax country. A country raising its profit tax rates may find itself losing rather than gaining tax revenue as MNCs adjust to the new rates.

Because the MNC functions in several countries (both developed and developing), it is a useful instrument for the transfer of technology between countries. It can also transfer capital and high-skilled labor from one country to another, and as such can be highly beneficial to the host country. Yet many governments are ambivalent in their attitude towards DFI. On the one hand, they offer MNCs a variety of tax concessions and other incentives to locate in their country; on the other hand, they place restrictions on MNC activities, known as "performance standards." For example, the host-country government may require any subsidiary of a foreign company to export a certain minimum proportion of its output, or to use a minimum proportion of local content (labor and materials) in the production process. Alternatively, governments may not permit production in certain sectors of the economy, such as high technology or energy, to be controlled by foreign interests. They may stipulate that the foreign subsidiary must take on a local partner who in turn would own a majority stake in the company. Some of these restrictions are subject to negotiations in the UR of GATT, with the intent of liberalizing them.

A few of these issues are represented in the five chapters on DFI. Chapter 15, by Professors Gray and Lundon of Rutgers University, deals with trade between units of the same MNC. The authors demonstrate that intrafirm trade can increase the efficiency of the global economy. They also articulate the main sources of such gains. Chapter 16, by Professors Movassaghi and Unsal of Ithaca College, shows that incentive schemes introduced by developing countries to attract DFI from abroad are generally ineffective. Foreign investors pay more attention to market size, availability of natural resources, and political stability in the host country than they do to incentives. In Chapter 17, Professors Chhachhi et al. study the effect on the return to stockholders of non-U.S. companies acquiring a U.S. subsidiary through merger. Chapters 18 and 19 deal with technology strategies. The first relates to developing countries. In it Professor P. Steidlmeier of SUNY-Binghamton explores possible conflicts between host-country priorities and the firm's mission. The second one by Professor Peters of Rensselaer Polytechnic Institute relates to Japanese subsidiaries and joint ventures in the United States. It inquires into the technology strategy of 100 such subsidiaries: to what extent is access to U.S. technology a motivation for locating in the United States? How many subsidiaries set up their own in-house research capability and why? How do research results flow between the subsidiary and the head office in the source country? These and related questions are answered through an interview study.

Part IV of the book contains four country studies. These were chosen not because of the importance of the country they represent; rather, they were selected because the feature or the policy they examine is of widespread interest.

In cases of quantitative import controls, governments sometimes wish to auction off the import licenses in order capture the quota rents that would otherwise accrue to private importers, or to measure the tariff equivalents of existing quantitative restrictions prior to a trade liberalization program. The experience of Colombia in introducing such a system is analyzed in Chapter 20, by K. Hallberg of the World Bank and Professor W. Takacs of the University of Maryland. The Colombian episode provided the country with information needed for its liberalization program, and the authors draw lessons for the design and conduct of license auction systems in other countries. In Chapter 21 Professor Yavas of California State University employs a statistical technique to identify the determinants of Turkey's exports. He finds that the GDP in the importing countries and the exchange rates are the significant variable. These results are applicable to other countries as well, where relative prices (namely, the country's competitive position) and the income of the importing countries are the main determinants of a country's exports.

Although Chapter 22 relates specifically to Iran, the analysis applies to any economy run strictly by the tenets of Islam. In it Professor Kavoossi of Howard University describes how the rules of Islam govern the Iranian economy, and the kind of adjustments a market economy needs to make to accommodate and live by Islamic rules. For example, because usury laws forbid interest payments, other forms of factor renumerations are used instead. Thus, interest-based securities are replaced by profit-sharing, interest-free instruments. In the final chapter, Professor Mueller of Friedrich-Alexander University in Germany deals with the economics of German unification. He examines the transformation of East Germany from a socialist to a market economy, assesses the budgetary cost of unification, and analyzes the effects of unification on the international and EC markets. Although these four chapters do not offer a panoramic view of the world, they deal with issues that transcend the specific country represented in the analysis.

Mordechai E. Kreinin
Michigan State University

NOTES

1. In the 1979 to 1988 period a total of 1833 antidumping cases were filed in the world, about evenly divided between the four regions mentioned in the text. The total number of countervailing duty cases was 429, of which 371 cases were filed in the United States. These numbers represent significant increases over earlier periods.

2. In a study of the trade effects of antidumping action initiated by the EC, it was shown that import of goods affected by the action declined by 18% in the first year, and by 50% 5 years later. The average antidumping duty in that study was 14%.

3. Less developed countries; the term is used interchangeably with the term *developing countries*.

4. See M. E. Kreinin, *International Economics: A Policy Approach,* Orlando, Fl.: Harcourt Brace Jovanovich, 6th edition, 1991, chapter 17.

5. The term *intra-industry* trade refers to a two-way trade in a similar commodity, such as the exchange of different car models between the United States and Canada. It is to be distinguished from *inter-industry* trade, which refers to the exchange between countries of totally different types of commodities, such as textiles and shoes for aircraft and computers, or the exchange of raw materials for finished manufactures.

6. The large members of this group are Thailand, Indonesia, Malaysia, and the Philippines.

Part One
General Commercial Policy

Chapter 1

The Uruguay Round—Phase II*

Mordechai E. Kreinin

Abstract *This chapter reviews the issues confronted in the Uruguay Round of GATT trade negotiations. It then considers why agriculture was such a major stumbling block in the Uruguay as against previous rounds, and examines difficulties other than agriculture encountered by the negotiators. Finally, the chapter considers possible outcomes of the round, and their consequences.*

INTRODUCTION

As of early 1993, the second phase of the Uruguay Round (UR) appears to be at an impasse. The UR is the eighth general round of GATT trade negotiations. It began in 1986 and was scheduled for completion by 1991. But the negotiators found themselves deadlocked at the end of 1990, and the UR was suspended. In early 1991 the U.S. Congress renewed the legislative negotiating authority for 2 years, a renewal that embodied fast-track consideration of the final agreement by the Congress (i.e., an up or down vote without amendments). The (second-phase) talks resumed in earnest almost immediately, but the impasse reappeared after less than a year of intensive bargaining.

Issues Addressed by the UR

It is not altogether surprising that the negotiations were deadlocked twice (even if a measure of success may emerge in the end). There was tough bargaining among 108 countries over issues that had never before been addressed in the GATT. Apart from the usual matters of tariff reduction, liberalization of NTBs, and the rules of GATT, the UR covers the following types of transactions:

1. Services. Services include insurance, banking, construction, transportation, tourism, telecommunications, data-based information, health,

---

*This chapter is an updated and expanded version of an article on the Uruguay Round prepared for the 1990 IFTA meeting and published in the proceedings. The early section also draws on Kreinin 1991, Chapter 16.

and education. Unlike goods, services cannot be stored and often require the simultaneous presence of the producer and the consumer. Government intervention in the service-producing sector is greater than in goods production. It usually takes the form of standards governing the conditions of competition and market access. Protective instruments are also different from those prevailing in commodity trade; there are no tariffs, quotas, or voluntary export restrictions, or VERs. Most frequently, protection takes the form of restrictions on the establishment of foreign suppliers (such as foreign law firms, banks, or insurance companies), or various kinds of discrimination in regulations.

2. Trade-Related Investment. Performance standards set by many host countries for foreign direct investment often require the local subsidiary of a foreign company to meet some or all of the following conditions: a minimum of 51% of the subsidiary must be owned by host-country nationals; the subsidiary must export a minimum proportion of its output; the subsidiary must use in production a minimum proportion of domestic materials and labor (local content requirement); and the subsidiary must employ a minimum proportion of domestic nationals in certain high-skill or managerial jobs. Because many of these provisions are trade related, they need to be incorporated into the GATT framework and subjected to GATT rules.

3. Patent Protection. The industrial countries want intellectual property rights negotiated under GATT auspices. The United States alone claims an annual loss of $60 billion from "pirating" of computer programs, drugs, tapes, books, and other items that are not protected by copyright laws in many countries. But many less developed countries (LDCs) object, regarding intellectual property rights as a public good.

4. Agricultural Protection and Subsidies. A group of 13 countries, known as The Cairns Group,[1] calls for liberalization of global agricultural trade. Drawing support from the United States, they attack the Common Agricultural Policy and export subsidies of the EC as well as agricultural protection in Japan.

In addition to these issues, the UR expected to liberalize trade in textiles by agreeing on a gradual abolition of the Multi-Fiber Agreement, and to liberalize VERs, which violate the rules of GATT.

In an oversimplified manner, a *Wall Street Journal* editorial (December 3, 1990) described the negotiations as a deal between the United States, Europe, Japan, and the LDCs:

> America wants freer trade in investment and services, and better protection for intellectual property. In return, it must stop protecting textiles. Japan and Europe want to protect free trade in manufactured goods, but they must quit mollycoddling farmers. The Third World wants access to developed world markets for its

While all the issues were difficult, the immediate cause of the 1990 failure and the 1992 impasse was the United States-EC deadlock over domestic support, market access, and export subsidies in agriculture. The United States demanded a 75% reduction in EC farm support and a 90% cut in export subsidies over the next 10 years, whereas the EC agreed to a mere 15% reduction by 1996. A Swedish compromise proposal, advanced in December 1990, would have cut domestic farm support, barriers to market access, and export subsidies by 30% over a 5-year period. While this would have still left agriculture as the most distorted sector in world trade, the text met a major U.S. demand by calling for specific cuts in each of the three types of subsidy, rather than leaving countries free to decide which subsidies to cut to meet some overall target. Yet even that proposal was rejected by the EC.

Agriculture—In the UR and in Previous Rounds

Agriculture was also a major stumbling block in previous rounds. Yet the negotiations never collapsed over the issue. Rather, in the Kennedy and Tokyo Rounds the United States finally withdrew its objections to an agreement without agriculture. Why did farm policy become an insurmountable sticking point at the Uruguay Round? Several possible reasons suggest themselves. First, the existence of an organized pressure group of 13 countries, the Cairns Group, in addition to the United States, added strength to the demand for farm-trade liberalization. Second, for the first time in GATT history the developing countries participated actively in the negotiations. And what the LDCs want most is access to developed-countries' markets for their farm products, as well as for textiles. For them agriculture had to be incorporated into the overall agreement if they were to agree to U.S. and EC demands in the areas of services, trade-related investment issues, and intellectual property rights. Testifying to the importance of this link is the fact that some LDCs threatened to walk out of the negotiations if no agreement could be reached on agriculture. As noted in GATT's newsletter *Focus* (November 1990, p. 1): "Agricultural reform is not just an EC-US issue—many countries had a fundamental interest in securing a successful outcome in the negotiations."

Thirdly, for the first time the cost of agricultural protectionism to the Organization for Economic Cooperation and Development (OECD) countries has been estimated and widely publicized. The staggering figure of $200–250 billion per year suggests that the EC may have intensified its intervention in the farm economy in recent years. Finally, there is the abiding need to reduce the U.S. budgetary deficit. And a prime candidate for expenditure cuts is the $55 billion agricultural support program. Although it is politically impossible for the United States to eliminate farm support unilaterally, it is likely that the U.S.

farm bloc could be induced to trade off domestic support for freer access to foreign markets, especially the markets of Europe and Japan. Thus a deal on agriculture may be viewed as a way to achieve a substantial cut in federal spending and an improvement in the efficiency of the U.S. economy. In fact half of the $14.9 billion cut in farm spending, obtained as a part of the 1990 deficit-reduction law, was contingent on success of the agriculture negotiations in the Uruguay Round.

Overlaying these specific reasons is the decline in the *relative* economic strength of the United States. This country can no longer afford to subordinate its commercial and economic interests to its political objectives.

These are possible reasons why agriculture loomed more important in the Uruguay Round than in previous rounds. Although the dispute over farm policy was mainly between the United States and the EC, Japan is just as reluctant to relax the tight controls on food imports such as rice (although the Japanese do not subsidize exports to third markets), and hence it sided with the EC in the dispute, as did Korea. Had a deal been struck with the EC, the focus would have shifted to Japan. And given the strength of its farm lobby (certainly no weaker than that of Europe), Japan's response could also have been negative.

Difficulties Other than Agriculture

Even apart from agriculture there are at least three other reasons that could have contributed to the second deadlock in the UR negotiations. First, the contemplated outcome of this set of negotiations embodies profound resource-redistributional effects within each country. The Uruguay Round represented the most ambitious (perhaps too ambitious) set of trade negotiations ever undertaken: it attempted to bring under the GATT umbrella sectors that have always been excluded from it.

World exports in 1989 as estimated by GATT (*International Trade*, 1989–1990) are shown in Table 1. Over $1.2 trillion in international trade are transactions not covered by GATT. Global service transactions add up to $680 billion annually, and amount to one fifth of merchandise trade. Bringing them under GATT rules is a difficult task. From the beginning the United States (which spearheaded the service negotiations) wished to exclude shipping and civil avia-

Table 1
World Exports 1989

Manufacturing (other than textiles)	$1965 billion	
Mining products	$415 billion	
Services	$680 billion	Not covered by GATT
Agriculture	$405 billion	
Textiles and apparel	$190 billion	

Source: GATT, International Trade 1989–1990.

tion, while France wanted to exclude films and television programs from any service agreement. Host-country performance standards imposed on direct foreign investment thwart investment activity. The multifiber textile agreement severely restricts trade in goods important to the LDCs and needs to be brought into conformity with GATT rules. And even within manufacturing, trade in many products is governed by "grey-area" measures, such as VERs, that are discriminatory in nature and not in conformity with GATT rules.

To the best of my knowledge none of these matters was fully settled by the end of 1990. This is highlighted in a statement by Arthur Dunkel, GATT's director general, published in *Focus,* November 1990 (pp. 1–4):

> In *services* there is a need to finalize the framework text, and reach decisions for its effective application to different sectors. In *textiles* and *clothing* it is necessary to determine the rate of progression for their integration into GATT, the criteria for the application of transitional safeguard measures, and the duration of such measures. In the case of the *subsidies code* the treatment of domestic subsidies is yet to be decided. No single text is available on *anti-dumping* measures, including the determination of injury and problems of circumvention of duties (it is feared that many LDCs will begin using anti-dumping laws). There is no decision on which *trade-related investment measures* are to be covered by the agreement, and whether such measures should be handled on a case-by-case basis or be subject to some blanket rules. In the case of *intellectual property rights* decisions still need to be taken on many issues such as the protection of computer programs, performers, and broadcasters under copyright, and the terms of protection for sound recordings and patents. The conferees are far from completing negotiations in the area of *market access* (tariffs and NTBs), where a formula approach to tariff reduction may be abandoned in favor of a product-by-product approach. And it has not been decided whether *safeguard* measures may be applied to individual sources of supply on a selective basis.

By winter 1992 the framework text of an agreement on services had been negotiated. It contains a list of about 150 services, and an array of ground rules (such as "national treatment") for service transactions. But the actual bargaining of "offers" and "requests" for individual service items has only begun, with very little actual liberalization taking place (see Hoekman, 1992).

Compared to the outcome of previous rounds, which resulted mainly in an expansion of intra-industry trade, an agreement covering all the UR topics would trigger a vast increase in interindustry and even intersectoral trade, and would represent a profound structural change. There would be huge "gains" and "losses." Even if it were possible to devise an accord that is well balanced for each major participant (or group of participants), the redistributional effects within each country could be immense. In the United States, for example, the financial services, agriculture, and high-technology industries would gain while textiles, certain services, and labor-intensive industries would lose. Such an expansion in international transactions would entail large internal adjustment costs in the participating countries.

A second possible reason for the collapse of the UR is the unified market program of the EC (EC-1992), which requires parallel steps in Europe at the same time that the UR was being negotiated globally. Apart from the European "policy overload" question, the need to absorb the Iberian peninsula and what was East Germany into the EC involves considerable structural adjustment in Europe. To cope with the new conditions, some country restrictions, especially against imports from the Far East (such as Japanese cars), would be converted to EC-wide restrictions. And that could force the Japanese to divert some exports from Europe to the United States, increasing the strains on the international trading system. In general, the adjustments within Europe could force the EC to alleviate internal difficulties by imposing restrictions against outsiders. The EC may also be expected to assume a more intransigent and less flexible attitude in the GATT negotiations.

A third possible reason is the overt import restrictions imposed by Japan in the areas of agriculture and some services (such as construction), and covert protectionism in manufacturing, creating resentment elsewhere at both the political and business levels. It is simply not possible to maintain a liberal trading system when such a major player plays by different rules.

Finally, on a technical level the negotiations are conducted by 13 separate working groups, each dealing with one issue. That makes it difficult to bargain concessions in one area (such as services) for equivalent concession in other areas (such as agriculture or textiles).

What Next? Consequences of the UR Collapse

At this writing there are three possible outcomes: a full-fledged success of the UR, a scaled-down agreement, or a complete collapse. Clearly a measure of success is important to the international trading system. But suppose we assume the worst-case scenario—what would be the consequences of a complete deadlock?

Although the collapse of the UR is certainly a great loss to be regretted by all concerned, I do not share the doom-and-gloom view of certain observers. This would not be the end of GATT and certainly not the end of the trading system. The agreements reached in earlier rounds would still be in force. It is feared by many that the collapse of the UR would precipitate a host of hostile bilateral trade measures, and that is certainly a possible outcome. However, the GATT discipline and the dispute-settlement mechanism remains in place, and can reduce the intensity of such conflicts. But the main anxiety is about the division of the world into three trading blocs: the EC, the Americas, and Asia.

Certainly one can expect some acceleration of the trend towards the formation of regional blocs. But the trend itself existed with or without a successful UR. The EC has already emerged as a unified market, and it might be extended in the future to incorporate EFTA. It may even be further augmented (perhaps in a loose form) by some east European countries. In North America, the U.S.-

Canada FTA is likely to be extended to Mexico, thus forming a three-country NAFTA, which would combine Canadian resources, U.S. technology, and Mexican labor. Negotiations with Mexico are difficult, given the disparity in living standards and labor costs. And organized labor in the United States is on record as opposing an FTA for fear of the loss of thousands of jobs. But it is not clear that there would be more than small (net) job losses and a mere transitional adjustment. First, in the absence of an FTA some U.S. jobs would flow to low-labor–cost countries in the Far East. Yet jobs shifted to Mexico, and the attendant economic gains there are more likely to be recycled back to the United States as income spent on goods and services than jobs shifted to Asia. Second, integrating manufacturing with Mexico will make U.S. firms more competitive in third markets, which in turn would create extra jobs in export industries in the United States. Finally, Mexican economic growth would lead to increased demand for U.S. exports. Once concluded, a North American FTA may be extended to incorporate certain South American countries. Formation of these two blocs could force the ASEAN group and the Asian NICs (and perhaps even Australia and New Zealand) to seek some form of association with the United States or with Japan.

Thus the emergence of a tripolar system: the Americas, Europe, and the Asian blocs are a much discussed and somewhat maligned topic in the literature. But this development is likely to have taken place even if the UR had succeeded. Furthermore, a superpessimistic view of this development is reached only by comparing a perfectly functioning global GATT system with "inward-looking," highly protectionistic, and discriminatory regional blocs. Yet the GATT system has never been perfect. Much of the world trade is not covered by GATT rules, while the sectors so covered contain many "grey-area" measures not sanctioned by GATT. The global landscape is filled with bilateral trade initiatives, such as the U.S.-Japan, U.S.-Korea and U.S.-Taiwan negotiations on various issues, while bilateral retaliations and counter-retaliations between the United States and the EC abound. Many trade disputes were resolved bilaterally. There has never been an all-encompassing, smoothly functioning GATT system.

On the other hand, regional blocs need not be "inward looking." Given their size and composition each can easily result in net trade creation, and many objectives unattainable on a global level can be achieved within a smaller region. In fact, fear that a "closed" bloc would have a domino effect on other blocs is the best insurance against a "fortress Europe" or "fortress North America" or "fortress Asia." Threats of retaliation by the "other" blocs may induce each bloc to maintain openness. Indeed past data show that for each of the three regions, extra-bloc trade is too important for it to be sacrificed by a closed arrangement. No region is in a position to severely curtail its relation with the rest of the world. Thus each of the regional blocs may provide a forum for "deep integration" where countries adjust to outside competition. Even some convergence of national policies can be effected within such groupings.

And the three regions may form the building blocks (rather than become stumbling blocks) which would subsequently be connected, albeit loosely, to a more open, integrated global system. GATT would have an important role to play in facilitating that transition. In addition to its traditional roles, GATT would need to ascertain that newly emerging regional blocs are "outward" rather than "inward" looking. But because GATT has no enforcement mechanism it would concentrate on surveillance, and much of the enforcement on each region would come from the counterweight exercised by the other regions.

The upshot of this argument is that movement towards liberalization of international transactions can proceed along two parallel tracks: deep integration within three or more regions, and more superficial integration on a global scale within the GATT system. But the regional integration movement would still have to meet the GATT rules with respect to customs unions and free trade areas, ensuring the relative openness of each bloc.

NOTES

1. The countries belonging to the Cairns Group are Argentina, Australia, Brazil, Canada, Chile, Colombia, Hungary, Indonesia, Malaysia, New Zealand, the Philippines, Thailand, and Uruguay.

REFERENCES

Hoekman, Bernard. "Market Access and Multilateral Trade Agreements: The Uruguay Round Services Negotiations" (Paper prepared for a conference on the Political Economy of International Market access, National Bureau of Economic Research, February 1992.)

Kreinin, Mordechai E. *International Economics: A Policy Approach,* 6th ed. (Orlando: Harcourt Brace Jovanovich, 1991), Chapter 16.

Chapter 2

Antidumping after the Uruguay Round: A Former Administrator's Perspective

*Alfred E. Eckes**

Abstract *In the absence of harmonized competition policies, vigorous national enforcement of the GATT Antidumping Code remains essential to protect producers against the harmful impact of predatory pricing practices in the evolving global economy. Rather than diluting existing rules approved in the Tokyo Round negotiations, GATT should seek to harmonize administrative procedures, improve transparency, and eliminate circumvention so as to heighten predictability and fairness.*

DEFINITION AND ENFORCEMENT HISTORY

Among economists many discussions begin with Jacob Viner's 1923 definition of dumping as "price-discrimination between national markets" (Viner, 1966). Useful as this language remains to focus the issue, one must approach the current policy debate through the language of GATT, which after all was written by diplomats and lawyers, not economists.

Article VI of GATT defines dumping as the introduction of the products of one country into the commerce of another at less than their normal value in the exporting country. It is important to note that Article VI authorizes the use of offsetting duties only when such dumping causes or threatens material injury, or materially retards the establishment of a domestic industry (GATT, 1979).

During the Tokyo Round, which concluded in 1979, GATT members drafted an Antidumping Code that elaborates on this language and seeks to harmonize certain procedures and practices. Subsequently, member nations, including the United States, took steps to bring their administration procedures into conformity with the code.

From the vantage point of the 1990s, the code launched a trade enforcement revolution. Prior to 1980, only developed countries, particularly the United

---

*Professor Eckes was a Commissioner on the U.S. International Trade Commission, 1981 to 1990, and Chairman from June 1982 to June 1984.

States, the European Community, Canada, and Australia, had employed anti-dumping measures, and these had done so irregularly. But in the 1980s these four countries initiated more than 1000 antidumping investigations, half of which led to dumping duties (*Financial Times*, 1989). And a number of developing countries (e.g., Mexico, Korea, and Brazil) also began to employ antidumping procedures, many of these against the computer and chemical exports of U.S. multinationals. As a result, supporters of more active enforcement would look back at the 1980s as a "golden era," whereas critics, from exporting countries and multinational firms, would view the trend as troubling evidence of an emerging procedural protectionism.

To understand the magnitude of the antidumping enforcement revolution, one must recall that there were few antidumping orders issued before the 1970s, even though Canada, Australia, and South Africa first enacted antidumping measures before World War I. For instance, in the United States, from 1955 to 1967 the Treasury Department and Tariff Commission, which had joint responsibility for administering dumping law, processed 371 complaints, but made only 12 dumping findings, a success ratio for domestic industries of 3% (Senate, 1968). As one critic observed in 1957, the "Antidumping act is about as near extinction as the whooping cranes . . . " (House, 1957).

Indeed, when U.S. administrators occasionally did issue dumping findings, the orders frequently were not enforced. During one 12-year period from 1946 to 1958, the Treasury collected only $370 in antidumping duties, an average of $31 per year (Senate, 1958). There are several obvious explanations for this lax enforcement pattern. For one thing, until the steep tariff cuts negotiated during the Kennedy Round of multilateral trade negotiations all took effect in 1972, tariffs on many manufactured items remained sufficiently high to discourage trade at either fair or unfair price levels. In addition, foreign policy considerations often militated against imposition of dumping duties, where the White House and State Department took the view that vigorous antidumping enforcement could jeopardize larger commercial, political, and military goals, most particularly the desire to facilitate reconstruction of Western Europe and Japan.

However, as import competition intensified in the 1970s, Congress grew increasingly restive with lax enforcement. In particular, the plight of domestic television producers gained considerable attention. Although this industry won an antidumping case against Japanese exporters in 1971, the Treasury Department declined to collect dumping duties. Indeed, in 1978, according to the General Accounting Office, an estimated $700 million in dumping duties remained uncollected (House, 1978).

From an administrative perspective, the Tokyo Round Antidumping Code inaugurated a more active era. In the United States, for instance, implementing legislation provided for timely, transparent, and reasonably predictable decision making. There were mandatory provisions, specific deadlines, and requirements for judicial review to ensure fairness. This system replaced discretionary administrative rulings that sometimes seemed to resemble star-chamber proceedings. Parties with complaints increasingly availed themselves of the quasi-judicial trade-remedy process. On December 31, 1990, the United States had 202 antidumping orders in place, up from 109 six years earlier. Only 44 orders dated from before 1980. It is also important to note that a substantial number (51) of the orders applied to Japanese products. Incidentally, this was more than from all members of the European Community (43).[1] Another 24 involved exports from China and Taiwan. Fifteen dumping orders applied to Canadian goods, but only three to products flowing across our southern border from Mexico (International Trade Commission, 1991).

ANTIDUMPING OPPOSED IN URUGUAY ROUND DEBATE

More vigorous administration of antidumping statutes produced a spirited debate in the first phase of the Uruguay Round negotiations, which concluded in December 1990. On one side, exporting nations, led by Korea, Hong Kong, and Japan, as well as a number of global corporations, sought to dilute the codes and to restrain aggressive enforcement.

Although some advocates of this position had a pecuniary stake in the outcome, such as traders and lawyers, others eager to dismantle the codes were old-fashioned free traders with a romantic vision of the global marketplace. For some of them antidumping was an anachronism of a less complicated era when internationally traded goods were produced wholly in one country and exported to another along the lines of comparative advantage. In such circumstances, the nation state could clearly identify with the interests of domestic workers, managers, investors, and consumers in its trade-remedy actions (Brunsdale, 1989).

But advocates of this position alleged that in the era of the global factory domestic interests were less easy to define and to regulate. A product with a U.S. label might consist of labor-intensive components produced in Singapore, capital-intensive components produced in Europe, with only final assembly in the United States. And a Japanese firm might perform that final assembly. In such circumstances, proponents of less regulation allege, natural market forces are surpassing the ability of trade administrators to regulate trade with simple straightforward rules. Thus, from this perspective the proliferation of national antidumping procedures threaten to stifle the benefits all enjoy from commercial innovation.

One example of this problem frequently cited involves antidumping duties imposed on computer chips from Japan. After authorities invoked duties, officials discovered that producers needing cheap chips simply moved assembly operations offshore to third countries where dumped chips could be obtained free from offsetting tariffs. Thus, from the free trade perspective, efforts to protect some domestic industries from unfair competition simply doomed others, the consumers of dumped inputs, to "second-rate status in the world market" (Brunsdale, 1989).

DUMPING ADMINISTRATION DEFENDED

On the other side of this issue, governments of the European Community and the United States remained staunch backers of active antidumping administration. In both economic regions, politically articulate producers of steel, textiles, automobiles, electronics, and other products mobilized their political resources. They considered antidumping one of the few mechanisms left to combat unfair foreign competition. These manufacturers took the position that the existing Antidumping Code should be strengthened, not gutted, to address new problems such as trade diversion and circumvention. Also, the code should be revised to include more transparent procedures to protect exporters against arbitrary and capricious administrative practices in developing countries. Some of these manufacturers conceded that in the 21st century the global economy might evolve to the point where common competition policies could substitute for national antidumping procedures, but in the interim they considered preservation of the present regime essential to their own competitive survival.

As one who has devoted 9 years to administration of U.S. antidumping law at the U.S. International Trade Commission (ITC) and has had the opportunity in the course of some 435 separate investigations to examine recent dumping practices closely, I find myself sympathetic to those who favor retaining and strengthening the Antidumping Codes.

Without a doubt, the pace of internationalization is raising a host of issues not anticipated when the dumping code was drafted. When I became an ITC Commissioner in 1981, most petitioners represented traditional domestic industries. And, in a typical case, American owners or American workers with American production facilities sought to invoke U.S. laws against foreign unfair trade practices. But, over the decade of the 1980s the cheap dollar and fears of U.S. protectionism helped trigger a surge of foreign investment, so that today a typical petitioner may have foreign ownership, and may seek to utilize U.S. laws against products manufactured or assembled abroad by U.S.-owned firms. Increasingly, then, it is difficult to identify the domestic industry, because many competitors, domestic and foreign, import components to take maximum advantage of favorable global sourcing patterns. Indeed, there are even instances where unions have identified with importer interests. Thus, from the standpoint of the government official it is not always easy to distinguish "Who Is Us" (Reich, 1990).

However, I find this difficulty a challenge to trade administrators, not a fatal impediment to the present regime. My greater concern is the meteoric growth of injurious dumping in the global economy. Some economists might think that with globalization dumping would become increasingly rare, for, after all, it depends on the presence of marketplace distortions, such as transportation costs and re-entry barriers. These prevent a buyer of dumped merchandise from reselling the item to consumers in the exporting country, and thus engaging in arbitrage. In point of fact, dumping appears to be increasing, a consequence of lower tariff barriers, improved transportation and communications, and a variety of new suppliers taking advantage of home-market barriers to dump abroad.

The motives for dumping vary widely. Some cases involve sporadic sales of surplus agricultural products, like raspberries, but the substantial majority appear to involve capital-intensive, oligopolistic industries. Firms in such industries frequently indulge in excess-capacity dumping, when supply exceeds demand, because they need to make regular payments on heavy fixed costs. Thus these producers dispose of surplus production in foreign markets at discount prices without regard to the impact of dumping on competition or on other firms. And, where the foreign producer is state subsidized, like European steel companies of the early 1980s, another motive for excess-capacity dumping may be political—to sustain home market employment in a cyclical downturn.

Japanese management consultant Kenichi Ohmae also apparently believes that globalization of competition will invite a proliferation of dumping. In his recent book, *The Borderless World,* Ohmae reminds us that to compete successfully in the global economy corporations must automate, and expand capacity. As a result, global corporations, whatever their ownership or nationality, are under increasing pressure to boost sales at any price so as to maximize marginal contributions to rising fixed costs (Ohmae, 1990).

Discussing the practices of Japanese businesses, Ohmae notes that when capacity exceeded growth in demand, Japanese firms cut prices to keep their factories growing. "This rapid erosion of prices knocked many American and European producers out of the industry entirely" (Ohmae, 1990). This pattern occurred with facsimile machines, photocopiers, office automation, watches, color televisions, automobiles, semiconductors, and shipbuilding. Peter Drucker also has observed the trend toward "adversarial" trade in which Asian competitors with closed home markets attack foreign markets for the purpose of driving competitors out of the market (Drucker, 1989).

Participation in ITC dumping investigations also introduced me to preemptive dumping, a phenomenon seen especially in new technologies, where products may have short life cycles, and the development of new products depends on experience with previous products or use of acquired skills. It is my impression that some Japanese producers have engaged in bargain-basement pricing to drive out or deter new competitors, and to achieve cost advantages from large volume production.

Thus, in the absence of a global competition policy, I do not believe the public interest is served in America, Europe, or elsewhere if companies with deep pockets and bountiful financial resources, combined with protected home markets, succeed in dumping. Such a result can only reduce the field of competitors, harm competition, discourage future investments, and, over time, drive up prices and harm consumer interests. In the present unstable world, the concentration of high-technology electronics production in one or two countries may be incompatible with the long-term security needs and interests of major industrial nations.

In my mind dumping in any form contributes to resource misallocations. Such price discrimination harms consumers in the exporting country, and enables foreign producers in protected home markets to generate profits and so subsidize export prices. For the importing country the short-term benefit to consumers of buying dumped products may conflict with the longer-term national and private interest, if it reduces the pool of competition or prevents a growth industry from developing the profitability and cash flow required to generate new product generations (Eckes, 1987).

Vigorous administration of existing antidumping laws is not procedural protectionism, in my view. Rather, the trade administrators are the real champions of free trade. For, in battling dumpers, they not only help sustain political support for an open global trading system, but they bring benefits to consumers as well as producers. I remember well how imposition of U.S. antidumping duties against Korean television makers prompted them to lower high home market prices in order to avoid the payment of U.S. dumping duties.

From my vantage point there is another persuasive argument for sustaining strong national antidumping procedures. The world political economy is in transition—but the future is unclear. In Eastern Europe remnants of central planning remain, even as market economies emerge. In Western Europe, Canada, and some other countries, governments continue to use subsidies for favored industries. And in Japan firms remain insulated from outside competition, and continue to attack the global market from a secure home base. Elsewhere, as in the United States, market forces are largely dominant. Given the diversity of national economic regimes, it is arguable that antidumping laws are needed to help mediate between economic systems and to prevent disruptive distortions (Jackson, 1989).

STRENGTHENING THE ANTIDUMPING CODE

In my view a successful outcome to the Uruguay Round, or some successor GATT negotiation, requires attention to several emerging problems. For one thing, under current circumstances, it is relatively easy for dumpers to outmaneuver government administrators. Flexible sourcing decisions often permit them to circumvent dumping orders in a variety of imaginative ways. Moreover, there is a need to address openly the problem of repeat offenders. And to facilitate the growth of international trade, particularly with developing countries, the GATT system needs to press forward with provisions to provide greater transparency and due process for firms caught up in national antidumping cases.

In my judgment, the judicial trade administration process, despite its flaws and costs, has proven preferable to the old system of capricious administrators and star-chamber proceedings.

NOTES

1. If the European Community is treated as a single economic unit, and duplicate orders against producers in individual nation states are consolidated, the United States has only 26 antidumping orders (not 43) outstanding against the European Community.

REFERENCES

Brunsdale, Anne E. "Global Industries and U.S. Trade Laws." Unpublished speech, International Trade Commission, 1989.

Drucker, Peter F. *The New Realities* (New York: Harper & Row, 1989).

Eckes, Alfred E. "The Interface of Antitrust and Trade Laws—Conflict or Harmony?" *Antitrust Law Journal* 56(2) (1987): 417–424.

Eckes, Alfred E. "Dumping Code: Time for Worry." *Journal of Commerce,* Oct. 29, 1990.

"GATT Warns on Use of Antidumping Measures." *Financial Times* (London), Dec. 12, 1989.

General Agreement on Tariffs and Trade. *Agreement on Interpretation and Application of Articles VI, XVI and XXIII of GATT* (Geneva: GATT, 1979).

International Trade Commission. *Operations of the Trade Agreements Program* (42nd Report) Washington, DC: USITC Pub. No. 2403, 1991.

Jackson, John H. *The World Trading System: Law and Policy of International Economic Relations* (Cambridge, MA: MIT Press, 1989).

Ohmae, Kenichi. *The Borderless World: Power and Strategy in the Interlinked Economy* (New York: Harper Business, 1990).

Reich, Robert. "Who Is Us?" *Harvard Business Review* 90 (1990):1, 53–64.

U.S. House of Representatives, Ways and Means Committee. (1957). *Amendments to Antidumping Act of 1921, as Amended* Hearings (84,1), p. 134.

U.S. House of Representatives, Ways and Means Committee. (1978). *Administration of the Antidumping Act of 1921* Hearings (95,2).

U.S. Senate, Finance Committee. (1958). *Antidumping.* Hearings (85,2), pp. 48–56.

U.S. Senate, Finance Committee. (1968). *International Antidumping Code.* Hearings (90,2), p. 71.

Viner, Jacob. *Dumping: A Problem in International Trade* (New York: Augustus M. Kelley, 1966).

Chapter 3

The Cost to Latin America
of Adopting Unfair Trade Policies

Julio Nogués

Abstract *The social costs of unfair trade policies to Latin America will increase in the upcoming years. During the 1980s, Latin America suffered significantly when industrial countries applied numerous unfair trade measures against its exports. For example, during those years the average antidumping duty applied by the U.S. against important export industries of Latin America was 32%, i.e. around ten times higher than the average duty paid on U.S. imports. These costs will continue to increase as numerous Latin American countries are themselves adopting unfair trade policies. In fact, there exists a systematic pattern that shows these policies to gain prominence as other protectionist policies are dismantled. Latin America should stop this process and consider instead the importance of protecting its industries with appropriate macroeconomic policies, realistic exchange rates, and eventually balanced safeguard measures.*

INTRODUCTION*

This chapter makes two points. First, during the 1980s the costs to Latin America of industrial countries' unfair trade policies were very high. Second, the forecast for the 1990s is one of continued high cost. Nevertheless, during this decade, as these countries become active users of unfair trade policies, the origins of these costs will probably shift from industrial to Latin American countries.

The next section presents some figures on the height of antidumping duties against Latin America's exports during the 1980s; the section following that one does the same with countervailing duties. Both sections conclude that Latin

---

*Many of the arguments presented in this and the next section are developed in Nogués (1991a).

American countries have suffered significantly from industrial countries' administration of these unfair policies. As Latin American countries have introduced trade liberalization measures, pressures from interest groups for introducing or activating unfair trade policies are mounting. The section also shows that Latin American governments are giving in to these pressures. Therefore, we may predict that during the 1990s these countries will introduce increasing unfair trade measures. The concluding sections remind policymakers that policy options exist for protecting domestic industries during the transition to more open and competitive economies. These options entail significantly lower social costs than those attributed to unfair trade policies.

DUMPING AND ANTIDUMPING INVESTIGATIONS

Economic and legal aspects

In international trade literature, dumping is usually identified with predatory pricing actions that seek to displace producers from a market in order to establish monopoly prices. Therefore, antidumping actions applied against predatory pricing are welfare-enhancing.

Article VI of the GATT defines dumping as occurring when the "products of one country are introduced into the commerce of another country at less-than-normal values." Normal value is the domestic sale price in the exporting country. Dumping, as defined by the GATT, can occur in several circumstances. It can occur in a recessionary period when low export prices can help to increase exports and cover fixed costs, when the exporter has its domestic market protected, when exports are subsidized, and when there is predatory pricing. Thus, the GATT definition of dumping is clearly biased towards protection. Furthermore, administrative regulations also facilitate the introduction of AD measures. For example, it has been noticed by Banks (1991), that the practice of constructing normal values as opposed to using market prices biases the estimates of dumping margins in favor of positive findings.

In short, given the conditions of strong competition prevailing in international trade of most goods, the possibilities of undertaking successful predatory actions are highly unlikely. This is particularly true of relatively small countries and enterprises. As Palmeter concludes " . . . predatory pricing schemes are rarely tried and [are] even more rarely successful . . . " (Palmeter 1988, p. 6).

Antidumping Actions Against Latin-American Countries

The statistics of the GATT shown in table 1 indicate that between 1980 and 1988 a total of 1689 antidumping investigations were initiated by industrial countries. This represents a significant increase over previous periods. For example, between 1975 and 1979, the United States initiated 97 antidumping cases, whereas during 1980 and 1988 the number of cases increased to 411. On an annual average basis, this represents an increase of 235%.[1]

Table 1

Import Relief Measures Initiated by Type of Policy and by Country, 1979–1988

Type of action	1979	1980	1981	1982	1983	1984	1985	1986	1987	1988	Total 1979–1988
World (percent of total)											
Antidumping	59.0	89.3	77.0	61.8	78.9	74.0	78.0	84.9	84.1	89.9	76.9
Countervailing duty	33.3	9.4	13.2	35.4	13.4	22.3	16.9	11.1	6.3	6.9	18.0
GATT safeguard	0.0	0.0	0.6	0.5	1.1	0.4	0.4	0.7	0.5	0.0	0.5
Escape clause	3.4	1.3	3.4	0.7	3.8	2.6	4.3	2.3	6.3	0.9	2.7
Other	4.3	0.0	5.7	1.6	2.7	0.7	0.4	1.0	2.9	2.3	1.9
World (number of actions)											
All actions	117	149	174	432	261	273	255	298	207	218	2384
USA											
Antidumping	16	24	15	63	47	73	65	70	14	40	427
Countervailing duty	37	11	22	145	22	52	38	26	5	13	371
GATT safeguard	0	0	0	0	2	0	0	0	0	0	2
Escape clause	4	2	6	1	5	6	3	3	2	2	34
Other	5	—	10	7	7	2	1	3	4	5	44
European Community											
Antidumping	53	26	47	55	43	42	35	31	34	40	406
Countervailing duty	2	0	1	4	3	1	0	0	2	0	13
GATT safeguard	0	0	0	1	0	1	1	2	1	0	6
Escape clause	0	0	0	2	5	1	8	4	11	0	31
Other	0	0	0	0	0	0	0	0	2	0	2
Australia											
Antidumping	N.A.	58	49	77	80	56	63	62	17	16	478
Countervailing duty	N.A.	0	0	3	7	6	3	3	0	0	22
GATT safeguard	N.A.	0	0	0	1	0	0	0	0	0	1
Canada											
Antidumping	N.A.	25	23	72	36	31	36	85	86	53	447
Countervailing duty	N.A.	3	0	1	3	2	2	4	6	2	23
GATT safeguard	N.A.	0	1	1	0	0	0	0	0	0	2
Developing countries											
Antidumping	0	0	0	0	0	0	0	5	23	47	75
Countervailing duty	0	0	0	0	0	0	0	0	0	0	0
GATT safeguard	0	0	0	0	0	0	0	0	0	0	0

Source: Messerlin (1990).

N.A. = not available.

Recently Finger and Murray (1990) have presented figures on U.S. anti-dumping cases; and those against Latin America are presented in table 2. According to U.S. legislation, an affirmative antidumping case can end with an undertaking or the imposition of antidumping duties. In an undertaking, the exporter usually agrees to raise its export price so as to eliminate the margin of dumping. As seen, most cases ended with undertakings but in the case of the smaller countries, they often ended with the imposition of antidumping duties.

Table 2
U.S. Antidumping and Countervailing Cases

	Antidumping					Countervailing				
	Restrictive			Not		Restrictive			Not	
	Under-taking	Other	Total	restrictive	Total	Under-taking	Other	Total	restrictive	Total
Argentina	0	2	2	3	5	0	4	4	2	6
Brazil	14	2	16	5	21	24	4	28	7	35
Chile	0	2	2	0	2	0	1	1	0	1
Costa Rica	0	1	1	0	1	0	2	2	0	2
Colombia	0	1	1	3	4	0	3	3	1	4
Ecuador	0	1	1	0	1	0	1	1	0	1
El Salvador	0	0	0	1	1	0	0	0	1	0
Mexico	3	2	5	1	6	6	21	27	2	29
Peru	0	0	0	1	1	0	2	2	2	4
Uruguay	0	0	0	0	0	0	1	1	0	1
Venezuela	10	1	11	1	12	8	1	9	0	9
Total	27	12	39	15	54	38	40	78	15	92

Source: Finger and Murray (Annex Tables, 1990).

More importantly, table 3 shows that the incidence of industrial countries' antidumping investigations against the highly indebted Latin American countries has grown at least until 1986.[2]

Given the legal definition of dumping, this increase in the incidence of antidumping cases against Latin American countries is not surprising. As stated, during those years, Latin American countries were undergoing a serious recessionary period. Therefore, these countries were vulnerable to the legal definition of dumping. In a world where sensible economics would have guided policy actions, unfair trade measures would not be applied against Latin Ameri-

Table 3
Percentage of Antidumping Cases
Against Highly Indebted Latin American Countries,
1980–1986

	Percentage (%)	
Country	1980–1981	1982–1986
EEC	2.7	7.1
US	2.7	16.5

Source: Nogués (1991a), Table 2.

can countries as it would have been unlikely to find these countries engaging in predatory pricing actions against the United States or other industrial countries.

Table 4 shows the range and simple average antidumping duties of U.S. investigations against Latin American countries. The figures show a range that goes from 2% in a case against Brazil to 119% in a case against Argentina. The simple average antidumping duty across countries is 32%. This average is nearly 10 times higher than the average duty paid by U.S. imports.

Unfortunately, there is yet no measure of the trade and resource allocation effect of U.S. antidumping actions against Latin America, but, for example, Staiger and Wolak (1991) have recently concluded that in the United States "imposition of [antidumping] duties leads to the expected negative impact on imports and positive impact on domestic output." It is also of interest to quote Messerlin (1988) when he analyzes the trade effect of the European Community (EC) antidumping actions. In his estimates, Messerlin shows that after the first year of initiating an antidumping action, imports of the goods affected by these actions declined by 18%. Five years later, these imports declined by 50%. This significant import-restricting effect of antidumping actions has taken place during a period (1980–1986) in which imports from outside the EC grew significantly. The average antidumping duty in Messerlin's study is 14%. In contrast, the average U.S. antidumping duty against Latin American countries is more than twice as high. Thus, by inference, it is likely that Latin American exports caught by antidumping actions have been seriously harmed.

To be sure, antidumping and countervailing duties have usually fallen on important export industries or on emerging ones with good export potential. Examples include orange juice exports of Brazil (Braga and Silber 1991), the cut flower industries of several countries including Colombia and Costa Rica

Table 4
Range and Average U.S. Antidumping Margins
Against Highly Indebted Latin American Countries*

Country	Range (%)	Simple average (%)
Argentina	69–119	94
Brazil	2–87	33
Chile	2–27	14
Colombia	4–83	27
Ecuador	3–19	9
Mexico	21	21
Venezuela	5–56	29
Sample	2–119	32

*Only affirmative antidumping investigations are included. The figures include 1980–1986 cases.
Source: Nogués (1991a), Table 3.

(Mendez 1991), Argentina's leather wearing apparel, etc. It has also been estimated that 9.5% of Brazil's exports pay antidumping duties in the United States and another 6.9% are affected by antidumping and countervailing undertakings (Bouzas 1991).

EXPORT SUBSIDIES AND COUNTERVAILING DUTIES

Legal and Economic Aspects of Countervailing Duties

Starting from the principle that there is unfair trade when exports are being subsidized, countervailing duties are used to compensate for the unfair edge provided by subsidies. Although the economic principle of countervailing duties is simple, in practice its application is not. Much of the real-world complications follow from the lack of a generalized agreement on what is a subsidy, and which are and are not countervailable.

For example, Article VIII of the Subsidy Code (formally the Agreement on Interpretation of Articles VI, XIV & XXIII of the GATT), asserts that countries that use subsidies should try to avoid injuring industries of other countries. But the Subsidy Code also recognizes the right of a country to introduce countervailing duties when a domestic industry has been injured by the subsidies. Thus, the language of the Subsidy Code is inconclusive, and the countries that negotiated this Code were only able to annex an "illustrative" list of subsidies that are not accepted in international trade.

Countervailing-Duty Cases Against Latin American Countries

Table 1 showed that between 1980 and 1988, industrial countries initiated 390 countervailing-duty investigations. Of this total, 334 were processed in the United States, 22 in Australia, 23 in Canada, and 9 in the EC. Therefore, among industrial countries, the United States is "the" countervailer.

As with the case of antidumping duties, the 1980s witnessed a significant growth in the number of countervailing-duty investigations. For example, between 1975 and 1979, the United States processed 104 countervailing-duty investigations, that is, an annual average of 21 cases. Between 1980 and 1988, the annual average increased to 43.

Why is it that the United States is by far the most important user of countervailing duties? One hypothesis is that countries that subsidize their exports have a higher tendency to sell in the U.S. market. Another hypothesis is that other industrial countries have more subsidy programs than the United States and, therefore, feel less inclined to use countervailing duties (Nam 1987). A less moral argument—and we need one in order to make room for U.S. agricultural export subsidies—suggests that other countries prefer to use antidumping investigations in order to countervail for subsidies.

Table 5 shows the range and simple average countervailing duties against Latin American countries. The range goes from 1% in a CVD case against

Table 5
Range and Average U.S. Countervailing Duty
Margins of Cases
Against Latin American Countries

	Range (%)	Simple average
Argentina	1–16	5
Brazil	3–25	12
Chile	12	12
Colombia	2–16	7
Costa Rica	15–20	17
Ecuador	1	1
Mexico	1–105	9
Peru	2–44	25
Uruguay	2	2
Venezuela	60–76	69
Total	1–105	15

Source: Nogués (1991a), Table 4.

Argentina, up to 105% in a case against Mexico. The simple average CVD rate across countries is 15%. This is more than four times higher than the weighted average tariff rate paid by U.S. imports. Again, it is reasonable to hypothesize that this level of countervailing duties must have had a serious impact on exporters who have been found to be receiving subsidies from their governments. Note that this average countervailing-duty rate is close to the average antidumping rate studied by Messerlin (1988) in the case of the EC. Also recall that Messerlin found a significant import effect on goods that had been affected by antidumping duties.

Before discussing the effects of export subsidies and countervailing duties, it might be of interest to comment on the likely reasons for the growth of U.S. countervailing duties during the 1980s. First, as discussed, one could attribute the growth of countervailing duty investigations to a higher tendency by other countries to subsidize exports to the U.S. market. In contrast it is reasonable to argue that the growth of countervailing cases could be accounted for by increasing protectionist pressures as well as an increasing willingness of governments to accept countervailing duty petitions. These are not opposing hypotheses, but I am inclined to believe that the latter provides an explanation that is closer to fact because Latin American export-subsidy programs of the 1980s are mainly a continuation of the programs that were introduced in earlier years.

If export-subsidy programs do not explain the growth of countervailing duties, then this growth must be accounted by domestic factors of industrial countries and in particular of the United States. In addition, as discussed, the growth of countervailing duties has been facilitated by legal changes. These legalities refer not only to the definition of subsidies, but also to changes in the rules making it easier to initiate countervailing duty investigations (Grinols 1988). For example, the Trade Agreement Act of 1979 shortened the period that the Department of Commerce has in order to decide whether or not to accept a countervailing duty petition. As I will argue, these changes have facilitated harassment against exporting countries.

Economic Consequences of Countervailing Duties and Export Subsidies

Finger et al. (1982) have presented quantitative evidence showing that "less-than-fair-value" policies including countervailing duties have been used as a protectionist instrument. More recently, Finger and Nogués (1987) have argued that the protectionist effects of countervailing duties are present even during the period when the investigation is being undertaken. For example, between 1980 and 1986, 35% of the countervailing duty investigations initiated in the United States had a positive preliminary outcome and a final negative; indeed, harassment appears to have been an extended practice. Furthermore, when countries are not signatories to the Subsidy Code or have not signed a bilateral agreement, the United States does not undertake the injury test in the countervailing investigations. Finger and Nogués (1987) have shown that such a test appears to have an important effect on the outcome of the final determinations. In any case, most of the Latin American countries are not signatories to the Subsidy Code, and we may conclude that harassment against these countries has been very easy.

On the other hand, export subsidies also have a negative economic effect on developing countries. For example, Latin American export subsidies are discriminatory and in general granted to products whose domestic markets are relatively more protected; usually these goods are of industrial origin (Nogués 1990a). Therefore, subsidies increase the social costs associated with protection. Second, additional welfare losses are incurred when resources are engaged in rent-seeking activities to preserve and increase export subsidies. Third, there is evidence that export subsidies have been used as an instrument for compensating declining real exchange rates or currency overvaluation. To this extent, the social costs of currency overvaluation should also be attributed, at least in part, to export subsidies (Nogués 1990b). Fifth, it is likely that social costs are incurred in the process of raising the funds to pay for export subsidies. Finally, social costs are also incurred in the presence of countervailing duties as resources are transferred from the treasury of the subsidizing country to that of the countervailing countries. Evidence that all of these factors have played a role in Argentina are presented in Nogués (1990b); the general hypothesis of this chapter is that subsidies have been anticompetitive and help to explain the economic decay of Argentina.

Adoption of Unfair Trade Policies:
The Case of Antidumping

The paper by Finger et al. (1982) predicted the dangers of antidumping and other administrative protection instruments. The experience of the 1980s proved this forecast to be correct. That paper showed that in the United States these policies have been easily captured by interest groups. The previous section argued that during the 1980s Latin American countries suffered significantly from them. Unfortunately, along this process, these countries learned how administrative protection operates, and how handy these instruments can be to provide import relief. Best of all, they are sanctioned by the GATT.

It is not surprising to observe that as the number of Latin American countries introducing trade liberalization measures increases, they become enthusiastic supporters of unfair trade policies. In recent years, Argentina, Brazil, Chile, Costa Rica, Colombia, Jamaica, Mexico, Peru, and Venezuela have all introduced or activated antidumping legislation. Several other countries including Bolivia, Ecuador, Guatemala, Panama, and Trinidad are also considering implementing similar legislation.

The use of these instruments has not reached the level observed in industrial countries. Yet a few examples of what is happening might illustrate the potential costs to Latin America of using antidumping regulations.

Argentina. The antidumping mechanism of this country violates the most basic rules of the GATT and the antidumping code. The existing legislation of Argentina is in total contradiction to the GATT. Article 717 of the Customs Code (Codigo Aduanero) states that " . . . except for evidence to the contrary, it will be presumed that there is injury to a domestic industry when the price in the international market of the imported merchandise is 15% below . . . the price of the identical domestic product . . . " (author's translation). A couple of comments: first, the legislation simply ignores the need to prove the existence of a margin of dumping, i.e., export prices below domestic sale prices in the country of export. Second, with this definition of injury, any domestic product is a potential candidate for receiving antidumping protection simply because transport costs presumably put Argentina's internal prices 15% above international prices. Resolution No. 405 of 1987 made things worse. According to this legislation, authorities can establish ex-officio " . . . a minimum export price below which antidumping duties can be automatically introduced . . . " (author's translation).

Brazil. Unlike other countries that have recently introduced antidumping mechanisms, until very recently Brazil had not introduced trade liberalization measures. This country introduced antidumping legislation because it was pressed by trading partners to dismantle some of its nontariff instruments including "pauta de valor minimo" (PVM) and "precious de referencia" (PR). These instruments had been in existence since decree-law 1111 introduced them in 1970 and were used quite often.

At the Committee on Customs Valuation of the GATT, Brazil's trading partners and particularly the USA complained that PVM and PR were inconsistent with rules on valuation. As a consequence, the committee ruled that Brazil had to dismantle these instruments. At that time, Brazil's policymakers decided that the best course of action would be to introduce an antidumping mechanism. Furthermore, it was decided that the GATT antidumping code could serve as an appropriate domestic legislation. Decree No. 93,941 of January 1987 promulgated the Agreement on Implementation of Article VI of the GATT, usually known as the antidumping code.

It is clear that Brazil's antidumping legislation has been introduced as a substitute for other protectionist instruments and that such protection will be provided if deemed necessary. As a matter of fact, recent newspaper articles report that Brazil has initiated a number of unfair trade actions against Argentina. The latter country also has cases against Brazil.

Chile. Among Latin American countries, Chile was the first country to introduce a successful liberalization program. Yet, during the early 1980s, it faced a severe economic crisis. At this time the uniform tariff was raised from 10% to 35%. In spite of this, continued pressures led policymakers to introduce minimum import prices to industries complaining of dumping. Corbo (1991) has shown that these measures continued to be used in spite of the excellent performance in the second half of the 1980s. Chile's experience corroborates just how difficult it is to stop using these instruments once they have been introduced.

Costa Rica. To my knowledge this is the only country whose legislation has created a double antidumping mechanism: one for agricultural and another for manufactured goods. Both mechanisms are managed independently by different ministries. This legislation dates back to the late 1950s, but it has remained dormant for most of this period. It is only in recent years when trade liberalization measures were introduced that requests for antidumping protection has started. The available evidence shows that this mechanism has already been captured by interest groups (Nogués 1991b).

Mexico. Of the five countries discussed here Mexico is the one that most recently began introducing trade liberalization measures. When this liberalization process started, the complaints of highly inefficient industries prompted the government to reinforce the system of official reference prices in many of the tariff lines for which nontariff protection had been lifted. Because Mexico had also joined the Customs Valuation Code and the Antidumping Code of the GATT, it was urged by trading partners to dismantle its reference prices. By the time this occurred in December of 1987, Mexico had started to make use of antidumping measures.

In late 1988, Messerlin (1988) provided an evaluation of Mexico's antidumping measures. The following findings emerge from his analysis:

(1) In the first year, Mexico initiated more antidumping cases than the United States and 55% as many as the EC;

(2) Sectors that are particularly concerned with trade liberalization are rapidly becoming petitioners of antidumping measures;

(3) The dumping test is not undertaken appropriately and the criteria for the injury test are extremely vague;

(4) In comparison to industrial countries where approximately 30% of the cases end with a negative finding, in Mexico it is only 8%;

(5) The unweighted average ad valorem duty is extremely high;

(6) The petitioners generally represent close to 100% of their respective markets.

As consequence, Messerlin (1988) concluded that the " . . . Mexican antidumping system is being captured by some large firms" (p. 9).

In summary, this section has presented evidence that the antidumping mechanisms of developing countries works in much the same way as those of industrial countries, that is, they grant protection to the domestic producers. Thus, trade liberalization measures introduced by these countries are threatened by the introduction and activation of antidumping measures.

CONCLUSION

Economic analysis has demonstrated convincingly that unfair trade policies provide protection. For example, under conditions of high competition in international trade, the likelihood of successful predatory actions is minimal. Therefore, our first policy lesson is that the best defense against these actions is precisely to maintain a high degree of international competition and not to resort to antidumping actions.

Unfortunately, this is a lesson that industrial countries refused to learn. For their part, during the 1980s and following sound policy prescriptions, numerous Latin American countries have introduced far-reaching liberalization measures. Unfortunately, the resistance to these policies put forward by interest groups plus the fact that unfair trade policies provide protection that is sanctioned by the GATT have prompted the governments of these countries to introduce or activate antidumping legislation.

The brief experience shows that in Latin America, unfair trade policies are being captured by interest groups. Therefore, during the 1990s, it is likely that the costs to these countries from unfair trade measures will come more from the actions initiated by them then by other countries, including industrial countries who hit them so hard during the 1980s.

What can be done? Our policy recommendation is that the best measures to protect domestic industries come from a stable macro-economy and a realistic exchange rate. Currency overvaluation heeds protectionist pressures and instability of real exchange rates retards exports (Corbo and Caballero 1988). In Latin America much remains to be done on this issue.

Finally, if for political and economic reasons special protection should be provided during a liberalization program, the adoption of safeguard mechanisms should be considered. Safeguards unlike unfair trade policies are applied on a "most favored nation" basis. But such safeguard mechanisms should be operated in a democratic fashion, meaning that those that might get hurt by these measures have voice and vote at the time of deciding on their introduction (Nogués 1991b).

NOTES

1. Because of data availability, from here on most of the empirical findings refer to U.S. unfair trade cases.
2. The lists of highly indebted countries are those of the World Bank.

REFERENCES

Banks, Gary, "Australia's Antidumping Experience," The World Bank, PRE Working Paper No. 551, December 1991.

Braga, Carlos and Silber, Simao, "Brazilian Frozen Concentrated Orange Juice: The Folly of Unfair Trade Cases," The World Bank, PRE Working Paper No. 687, May 1991.

Bouzas, Roberto, "A U.S. Mercosur Free Trade Area: A Preliminary Assessment," Facultad Latinoamericana de Ciencias Sociales (mimeo), 1991.

Corbo, Vittorio and Caballero, Ricardo, "Export Pessimism Empirical Evidence of the Role of Uncertainty and Imperfect Competition," The World Book (mimeo), 1988.

Corbo, Vittorio, "Chile's Trade Policies: An Update," The World Bank (mimeo), 1991.

Finger, J. Michael, Hall, H. Keith and Nelson, Douglas, "The Political Economy of Administered Protection," *The American Economic Review,* June 1982.

Finger, J. Michael and Nogués, Julio, "International Control of Subsidies and Countervailing Duties," *The World Bank Economic Review,* September 1987.

Finger, J. Michael and Tracy Murray, "Policing Unfair Imports: The United States Example," *Journal of World Trade,* August 1990.

GATT, *Agreement on Implementation of Article VI of the GATT,* GATT, Geneva, 1986.

GATT, *Agreement on Interpretation and Application of Articles VI, XVI and XXIII of the GATT,* GATT, Geneva, 1986.

Grinols, Earl, "Procedural Protectionism: The American Trade Bill and the New Interventionist Mode," National Bureau of Economic Research for the International Seminar in International Trade (mimeo), 1988.

Havrylyshyn, Oli, "The Experience of Yugoslavia," in vol. 3, *The Experience of Israel and Yugoslavia,* in series *Liberalizing Foreign Trade* ed. by D. Papageorgiou, M. Michaely, and A. M. Choksi, Oxford: Basil Blackwell, 1990.

Mendez, José A., "The Developments of the Colombian Cut Flower Industry," The World Bank, PRE Working Paper No. 660, May 1991.

Messerlin, Patrick, "Antidumping Laws and Developing Countries," The World Bank, PRE Working Paper WPS 16, June 1988.

Messerlin, Patrick, "Antidumping," in Jeffrey Schott, *Completing the Uruguay Round,* Institute for International Economics, 1990.

Nam, Chong-Hyun, "Export Promoting Subsidies, Countervailing Threats and the General Agreement on Tariffs and Trade," *The World Bank Economic Review,* September 1987.

Nogués, Julio, *Latin America's Experience with Export Subsidies,* PRE Working Paper 182, The World Bank, International Economics Dept., Washington, D.C., processed, 1989.

Nogués, Julio, "Latin America's Experience with Export Subsidies," *Weltwirtschaftliches Archiv* (Review of World Economics), Band 126, Heft 1, 1990a.

Nogués, Julio, "Observations on the Links Between Subsidies and Economic Decay in Argentina," *Desarrollo Económico,* April–June 1990b.

Nogués, Julio, "Less Than Fair Trade Cases Against Latin-American Countries," *The World Economy,* September 1991a.

Nogués, Julio, "Antidumping vs. Safeguards During a Trade Liberalization Process," The World Bank (mimeo), 1991b.

Palmeter, N. David, "The Capture of the Antidumping Law," *Yale Journal of International Law,* 1988.

Rajaram, Anand, "Tariff and Tax Reforms: Do Bank Recommendations Adequately Integrate Revenue and Protection Objectives?" The World Bank, Country Economic Dept., Washington, D.C., processed, 1989.

Staiger, Robert and Wolak, Frank. "The Determinants and Impacts of Antidumping Suit Petitions in the United States: An Industry-Level Analysis," Stanford University (mimeo), 1991.

Chapter 4

The World Bank's Experience with Trade Liberalization: Some New Light on Old Questions

John Nash

Abstract *Trade policy regimes in most developing countries were quite protectionist as of the early 1980s. In the decade of the 1980s, however, many of these countries embarked upon structural adjustment programs including trade policy reform. Reforms tended to be strongest in reducing nontariff barriers to trade and correcting overvalued exchange rates. Fewer countries significantly reduced tariff protection. Where reforms were reasonably strong and sustained, economic performance generally improved—growth of exports and GDP rose, while inflation and deficits (fiscal and trade) declined, relative to non-reforming countries. This study highlights some of the policies—with respect to exports, imports, and relations with trading partners—that have contributed to successful reforms.*

INTRODUCTION

In spite of a large body of theoretical and empirical research over many years, a number of questions about trade policy reform remain unanswered. The 1980s was a decade during which many countries undertook reforms, most with the support of the World Bank. The Bank has recently completed a study to assess the experience of countries liberalizing their trade regimes, especially those that did so in this decade (Thomas and Nash, 1992). The objectives of the study were to shed light on the unanswered questions and to identify those issues most in need of further research. This chapter discusses the conclusions of this study, how they relate to the extant literature on the subject, and the implications for future reform programs.

PREREFORM POLICIES

It is well known that the trade policies of most developing countries have been shaped by the objectives of increasing self-sufficiency and conserving foreign

51

exchange through import substitution. Policies have relied on both tariffs and nontariff barriers (NTBs) to imports. Quantifying their total effect is difficult, since it is difficult to know how much of a wedge they drive between domestic and international prices. Furthermore, their effect changes from year to year as authorities tighten or loosen restrictions. In spite of these shortcomings, tariff levels and NTB coverage are useful indicators because they are available for many countries, because they render it convenient to monitor changes in any given country over time, and because they are believed to correlate at least roughly with protection. By these measures, protection in the early to mid-1980s was much higher in developing than in high-income economies. Charges for imports in a sample of 50 developing countries averaged around 30% (compared to around 5% in OECD countries), and more importantly, NTBs covered about 40% of all tariff positions (compared to around 15% in OECD countries). Undoubtedly, these figures understate protection, since they are unweighted averages of all tariff positions, whereas protection tends to be concentrated in products where domestic production is most important.

WHAT REFORMS WERE IMPLEMENTED

Most countries that have carried out trade policy reform have done so in conjunction with adjustment loans from the World Bank, although a few major reform efforts have not been associated with such loans (e.g., Haiti, Bolivia). Our study compared 47 countries that had not received trade adjustment loans to 40 that had, and found a dramatic difference in the behavior of the real exchange rate: the unweighted average real exchange rate index for the former groups depreciated by about 4% from 1980 to 1988, while for the latter countries it depreciated by about 30%. When we looked carefully at a sub-sample of 24 loan recipients, it appeared that commercial policy reform in most countries moved at a much slower pace than exchange rate reform in the 1980 to 1987 period. In a third of these countries, little or no policy reform was actually implemented, or the reform program was substantially reversed. In a fourth of the sample (Chile, Jamaica, Korea, Mauritius, Mexico, and Turkey), reforms were quite substantial.

In general, more significant changes were made in policies related directly to exports than in import-related measures. Taxes on exports were reduced, prohibitions and licensing requirements were lifted, and a number of countries began or improved systems to exempt exporters from restrictions and tariffs on imported inputs. Next to exchange rate and export measures, the most common type of reform was to reduce the number of products subject to nontariff barriers (bans, licensing requirements, official import prices, explicit quantitative quotas, etc.), often in conjunction with increases in tariffs to at least partially compensate for the effects of reducing nontariff barriers. Only in a handful of countries were tariffs significantly reduced or made much more uniform.

It would be desirable, of course, to have detailed measures that would allow us to assess what happened to the antiexport bias in these countries over the course of the reforms. Unfortunately, though, such measures are available in only a few countries. Measures on aggregate imports show that as a percentage of GDP, imports fell less in adjusting countries than in nonadjusters, which could be taken to mean that import penetration increased as a result of a fall in protection, but could also just reflect the availability of financing. The composition of nonfuel imports may be a better indicator: since consumer goods are generally more highly protected, if protection had really declined, their share should have increased in adjusting countries. Instead, it fell. Overall, the preponderance of both direct and indirect evidence points to a conclusion that in most countries, protection was only modestly decreased. This seems to be especially true in sub-Saharan Africa. On the other hand, a few countries (e.g., Chile and Mexico), have substantially reduced all forms of protection, now have trade regimes almost as open as OECD countries, and are beginning to address second-order problems that interfere with the effectiveness of trade reforms (regulatory issues, port conditions, etc.).

OVERVIEW OF PERFORMANCE OUTCOMES

A strong empirical link between GDP and export growth has been demonstrated in many previous studies and this study again confirmed this connection in our sample of 87 countries. It has sometimes been argued, incorrectly in my view, that this empirical link is a statistical identity because export production is a component of GDP.[1] However, in our sample, the link holds even when exports are subtracted from GDP. There is also a strong link in our sample between receipt of a trade policy loan and export performance. Comparing the period from 1985 to 1987 to a base period from 1981 to 1983, the growth rate of manufacturing exports rose from 5.8% to 11.9% for the 40 recipients and fell from 8.8% to 4.2% for the 47 nonrecipients. In the same period, GDP growth rates almost doubled for recipients, while falling by about a quarter for nonrecipients (table 1). When 26 pre-1986 recipients were compared to nonrecipients using nine performance indicators (GDP growth, investment/GDP, real exchange rate, manufacturing export growth, import growth, resource balance/GDP, inflation, external debt/exports, and debt service/exports), the recipients outperformed the nonrecipients in every indicator, although the difference in means between the two groups was statistically significant for only some variables. The difference was quite consistent; when each country-indicator pair was counted as an observation, recipients outperformed nonrecipients in 76% of these observations.

This study did not generate new evidence on the connection between trade policy reform and employment. A fair amount of evidence already exists that generally outward orientation increases employment (e.g., Krueger 1978), consistent with the a priori expectation that exports from countries where wages are low would tend to be labor intensive. Systematic cross-country evidence on the

Table 1
Growth Rates of Export Volume and GDP for Selected Country Groupings

	1980	1981	1982	1983	1984	1985	1986	1987	1988
Manufacturing exports									
Developing countries	18.4	9.7	1.2	11.2	9.8	10.6	7.2	5.5	10.7
10 intensive trade loan recipients	26.8	20.2	−3.8	15.6	11.9	9.5	10.2	13.7	17.2
40 trade loan recipients	25.6	6.5	0.6	10.3	7.4	14.1	11.6	9.9	13.7
47 nonrecipients	11.9	12.6	1.7	12.1	11.8	7.4	3.5	1.7	7.9
GDP									
Developing countries	3.6	3.4	1.8	1.2	2.5	3.1	3.2	2.3	3.3
10 intensive trade loan recipients	0.2	2.4	1.1	0.2	2.1	2.7	3.8	4.2	4.1
40 trade loan recipients	2.7	2.8	0.3	0.4	2.2	3.5	3.9	3.2	3.6
47 nonrecipients	4.4	3.9	3.1	1.9	2.8	2.7	2.6	1.6	3.0

Source: World Bank data.

effect of *changes* in trade regimes on employment is rarer. Anecdotal evidence alludes to increasing short-term unemployment from trade policy reforms, and indeed one would expect some dislocations when relative prices change substantially. However, the issue is difficult to examine empirically because most serious trade policy reforms have been associated with stabilization measures, which are likely to produce some unemployment. A study of 18 episodes of trade liberalization in the late 1960s through early 1980s failed to find a causal link to unemployment (Papageorgiou et al. 1990). In eight episodes unemployment fell during the episode, whereas in the other 10, absorption-decreasing macro policies or worsening of external terms of trade made it difficult to attribute increasing unemployment to trade policy. The study's authors concluded that perhaps more than is generally realized, adjustment to changes in incentives takes place within sectors or even within firms through changes in product lines or techniques, thereby minimizing displacement of employees.

Although most countries that liberalized trade policies increased GDP and export growth, some did not. This is sometimes referred to as a weak "supply response," and a number of factors can be identified that have constrained the supply response in particular cases. First, to create the behavioral changes that generate the supply response, reforms must be credible and expected to last. Enterprise surveys in Mexico indicated that one reason why investment in export industries lagged behind the reforms was that businessmen doubted they would last, which was not surprising, considering earlier policy reversals. Domestic regulatory policies, particularly those that restrict hiring and firing and company reorganization or that increase transport costs, are often problems. Public sector policies related to central allocation mechanisms in socialist economies, to monopolies of state-owned enterprises, and to inefficient or corrupt customs services sometimes keep firms from responding to changing incentives. Other problems have included insufficient attention to exporters' institutional requirements, inadequate infrastructure, and protection in the markets of developed countries. Finally, especially in some African countries where policies have been inimical to the private sector (especially merchants) for decades, a supply response may require a rebuilding of the entrepreneurial class.

MACROECONOMIC POLICY AND TRADE POLICY REFORMS

It is not purely by chance that many of the countries with the most restrictive trade regimes also suffered from severe macroeconomic disequilibria in the 1980s. Such restrictions, as well as domestic regulatory policies, made economic structures rigid and slow to adjust to shocks in the terms of trade and reduction in external financing, resulting in rising deficits and inflationary finance. Balance of payments crises brought about by the macro imbalances were dealt with by increasing import restrictions, and trade taxes were raised to try to reduce fiscal deficits. Thus, the links between trade restrictions and macro imbalances run both ways.

Often, therefore, there is a need for both stabilization and trade policy reform. Of the 40 countries receiving trade adjustment loans from the Bank between 1979 and 1987, four began with inflation of 100% a year or more, five with 40% to 99%, and six with 20% to 39%. This raises the question of whether both can be undertaken simultaneously. As is commonly recognized, there is potential for conflict. Tariff reductions can exacerbate fiscal deficits; increases in real interest rates and cuts in public investment that sometimes accompany stabilization programs may reduce the supply response to trade policy reform; high inflation obscures relative price changes from reforms. Perhaps the most important source of tension is that successful trade liberalization generally has to be supported by a real depreciation of the currency, while disinflation can cause the real exchange rate to appreciate.

Although concerns about such conflicts are valid, they cannot generally justify delaying trade policy reform. First, many of the concerns simply argue that stabilization measures may keep the reforms from working as quickly as they would under optimal conditions. This may be true, but postponing the reforms would postpone their effects even more. Second, many problems can be mitigated or avoided entirely by appropriate design of the stabilization and reform programs. Many trade policy reforms are revenue-gaining, including those that get rid of prohibitions, relax quantitative restrictions, eliminate exemptions, and raise low tariff rates on imported inputs. (Usually exemptions and low duties apply to imported inputs that do not compete with domestic production, so these last two steps reduce effective protection as well as raise revenue.) These steps can be combined with reductions in high tariffs to produce a reform program that causes little or no reduction in revenue, or increase in the fiscal deficit. Likewise, expenditure can be reduced in ways that encourage or at least do not interfere with the supply response (e.g., by concentrating cuts on consumption, transfers, and the public sector wage bill). Or the cuts in tariff revenue can be offset from other revenue sources, preferably in ways that would increase efficiency (e.g., increases in underpriced public sector services), but as a last resort by substituting less distortive taxes. Exchange rate policy can support reforms by not using the nominal exchange rate to "anchor" prices (which seldom works well anyway) or at least by deeply devaluing in the period before the anchor is deployed (as Mexico did in 1985–1987). Import liberalization can dampen inflationary expectations by lowering import prices. Crawling pegs have been effective in achieving both devaluation and disinflation simultaneously. At least 10 countries have cut moderate or high inflation rates in half (or more) within 3 years, while devaluing the real exchange rate.

Whatever the theoretical arguments, in practice countries have been able to carry out trade policy reforms and improve macroeconomic performance simultaneously. In a subset of 24 countries for which detailed data was analyzed, the significant trade policy reformers generally improved their macroeconomic performance indicators relative to mild or nonreformers (table 2). So the answer seems to be that, in general, trade policy reforms and stabilization *can* be

Table 2

Macroeconomic Indicators Before and After Reform in Trade Adjustment Loan Countries

	3 years before	2 years before	1 year before	Year of program	1 year after	2 years after	3 years after
Inflation rate							
Significant reform	31.5	34.3	30.6	55.5	25.9	22.9	22.6
Moderate reform	12.4	11.8	12.3	9.3	8.9	8.1	7.6
Mild reform	15.5	15.7	15.3	17.4	14.8	16.9	19.3
Fiscal balance/GDP							
Significant reform	−4.8	−6.4	−7.8	−7.2	−6.1	−4.4	−4.6
Moderate reform	−7.2	−7.8	−6.0	−5.8	−5.4	−5.1	−4.7
Mild reform	−8.0	−6.8	−8.6	−8.9	−8.4	−8.0	−13.8
Resource balance/GDP							
Significant reform	−5.2	−3.4	−2.5	−1.5	0.4	−0.7	−1.1
Moderate reform	−8.8	−8.6	−7.1	−6.4	−7.1	−6.0	−4.4
Mild reform	−6.2	−9.9	−7.5	−7.8	−6.4	−6.4	−3.2

Note. Group includes 24 countries for which implementation data are available. The extent of reform (1980–1987) is based on a combination of changes in policies (high, moderate, or low) with respect to the exchange rate (depreciation) and commercial policy. Countries in each group are as follows: significant (high in both categories or high in one and moderate in the other): Chile, Colombia, Ghana, Jamaica, Korea, Mauritius, Mexico, and Turkey; moderate (moderate and moderate, or high and low): Bangladesh, Madagascar, Morocco, Pakistan, Panama, Philippines, and Thailand; and mild (others): Côte d'Ivoire, Guyana, Kenya, Malawi, Senegal, Togo, Yugoslavia, Zambia, and Zimbabwe. (Countries that reversed reforms are included in the mild reform category.)

Source: World Bank data.

undertaken together without jeopardizing either. Under some special circumstances, of course, it may not make sense to do so; for example, when "noise" from a hyperinflation completely drowns out relative price changes, reducing protection may not be sensible (Fisher 1984). To say that reforms and stabilization *can* be carried out jointly is not to say that this has always been successfully done. Some reforms have been reversed because they adversely affected fiscal deficits, as in Morocco (a partial reversal), for example. But the lesson to be learned from these episodes is that more attention should be paid to potential conflicts so that the program can be designed to circumvent them in the ways outlined above.

EXPORT POLICY

Widespread recognition of the advantages of outward orientation combined with the need to generate foreign exchange to service foreign debt resulted in a renewed interest in expanding developing country exports in the 1980s. Exports from developing countries continued to grow in the 1980s, although the growth rate was below that of earlier years. The average growth rate of volume was 4.3% in 1981–1987, compared to 6.2% in the preceding 7 years. Manufactures continued to be the fastest-growing merchandise export sector (9.4%, compared to 13.4% in the earlier period), with foods and beverages second (3.4%, compared to 4.6%). Nonfactor service exports (e.g., tourism and transport) also grew rapidly, and by 1987 held a sizable share (18%) of exports of goods and nonfactor services.

Yet tempering this optimistic story is the fact that export performance was quite weak in many countries, especially the poorest. Thus, the question arises of whether some countries did something right and others wrong (and, if so, what); or whether the success of some and failure of others was due to circumstance. The answer, of course, is that virtually all successful exporters have some things in common. One central pillar of success has been macroeconomic stability coupled with a favorable exchange rate. This has been common to the earlier East Asian success stories of Hong Kong, Japan, Korea, Malaysia, and Singapore, as well as more recent ones like Thailand and Indonesia.

The other central pillar is an efficient system to provide exporters with quick access to imported inputs at tax-free international prices so they can compete on an equal footing with competitors in world markets. One way to do this is to provide free trade zones (sometimes called "in-bond systems" or "export processing zones"), where exporters are exempt from all duties (and domestic indirect taxes) and restrictions on imported inputs. The most successful way to do this is to make the whole country a free port (e.g., Hong Kong, Singapore). When there are no tariffs or restrictions on any imports, there is no need for the costly (for exporters and government) procedures otherwise necessary to guard against "leakages" of duty-free inputs to nonexport production; there is also no antiexport bias in the incentive structure. If the free trade zone does not include the whole country, it is important to minimize the trouble and expense of clearing input shipments through customs. It also helps if the zones are flexible in location to suit the individual exporter; Mauritius's system is based on a streamlined in-bond procedure that functions wherever an exporter wants to locate. The best of these zones—some public and some private—have done well, but many others have suffered from poor choice of location, excessive investment costs, mediocre management, or uncooperative customs officials.

Free-trade zones are only used for producers that export 100% of production. Other mechanisms must be applied to manufacturers that sell in both domestic and international markets. Korea and Taiwan pioneered the use of such schemes. The successful ones provide automatic exemption from restrictions as well as exemption from or rebate of duties on inputs for the exports produced. They are generally based on some standard technical coefficients that provide a quick and easy guide to how much of each imported input is used for a given quantity of exports. Such schemes are now used in a number of countries, including Mexico, Morocco, Indonesia, and Thailand. It is also very helpful to extend the treatment to "indirect exporters," that is, local suppliers to direct exporters.

Export subsidies in various forms—including income tax rebates—have been used in many countries to try to compensate for the antiexport bias created by high protection to import substitutes. They have seldom been successful, often result in fictitious exports and cheating (e.g., during a period of high export subsidies, one of Turkey's major export markets was reportedly Luxembourg, because of its lax procedures to verify claimed values of shipments), and can have adverse fiscal and macroeconomic effects, as in Yugoslavia (Havrylyshyn 1990), or burden efficient export sectors with the taxes needed to pay for them, as in Argentina (Nogués 1989).

A few countries have successfully used export subsidies to offset high import tariffs, notably Korea in the 1960s and 1970s. Korea's case was unusual, however, in a number of ways. (1) The authoritarian nature of the regime and a wide consensus on goals allowed a single-minded pursuit of export growth and the repression by labor or management of any activity considered incompatible with this. It is probably not a coincidence that liberalization of the political regime has gone hand in hand with accelerated economic liberalization in the 1980s. Because economic policy instruments are inherently vulnerable to populist pressure and misuse in democratic political systems, the fewer the better. (2) The real exchange rate was kept very competitive and stable. (3) Both the specific incentives and the policies in general were time-bound. "Infant industries" that did not become efficient were allowed to die before becoming elderly. In the 1980s, protection has been drastically reduced along with export subsidies. (4) Export incentives were not generally targeted to specific industries, but were available across the board. (This last policy was changed during the Heavy and Chemical Industry drive of 1973–1979, with a number of adverse consequences, but the mistakes were recognized and corrected and were a major reason for the government's decision to liberalize in the 1980s.) Because few countries have the political and economic conditions that permit these actions for offsetting the problems of a strategy of high import protection cum export subsidy, this policy seems generally inadvisable. This conclusion is strengthened by the facts that (1) many countries have unsuccessfully tried variants of the strategy and (2) one of Korea's main instruments—direct export subsidies—would be countervailable under current GATT rules if used today.

Developing countries have seldom been as concerned with primary as with manufactured exports. Typically, primary export sectors have been looked upon as cash cows to be milked as much as possible through direct or indirect taxes, and further burdened by the antiexport bias from protecting import substitutes. Programs to develop primary exports have been generally quite modest, but even when they have just consisted of reducing export taxes and establishing a supportive macroenvironment, results have been quite good. Chile's agricultural and wood exports grew from $44 million in 1972 to $1.1 billion in 1986. More recently, Nigeria's exchange reforms in 1986 combined with abolition of marketing boards for all export corps led to a 6% increase in production in spite of bad weather. Overall, cross-country evidence suggests an exchange rate supply elasticity of primary exports of 0.68 (1.35 in sub-Saharan Africa), which is almost as large as or larger than the elasticity for all merchandise exports (which is 0.77 in all developing countries and 1.01 in Africa; Balassa 1987).

IMPORT POLICY

By this time, most economists and policymakers have come to the conclusion that protection of import substitutes needs to be reduced. From the World Bank's point of view at least, the basis of this conclusion is not so much theoretical as pragmatic. Development strategies based on import substitution have not succeeded as well as outward-oriented strategies. Although one can certainly come up with circumstances under which temporary protection of infant import-substituting industries might be justified in theory, the truth is that such protection is almost never temporary and has generally been associated with heavy costs. It is of special concern that this penalizes infant export industries, which in the long run form a better foundation for sustained growth.

But, given acceptance of the general goal of reducing protection, there remain unanswered questions about what the exact targets should be, how to go about reaching them, at what pace, and in conjunction with what other policies. To take the first issue first, there is no real justification in basic trade theory for a small open economy to have any level of protection at all, so a first approximation of an optimal target level is 0. This conclusion, of course, may be tempered by a need to have a diversified revenue base. In practice, even strongly committed reformers have not reduced protection to 0, with the exception of Hong Kong and Singapore, who have had this policy for a long time. However, several countries have come fairly close: Korea's tariff range is now about 0%–30% (average 18%), with 5% of imports still controlled by NTBs; Chile has a uniform 15% tariff with no NTBs; Bolivia's range is 5%–17% (14% average) with no NTBs; Mexico's is 0%–20% (4% average), with 20% of local production having NTB coverage; and Ghana's is 0%–35% with no NTBs. It is also important that the target be a uniform tariff structure. Although the theoretical case for tariff uniformity is not airtight, the case is strong based on both efficiency and political economy grounds. Uniformity is important not only among final goods, but between final goods and inputs (for a cautionary note, see below). Even relatively low rates of nominal protection on final goods, combined with even lower input protection, create very high effective protection and strong incentives for rent-seeking.

The steps taken to reach the target are by now fairly standard, and this study found no reason to question them. The first order of business should be to reduce significantly or eliminate the coverage of nontariff barriers. This has important economic benefits and also serves as a signal of a serious policy change. Most sustained reforms have been associated with strong up-front action in this area. Exchange rate policy can play an important role here: devaluation, by raising domestic prices, may make NTBs redundant or at least reduce the shock of their removal. Tariffs may also be raised on items from which NTBs are removed, to cushion the blow, but they should not be used to try to replicate the protection level of the NTBs, both because of the pragmatic difficulty of calculating the right tariff levels and the fact that some "up-front" reduction in protection helps to get the resource reallocation started. The next stages of reform deal with tariff policy, the objective being to reduce effective protection. Reduction of high tariffs is the most obvious way to do this, but elimination of exemptions and raising low tariffs on imported inputs can also play an important role. Often, inputs that are not produced domestically are the ones with lowest tariffs, so raising these will not misallocate resources. There will be some adverse effect on exportables, however, through the effect on the real exchange rate and (if no effective duty drawback or similar scheme is operational) through increased cost of production. These negative effects should be weighed, but analytical results indicate that in the circumstances characterizing most developing country tariff regimes, they are more than offset by the positive welfare effects of raising input duties.

Furthermore, an additional advantage of raising low tariffs and eliminating exemptions is that these steps raise revenue and therefore allow high tariffs to be reduced more when revenue is a constraint. This brings us to the more general unresolved (and infrequently addressed) issue of how other policies interact with trade policy reform. This study and other recent work at the Bank have identified the failure to address complementary policies as one of the greatest shortcomings of reform packages. One example is fiscal policy (Rajaram 1989), as illustrated by the example of Morocco.

But a variety of other policies can either magnify or diminish the effects of trade policy reforms. In a nutshell, any reforms that make it easier and cheaper to transfer resources among firms or sectors improve the supply response. Reducing direct regulation of market entry and exit falls in this category, as does getting rid of the central allocation mechanism in socialist economies. This also includes reform of most labor market regulations, which make it costly to lay off employees. In Barbados, firms laying off workers may be required to make severance payments averaging 20 months' pay per worker or more. This not only forces some firms into bankruptcy that could otherwise survive, but also makes expanding firms reluctant to hire permanent workers. Inefficient or corrupt customs services or excessive customs regulations have also been major constraints in some countries; schemes to insulate exporters from input tariffs are susceptible to this problem. (In Madagascar, temporary admission of inputs requires 51 documents to be stamped and verified three times.) Transport regulations, public sector investment policy, and state-owned enterprise pricing policies are among the myriad other areas where reforms could help. Obviously, administrative capacity and political opposition constrain the ability to carry out all reforms simultaneously. But, at the least, more thought should go into how trade policy reforms can be dovetailed with a few other critical reforms to encourage maximum supply response. One factor contributing to Chile's rapid and sustained supply response was reform of labor market regulations. In contrast, regulations governing entry and exit of firms and transportation delayed Mexico's response, although many of these issues have now been addressed.

TRADE POLICY REFORM AND TRADING PARTNERS

Export growth in developing countries is determined not only by internal policies but also by the policies of trading partners. Protectionism has been a constraint to both North-South and South-South trade. The importance of the latter is indicated by the growing share of total developing country exports that go to other developing countries—32% in 1985 as compared to 21% in 1965. Both tariffs and nontariff barriers in developing countries are concentrated in South-South traded products, so trade policy reform would encourage growth in this even more than in North-South trade (Erzan 1989).

The rapid growth of OECD countries, combined with deep reduction in tariffs, has had a major positive influence on developing country exports to these countries. Average MFN tariffs have been reduced from about 40% in the late 1940s to a little over 5% today. Unfortunately, nontariff barriers in the North have in recent years increasingly been applied to products that are exported from the South. Conservative estimates are that these restrictions reduce developing country exports by 10% and GNP by 3% (Finger and Messerlin 1989). These restrictions are especially burdensome for agricultural products: over 90% of OECD food imports face some NTB. These depress producer prices in developing countries, with the impact falling most heavily on the rural poor (Valdes and Zietz 1980), and dramatically increase the variability of world prices. Developing countries thus have a major interest in the multilateral trade negotiations although only a few have any real leverage. But regardless of whether the Uruguay Round produces significant results, a number of countries have found that a commitment to the GATT framework is useful to lend credibility to their reform programs.

Many developing countries have pinned their hopes for trade expansion on regional integration schemes that usually involve trade preferences for neighboring countries, sometimes along with a unification of tariffs and nontariff barriers toward imports from nonmembers. The idea behind the schemes is that the regional market can allow industries to take advantage of economies of scale, and potential exporters can learn exporting skills in protected regional markets until they become sufficiently competitive to make the leap into the international market. In the long history of such efforts, few (apart from the EEC) have significantly expanded trade among members. The greatest success has seemed to come to groups like the EEC and ASEAN, where countries are fairly well-developed and outwardly oriented; otherwise experience has shown that high-priced regional products create resentment among regional partners, and balance-of-payment problems lead to a breakdown of trade, especially among countries with nonconvertible currencies. There are few success stories of industries that started exporting into regional markets and later became internationally competitive. On balance, regional schemes are likely to be more useful in other areas (e.g., to arrange joint infrastructure projects or negotiate jointly in international fora) than in trade policy.

NOTES

1. The reason the view is incorrect is that it looks upon export sector and nonexport sector growth as independent random variables. Thus the expectation of the sum of the two (GDP growth), conditional upon a high value for export growth, *must* be greater than the unconditional expectation, even though export growth may not increase productivity. The problem with this line of reasoning is that for a given production possibility frontier (or a given rate of expansion), more (or a higher growth of) exports must come at the expense of less (or slower growth of) nonexport production. Thus, more exports are not necessarily associated with more GDP; this association is more likely if something is expanding (or increasing the rate of expansion of) the frontier. This does not say anything about causation, however.

REFERENCES

Balassa, B., "Economic Incentives and Agricultural Exports in Developing Countries," 1987, Washington, D.C.: World Bank, Report DRD250, 1987.

Erzan, R., "Would General Trade Liberalization in Developing Countries Expand South-South Trade?," Washington, D.C.: World Bank, PPR Working Paper Series 319, 1989.

Finger, J. M., and Messerlin, P. A., *The Effects of Industrial Countries' Policies on Developing Countries,* Washington, D.C.: World Bank, Policy and Research Series 3, 1989.

Fisher, S., *Real Balances, the Exchange Rate and Indexation: Real Variables in Disinflation*, Cambridge, Mass.: NBER Working Paper 1497, 1984.

Krueger, A. O., *Foreign Trade Regimes and Economic Development: Liberalization Attempts and Consequences* (Cambridge, Mass.: Ballinger Publishing Co., for NBER, 1978).

Papageorgiou, D., Michaely, M., and Choksi, A. M., eds., *Liberalizing Foreign Trade* (esp. vol. 7 *Lessons of Experience in the Developing World*), Oxford: Basil Blackwell, 1990.

Thomas, V., Nash, V., and Associates, *Best Practices in Trade Policy Reform*, New York: Oxford University Press, 1992.

Valdes, A., and Zietz, J., *Agricultural Protection in OECD Countries: Its Costs to Less Developed Countries*, Washington, D.C.: International Food Policy Research Institute, 1980.

Chapter 5

Super-301 and Japan—A Dissenting View

*Mordechai E. Kreinin**

Abstract *This chapter develops a view that the "Super-301" provision of the 1988 Trade Act is a useful instrument in the hand of American negotiators dealing with Japan on trade matters. After demonstrating the relatively "closed" nature of the Japanese market and the relative paucity of intra-industry trade, it assesses the cost of Japan's business behavior and "administrative guidance" to the United States. This cost is weighed against the cost of taking retaliatory trade action or offering a credible threat. It is likely that the cost of benign neglect exceeds that of a credible threat. Superficial appearances to the contrary, Europe also pursues a policy of credible threats towards Japan.*

INTRODUCTION

A most controversial component of the 1988 Omnibus Trade and Competitiveness Act is the so-called "super-301" provision. It required the administration to determine and list publicly countries that "trade unfairly" with the United States, negotiate removal of such practices within 3 years, and take retaliatory action if the negotiations fail. A 1989 GATT report was highly critical of the 301 provision, as were many academicians on both sides of the Atlantic.

Equally controversial was the application of this provision to Japan. Japan was designated as an "unfair trader" in May 1989 (along with India and Brazil) for refusal of its public authorities to purchase American commercial satellites and supercomputers, and for stringent import requirements that keep out forest products manufactured in the United States. The designation triggered a series of negotiations that covered a wide range of "structural impediments" to trade (hence its title, the "structural impediments initiative," or SII), such as wholesale and retail redistribution systems in Japan that keep out imports, pricing mechanisms, business practices, bid rigging, market allocation, group boycotts, industrial organization (such as groups of companies with interlocking director-

---

*The author is grateful to the International Business Center at Michigan State University for a financial grant in support of this project, and to Professor Leonard Cheng for helpful comments.

ates known as *keiretsu*), land use, and savings and investment patterns thought to be a cause of the trade imbalances. Although Japan was dropped from the list of unfair traders in May 1990, the SII discussions continue.

An additional approach that may be usefully adopted by the United States is a direct appeal to Japanese consumers (and voters), whose standard of living is often impaired by business and government practices that keep out imports. (Certainly Japan's living standard is lower than what would be justified on the basis of its high level of productivity.) This would be in full conformity with GATT principles.

But beyond such an innocuous step, should the United States apply pressure on Japan's government to open up its markets to foreign goods? Should it insist on the removal of "administrative guidance" procedures and business practices that reduce imports? Should credible threats and even retaliation be employed in that effort, as mandated by super-301? Most economists answer these questions, and especially the last one, in the negative, falling back on the time-honored tradition of free trade, and on the proven proposition that free trade is a country's welfare-maximizing policy no matter what its trading partners do. But these propositions were developed in the context of perfect competition in all product and factor markets, and may not be the best guide to the current U.S.-Japan scene, which is dominated by oligopolistic firms. In oligopolistic markets, where strategic interactions between firms are present, and where government policies affect actions taken by firms, the cost of acquiescing to Japan's behavior may exceed the cost of employing credible threats, threats backed by the possibility of retaliation or other measures of activist commercial policy. This chapter examines the costs and benefits of a policy of exerting such pressure on Japan.

JAPAN'S IMPORT REGIME

Much as been written about the alleged relative closedness of Japan's market to foreign goods. It is well known that agricultural imports are tightly limited by quotas and other governmental controls. In the service sectors, a variety of regulations restrict access to the market. For example, despite years of negotiations, American construction companies are still not allowed to bid on public construction projects in Japan (such as the massive Osaka airport or the Tokyo bridge) although exceptions were negotiated for bids submitted jointly by U.S. and Japanese companies. Restrictions exist in the financial sector and a variety of other service industries. For example, although the United States and Japan have been holding talks on financial services since 1984, the Japanese market remains closed to U.S. financial institutions, and in October 1991 the U.S. negotiator expressed in public his exasperation with the slow progress of the negotiations.

But what about the important manufacturing sector? Here there are no overt governmental import restrictions, and tariff rates are low. Yet it is often claimed that business practices, social pressures, taste, tradition, and perhaps "administrative guidance" by the government limit imports. It is also alleged that Japan engages in far less intra-industry trade than do other industrial countries.

A common means of assessing the degree of intra-industry trade is by use of a formula developed by Grubel and Lloyd:

$$\frac{\sum_{i=1}^{n} (X_i + M_i) - \sum_{i=1}^{n} |X_i - M_i|}{\sum_{i=1}^{n} (X_i + M_i)} \cdot 100$$

where X_i and M_i refer to the country's export and import of commodity category i, and n is the number of commodity categories. The smaller the proportion of the intra-industry trade in total trade, the lower the resulting index. At the extreme, if a commodity is either exported *or* imported (but not both), so that there is no intra-industry trade, the numerator is zero. Computing this index for 1989 manufacturing trade, based on four digit SITC groups, yields the results shown in table 1:

The high proportion of intra-industry trade for Germany possibly reflects the importance of intra-European trade in its total trade. Given the similarity of factor endowments and technology among the EC countries, much of that trade is expected to be of the intra-industry variety. At the other extreme, Japan clearly engages in less intra-industry trade than either the United States or Germany, a phenomenon that is particularly pronounced in SITC 7—machinery and transport equipment. Similar results were obtained by the use of an alternative formula (developed by Balassa), with a higher degree of commodity aggregation.

As a specific example of this phenomenon, table 2 presents international trade in machine tools in six major industrial countries. The United States and European countries both import and export machine tools. By contrast, in the case of Japan the export-to-import ratio is about 11:1. It appears from other

Table 1
Indices of Intra-Industry Trade, 1989

SITC	Japan	U.S.	Germany
5–8	30	61	64
5	65	63	67
6	31	53	70
7	25	70	60
8	30	42	77

Table 2
Exports and Imports of Machine Tools, 1983 ($ Millions)

	U.S.	Germany	Japan	U.K.	France	Switzerland
Exports	355	1,440	1,178	263	242	603
Imports	799	348	105	224	330	102

Source: The Economic Handbook of the Machine Tool Industry,
National Machine Tool Builders Association, Arlington, VA.

sources that Japan imports only highly specialized machines tools that are not produced locally.

What about the general level of manufacturing imports into Japan and how do they compare to those of other industrial countries? Several statistical studies of the matter reached conflicting results. Some found that Japan's trade conforms to the expected pattern; namely, Japan's imports do not deviate from what they would have been had her market been as open as that of other industrial countries. By contrast, other studies conclude that Japan's imports are far too low relative to the expected pattern—up to 40% less than that of other developed countries, allowing for intercountry differences in the various variables that determine trade. The approach employed in all these studies requires a variety of simplifying assumptions and places a heavy reliance on the theory selected to explain trade.

To avoid reliance on such models and their simplifying assumption, and to compile a more direct yet systematic body of evidence, I conducted a comparative survey of 62 subsidiaries of Japanese, American, and European companies in Australia, plus two governmental organizations (one Japanese and one Australian) concerned with purchases by foreign subsidiaries of materials and machinery. The focus of the study was on purchasing procedures of capital equipment acquired *outside* Australia and the sourcing of such equipment. The concluding paragraph states:

> Based on a survey of 62 companies in Australia, the purchasing behavior of Japanese-owned subsidiaries is definitely different from that of their American-owned and European-owned counterparts. They are tightly controlled by the respective parent company, procure their equipment mainly in Japan and own and operate mainly Japanese machinery. By contrast, "Western" firms (with the possible exception of a minority of the German firms) have a great deal of autonomy to make purchase, sourcing, and other decisions, procure most of their capital equipment by international competitive bids and own machinery made in three continents and six to eight countries without a preponderance of any particular source. *To a large extent this reflects the buying behavior and machinery ownership of the parent and sister companies worldwide* (Kreinin 1988).

Reasons for the differential behavior of Japanese firms include loyalty to traditional Japanese suppliers and industrial organization in Japan where the company procures machinery from other companies within the same corporate group. Although the survey did not include Japanese companies in Japan, and hence does not bear directly on Japan's imports, respondents suggested that the parent companies behave in a manner similar to their subsidiaries. Still, this constitutes only indirect evidence concerning the relatively low level of Japan's imports.

To a large extent, the preference for Japanese suppliers can be explained as the profit-maximizing behavior of corporate groups (keiretsu) by which a large segment of Japan's industry is organized (Cheng and Kreinin 1992). And indeed there is evidence that some U.S. industries are moving to create their own keiretsus (*Business Week*, Jan. 27, 1992). But not all Japanese firms are so organized, and respondents to the Australian survey gave a variety of reasons for their behavior, unrelated to the form of industrial organization.

Industry studies also demonstrate Japan's targeting of high technology industries and its habit of insulating the home market as a sanctuary for domestic firms struggling to achieve economies of scale and reduce costs. One study (Mastanduno 1992) documents such recent behavior in the areas of optical fiber, software, satellites, supercomputers, as well as more traditional industries such as wood products. Various anticompetitive practices are also documented. Even in products such as supercomputers, in which the United States dominates the world export markets, it has only a small share of Japan's market.

Although Japan's imports may be increasing, there is ample anecdotal and systematic evidence that imports are restricted through a variety of mechanisms. This is especially so in the area of high technology and other advanced manufacturing, and where sophisticated processes are required. Indeed, the composition of Japan's imports is just as important as its aggregate value. The fact that in his January 1992 visit to Japan President Bush publicly opened an American toy store in Tokyo is symbolic (apart from the fact that most of the toys are made in Asia): 30 years ago Japan was a toy exporter to the United States.[1]

WHO GETS HURT?

Japan itself is the most likely loser from its import restrictions, whether imposed by the government or generated by business and consumer behavior. This is particularly true in the short run. By restricted access to foreign goods, the population is denied the enjoyment of a living standard commensurate with its high level of productivity. But this is no reason for threat of retaliatory action by its trading partners. Here the critical question is: do these practices hurt the United States?

There are several channels (not necessarily mutually exclusive) through which the United States may be affected. The first channel is deterioration in its terms of trade caused by the "artificially" reduced demand for American products. Total U.S. imports of manufacturing in 1989 amounted to $366 billion, of which $95 billion came from Japan. Most of the imports from Japan were in the machinery and transport equipment sector. A 10% deterioration in the U.S. terms of trade with Japan costs this country $9.5 billion a year. This is apart from the more serious deterioration in the terms of trade that would be required to generate a trade surplus large enough to service the U.S. foreign debt.[2]

More serious effects flow from the type of manufacturing that Japanese firms, aided by government "administrative guidance," tend to appropriate for themselves. These are largely high-technology products, where firms in oligopolistic industries tend to be subject either to economies of scale or to "learning by doing," and most often to both. To the extent that the United States is denied producing in these areas through the behavior of Japanese firms, with or without government support, the U.S. growth prospect could be damaged.

It is not necessary to enter the debate over industrial policy and the role of the Japanese government in promoting or "targeting" certain industries and manufacturing processes through "picking winners." We know that in certain areas (such as supercomputers, high-definition television, and superconductivity) the Japanese government serves as a catalyst and even as a coordinator for the research and development efforts of private firms or industrial groups. But even if the government role were minimal, the private industrial sector appears to be guided towards the types of industries that display the above characteristics. We are certainly not facing a totally competitive industrial sector concerned only with short-term profits, where profits are competed away in the long run. Rather, these are oligopolistic firms or industrial groups that often sacrifice short-term gains for what they perceive to be long-term profits and secular growth.

In addition to economies of scale and "learning by doing" considerations, Japanese firms would also appropriate for themselves a higher share of global economic profits, in a manner described by the new theory of strategic behavior.

There is an additional, yet intangible, cost attributable to Japan's business and government behavior. Their practices create resentment at both the political and business levels in the Unites States and Europe, and intensify the pressure for protectionism. It is very difficult to maintain and operate a liberal trading system when such a major player plays by different rules.

At the present time, the formal theoretical literature on trade, inventions, and growth is at its infancy so it is not possible to measure empirically the impact of the Japanese practices on U.S. long-term growth, and the profitability of American firms. But one suspects that the impact could be considerable. These would be the costs to the United States (as well as other countries) of not responding in any way to those Japan's business practices that reduce imports and artificially enhance Japan's own share in global output of high technology products.

COMPARATIVE COSTS OF RESTRICTIONS
AND OF BENIGN NEGLECT

Against the cost of treating Japan's practices with benign neglect, we must consider the costs of responding by a credible threat of retaliation, which may lead to restrictions on Japanese imports. Here it is possible to estimate the static welfare loss from trade restrictions. In the case of the automobile VER, the most glaring example of restrictions imposed by the United States on Japanese imports, the annual welfare cost to the United States was estimated at $5.8 billion in 1984; the machine-tool VER cost the United States about $100 million per year, and the cost of steel import restrictions (on all sources of supply) was estimated at $1.7 billion per year (Dinopoulos and Kreinin 1988, 1991; Melmo and Tarr 1989). These figures may be magnified by various dynamic and X-efficiency considerations. Presumably the restrictions imposed by the EC on imports from Japan are more severe (although introduced and enforced with far less fanfare), and therefore more costly in terms of European welfare.

Japanese goods sell well in the American market because consumers choose to purchase them over alternative products; consequently, import restrictions carry a welfare cost. Yet years of negotiation with Japan in successive attempts to bring about the opening of its market yielded very few results, which shows that American negotiators need to be backed by a credible threat that failure to bring about a demonstrable change would trigger U.S. response in the form of import restrictions. That is what the super-301 provision is designed to do. But the cost of such restrictions in terms of U.S. welfare may be on the order of $15–$20 billion per year, leading many observers to oppose these restrictions. Indeed in most cases it has been shown that the annual cost of saving one job via protection is a multiple of the wage rate in the particular industry. But the purpose of a possible American response is not to save jobs; rather, it is to provide a negotiating tool designed to pry open Japan's market, because its closed nature is also costly to the United States and may be far more costly than a retaliatory act. Finally, the opening of Japan's market would benefit all trading nations, not just the United States. Thus a recent article concludes that "in the context of multilateral negotiations between the EC, the United States and Japan, the EC and United States do gain significantly compared to the status quo by having these negotiations occur with the threat of a retaliatory trade war" (Harrison and Rutstrom 1991, p. 434).

In other words, doing nothing is also costly to the United States: there is possible loss of trade and probable loss of future economic growth, to the extent that the United States loses output in industries in which decreasing costs and learning by doing are prevalent. There is also a loss of economic profits in oligopolistic industries (before they are competed away), as well as a cost to the international trading system. Just because these costs cannot be measured does not mean that they are trivial. They may well be more substantial than the static cost of protectionism. These considerations justify arming our negotiators with the provision of "super-301."

Does "super-301" constitute a credible threat that can have an effect on the behavior of foreign countries? Two pieces of evidence suggest that it does. First, countries like Korea and Taiwan took steps to liberalize their imports in order to avoid being included on the U.S. list of unfair trades. Second, such trade liberalization as occurred in Japan took place *because* of American pressure. A recent study (Bayard and Elliott 1992) suggests that U.S. negotiating objectives were achieved at least partially in over half the cases. Whenever that pressure is relaxed, trade and service restrictions seem to tighten. Formalizing and codifying the pressure in legislation can only help.

If the probable costs of benign neglect are so serious, one might ask why are not the Europeans considering legislation that would enable them to retaliate against the Japanese. The answer is that Europe applies far stricter limitations to Japan's imports than does the United States. For example, Japanese cars allowed annually into Italy, France, and the United Kingdom are 2300 units, 3%, and 10% of the market, respectively. After the Unified Market takes effect on January 1, 1993, imports of cars from Japan to the entire EC will be frozen at the present level of 1.23 million per year for a 7-year period. Furthermore, the principle of bilateral reciprocity adopted by the EC Unified Market program (EC 1992) with respect to the service sectors was allegedly aimed mainly at the Japanese. A recent paper about Europe's computer and electronics industry by the European Commission's information technology directorate "calls for the EC to get tougher with Japan about the removal of supposed trade barriers and to consider using more anti-dumping measures against Japan's exports" (*The Economist*, Feb. 16, 1991). But in general, Europe's market is far less open than that of the United States; the Europeans impose trade restrictions without the legislative fanfare that is typical of the United States. With many of their industries reasonably protected, the Europeans are not compelled to request anything of the Japanese. A U.S. super-301, aimed at opening up Japan's market to goods and services from all countries, may be more helpful to the promotion of a liberal international trading system than the policy pursued by Europe.

NOTES

1. Another interesting episode happened in the same month. The city of Los Angeles decided to award a major contract for railroad cars to a Japanese company, even though an American company's bid was lower (that decision was later reversed as a result of public pressure). The reason given was the technological superiority of the Japanese manufacturer. In contrast, a few years earlier Japan's air force was in the market for a jet fighter, an area in which the United States had distinct technological superiority. Rather than purchase the U.S. F-16, the Japanese government decided first to develop its own aircraft, and later (under U.S. pressure) to co-produce the plane and share in the technology.

2. In its origin in the first half of the 1980s—the U.S. trade deficit was a macro-

economic phenomenon, in the sense that the excess of domestic investment over savings (including the government budgetary deficit) had to decline in order for the trade deficit to shrink. But in the early 1990s, with vast unemployment, the export identity $I - S = M - X$ no longer implies a causal relationship. The line of causality can be reversed: a rise in exports (caused, say, by depreciation of the dollar) would raise income, which would in turn increase savings.

REFERENCES

Bayard, Thomas O., and Elliott, Kimberly A., "Evidence from Section 301 on the Utility of 'Aggressive Unilateralism' as a Trade Policy Tool." Prepared for a conference on The Political Economy of International Market Access, National Bureau of Economic Research, February 1992.

Business Week, "Learning from Japan: (How a Few U.S. Giants Are Trying to Create Homegrown Keiretsu)," January 27, 1992.

Cheng, Leonard K., and Kreinin, Mordechai E., "Supplier Preferences and Dumping: An Analysis of Japanese Corporate Groups," 1992.

Dinopoulos, Elias, and Kreinin, Mordechai E., "Effects of the U.S.-Japan Auto VER on European Prices and on U.S. Welfare," *Review of Economics and Statistics,* November 1988.

Dinopoulos, Elias, and Kreinin, Mordechai E., "The U.S. VER on Machine Tools: Causes and Effects," in R. E. Baldwin (editor), *Empirical Studies of Commercial Policy,* University of Chicago Press, 1991.

The Economist, February 16, 1991, p. 57.

Harrison, Glen W., and Rutstrom, E. E., "Trade Wars, Trade Negotiations, and Applied Game Theory," *The Economic Journal,* May 1991, pp. 420–435.

Kreinin, Mordechai E., "How Closed is Japan's Market?" *The World Economy,* December 1988, pp. 529–542.

Mastanduno, Michael, "Setting Market Access Priorities: The Use of Super 301 in U.S. Trade With Japan." Prepared for a conference on the Political Economy of International Market Access, National Bureau of Economic Research, February 1992.

Melmo and Tarr, "Welfare Costs of U.S. Quotas in Textiles, Steel and Autos," mimeo, 1989.

Chapter 6

Domestic Institutional Barriers
to Increased U.S. Exports

James O. Luke

Abstract *Discussions of export promotion usually focus on overcoming three types of export barriers: macroeconomic factors, foreign nation protectionist policies, or domestic firm management policies. Further, active export promotion policies are often viewed as trade-distorting market subsidies. This chapter argues that a market-failure rationale exists for government export promotion policies, but that existing U.S. policies toward export promotion are inherently and structurally weak and/or ineffective.*

INTRODUCTION

"Export-led growth may be the only feasible strategy for the U.S." to achieve and maintain positive real economic growth in the 1990s due to limitations on the feasibility of traditional fiscal and monetary policy tools (Bergsten, 1991). The potential for such export-led growth certainly exists, especially among small- and medium-size businesses. According to the U.S. Small Business Administration, U.S. small- and medium-size businesses "under-export" by exporting only 6% to 7% of output compared to the 15% to 20% exported by their German or Japanese counterparts (Eason, 1984). Achieving this export potential requires lowering or eliminating all barriers to improved U.S. export performance. This chapter suggests that, in addition to the much-discussed typical export barriers, such as macroeconomic variables, foreign protectionist policies, and business firm management policies, domestic institutional barriers to improved export performance exist in the inherent structure of U.S. export promotion programs. A possible policy direction is suggested by comparison to structure and policy of a high-performing exporting nation such as Germany.

BACKGROUND: TYPES OF BARRIERS TO EXPORTS

Theoretical discussions and policy debates about U.S. export performance typically focus on one or more of three types of barriers to increased exports. First are explanations revolving around exchange rates and macroeconomic policies. Such models emphasize the role of macroeconomic policy variables (money supply, etc.) in determining exchange rates, which in turn determine export prices. Several authors have noted, however, that exchange fluctuations affect U.S. exports only after a large time lag (Rosensweig and Koch, 1988).

A second cause mentioned in debate on export performance is foreign protectionist policies. However, although foreign protectionist policies no doubt play a part in limiting U.S. export opportunities, they do not appear to explain fully recent U.S. performance. Further, as the difficult GATT negotiations attest, lowering these barriers is a laborious process.

A third type of barrier to U.S. exports is widely perceived to lie in the attitudes or inadequacies of U.S. firm managers, including apathy, antiforeign biases, and short-term orientation. This barrier is frequently cited by officials and policymakers in the export promotion field (Schares et al., 1991; Holstein, 1991). Although such a barrier may in fact exist, it is difficult to explain in terms of economic theory. Indeed, to attribute poor U.S. export performance to management bias against exports requires one to envision large numbers of businesspeople irrationally forsaking profitable opportunities abroad so that they might indulge their preferences for weaker sales in their "comfortable" domestic market. Real managers may not be profit maximizers, but it is unlikely that they are profit avoiders.

In addition to these three types of export barriers, the institutional nature of U.S. export promotion policies is itself a significant barrier to increasing U.S. exports. Although government-supported export promotion may be economically justified, the institutional nature of the policy must be altered for such policy to be effective.

RATIONALE FOR PUBLIC EXPORT PROMOTION POLICY

Unlike market-distorting export subsidies, public export promotion programs can be justified on economic grounds. Empirically, it is shown that such programs can be cost effective (Webster, Mathis, and Zech, 1990). Coughlin, Cetus, and Cartwright (1987a, 1987b) found that $1000 of state-level export promotion expenditures yield $432,000 of increased manufactured exports. But besides such empirical justification, theoretical support exists as well without resort to "managed-trade" or "strategic trade" arguments.

A market failure due to imperfect information and high initial costs of obtaining information exists in this area. Sales and marketing activities are costly and information intensive, and international distances exacerbate these costs. Export expansion decisions are made by profit-maximizing managers by equating expected marginal benefits to expected marginal costs. But information and expectations are asymmetric between costs and benefits. Whereas the marginal costs of international marketing activities are usually inflated by high travel, communications, transport, translation, and other costs, the marginal benefits from international sales are discounted because they are either unknown or are uncertain; information about them cannot be obtained without incurring significant initial research costs. The obvious marginal costs of learning about each new market can easily appear to exceed the uncertain marginal benefits, thus rationally discouraging efforts at export exploration. Yet, even the uncertain marginal benefits may outweigh marginal costs if the costs of producing information can be shared or distributed. Collectively, international market research is rational; individually, it is not.

This is a good example of the type of incomplete market/imperfect information market failure that Stiglitz (1989) and others have argued justifies public-policy intervention. Timely information on foreign markets may be considered a quasi-public good, and private efforts will be suboptimal for all but the largest exporting industries.

Survey research of small- and medium-size businesses confirms this view. A study conducted on 309 Michigan-area nonexporters who expressed a desire to export revealed lack of knowledge and lack of human resources (resources for acquiring information) as the two primary reasons for not exporting (Braniecki and Williams, 1990). Other studies have reached similar conclusions, including one that quoted an Ohio businessman as saying: "If I could identify foreign customers . . . and agents . . . I would export. The time and expense doesn't seem warranted." (Kedia and Chhokar, 1986; Howard and Herremans, 1988). Thus there is a role for government to ensure the availability of timely, detailed, accurate marketing information.

INEFFECTIVENESS OF U.S. EXPORT PROMOTION POLICY

The centerpiece of U.S. export promotion policy is the U.S. Foreign and Commercial Service in the International Trade Administration. The U.S.F. & C.S. emphasizes one-on-one counseling with businesspeople by individual "trade specialists" at 68 field offices. The trade specialists are backed up by a computerized data base of international trading information gathered from overseas offices.

These efforts have been weak and ineffective in fulfilling the critical information provider role. Recent studies by Congressional subcommittees, the General Accounting Office, and other critics have been unfavorable evaluations, characterizing the Commerce Department's export promotion efforts as "in disarray," "unfocused," "inefficient," inaccurate, and out of date (Rosenthal, 1989; Robichaux, 1990; Schares et al. 1991; Holstein, 1991).

Why are these U.S. efforts ineffective? Many critics have argued that the United States greatly underspends on export promotion relative to its industrialized rivals. Canada, for example, spends 18 times the U.S. per capita for export promotion (Robichaux, 1990). But, regardless of the total amount spent on export promotion, the United States does not seem to obtain good returns on its expenditures.

The ineffectiveness of U.S. export promotion activities is inherent in their structure, organization, and culture. The approach to exporting decisions of a large, civil-service–based federal bureaucracy is at odds with that of the small- and medium-size business "clients" it attempts to serve.

"PLANNING TO EXPORT" OR "LEARNING BY EXPORTING"?

Charrier and Lauf (1990) offer a model of organization culture that clarifies the clash between U.S. export promotion programs and their small- and medium-size business clients. They identify two "world views" by which decision-makers may be classified. One group may be called the "Model E's." Managers in this group are compelled to move quickly to action based upon intuitive judgments of uncertain information, even at the cost of making mistakes. Their bias is to learn from actual experience, not from conceptual research or analysis. Such managers, characterized by the slogan "Ready, Fire, Aim," are frequently found in sales and marketing groups and in smaller organizations.

The other group are the "Model T's." Their need is for careful, studied research. Their main concern is to avoid wrong action, even if it involves delay, and they give priority to finding the "best" answer. Such managers, characterized by the slogan "Ready, Aim, Aim," are frequently found among the scientific, analytical, and staff ranks of large organizations.

In Charrier and Lauf's terms, U.S. export promotion programs are clearly "Model-T" oriented. The approach recommended by the U.S. Department of Commerce for "How to start exporting" is heavily biased towards heavy planning, analysis, and research activities up front before engaging in actual business transactions. Of the first four pages of the U.S. Department of Commerce's *A Basic Guide to Exporting* (1986), three pages push the merits and requirements of formally written planning. In another 10-page guide titled *A Short Course in Export Marketing* (1989), the first five of eight steps in starting to export involve heavy research, interviewing, analysis, and writing before ever talking to a potential customer. The motivation for such intensive planning is revealed in step 6: "Postpone irrevocable commitments in high-priority markets until you know what you are doing. Limit the effects of your inevitable mistakes." Commerce's approach to exporting is a "Model T."

By contrast, businesspeople involved with small or medium-size businesses are Model E types. They are action oriented and believe in "learning by doing." A McKinsey and Co. study of successful medium-size U.S. exporters found them "characterized by an attack mentality . . . these people are really entrepreneurs" (McClenahen, 1987). Bernard Tenenbaum of the Snider Entrepreneurial Center at the Wharton School notes that time and impatience are the major obstacles to writing plans for such entrepreneurs. "They want to get on with building the business." Another experienced consultant describes planning as a "tortuous activity" for such businesspeople (Thompson, 1988).

What managers of small- and medium-size businesses need to expand exports is specific, timely, detailed marketing and sales information (Kedia and Chhokar, 1986). Given their Model E view, such information is needed not to develop the best full-fledged export strategy, but rather to seize an acceptable export opportunity quickly. From the initial experience, the business will acquire more information and expand its efforts. Indeed, some business strategists advocate just such a strategy (van Mesdag, 1987).

Given their clients' view and resource constraints, U.S. export promotion efforts most likely discourage businesses from exporting. The emphasis on planning and research raises perceptions of both initial and marginal costs while doing little to raise perceptions of the marginal benefits. Indeed, the U.S. export promotion literature, written with a motivation to prevent failures, often brings more attention to the possibility of "mistakes" and thus heightens uncertainty. In fact, the Commerce Department has reinforced businesses' fears of foreign business transactions, fears rooted in a lack of information.

The importance of matching the decision-making style of the export promotion organization to the entrepreneurial style of small and medium-size businesses can be inferred by examining other nations' approaches. Despite having an economy roughly only one-fourth the size of that of the United States, Germany equals or exceeds the U.S. export volume. Most of the difference in performance is due to the higher export performance of medium-size German businesses (the "Mittlestand") versus their U.S. counterparts. In turn, much of the credit for the high German performance is attributed to the method of export promotion (Schares et al., 1991; Holstein, 1991). Seringhaus and Rosson (1991) and Camino (1991) observed that Germany's successful export promotion programs, although subsidized by the government, are actually managed and operated by private business-based organizations such as chambers of commerce, trade associations, and consortia. Sweden, Austria, and the Netherlands have programs that also emphasize the use of private business-based organizations to provide services. In Italy, where a mix of government and private organizations is used, businesspeople's performance ratings of the usefulness of private institutions' services was better than that of public institutions' services by a margin of 3 to 2 (Sbrana and Tangheroni, 1991).

CONCLUSIONS AND POLICY RECOMMENDATIONS

Bureaucracy and civil service requirements make staffing government-operated export promotion programs with experienced, entrepreneurial "Model E" people unlikely. Thus, increased funding and reorganization of the U.S. Foreign and Commercial Service is likely to be insufficient to make U.S. export promotion efforts more effective.

Instead, the following policy approaches should be explored:

1. De-emphasizing one-on-one counseling in favor of increased information research efforts and data base improvements. In addition to theory, casual empiricism of successful European export promotion efforts supports this approach. These programs place greatest emphasis on the provision of

accurate, timely, opportunity-specific marketing and sales data, not general consulting and planning services.

2. Privatization of export promotion efforts through grants and contracts to utility companies, telephone companies, chambers of commerce, trade associations, and private information providers.

3. Funding of international market information centers in public libraries, colleges, and universities.

Whatever approaches and programs are used, it should be remembered that to be effective, the government's role in export promotion is not that of export business consultant but to provide information so as to expand the marketplace.

REFERENCES

Bergsten, C. Fred, "Rx for America: Export-led Growth," *International Economic Insights,* 2: 1 (1991): 2–6.

Braniecki, Karen, M., and Williams, Sharon, "Development of a Plan to Increase Exporting in a Seven County Area" (Master's project, Livonia, Michigan: Madonna University, 1990).

Camino, David, "Export Promotion Policies in Spain and Other E.E.C. Countries: Systems and Performance," in F. H. Rolf Seringhaus and Philip J. Rosson, eds., *Export Development and Promotion: The Role of Public Organizations* (Boston: Kluwer Academic Publishing, 1991), pp. 120–138.

Charrier, George O., and Lauf, Richard I., "The Double-Barreled Organization," *SAM Advanced Management Journal,* 55: 2 (1990): Spring, 4–11.

Coughlin, Cetus C., and Cartwright, Phillip A., "An Examination of State Foreign Exports and Manufacturing Employment," *Economic Development Quarterly,* 1: 3 (1987a): 257–67.

Coughlin, Cetus C., and Cartwright, Phillip A., "An Examination of State Foreign Export Promotion and Manufacturing Exports," *Journal of Regional Science,* 27 (1987b): 439–49.

Eason, Henry, "Small Firms Could Miss the Boat on Export Profits," *Nation's Business,* 72: 11 (1984): 62–64.

Holstein, William J., "Why Johann Can Export, But Johnny Can't," *Business Week,* November 4, 1991, pp. 64–65.

Howard, Donald G., and Herremans, Irene M., "Sources of Assistance for Small Business Exporters: Advice from Successful Firms," *Journal of Small Business Management,* July 1988, pp. 48–54.

Kedia, Ben L., and Chhokar, Jagdeep S., "An Empirical Investigation of Export Promotion Programs," *Columbia Journal of World Business,* 21 (1986): 13–20.

McClenahen, John S., "How U.S. Entrepreneurs Succeed in World Markets," *Industry Week,* May 2, 1987.

Robichaux, Mark, "Exporters Race Big Roadblocks at Home," *The Wall Street Journal,* November 7, 1990, p. B1–2.

Rosensweig, Jeffrey A., and Koch, Paul D., "The U.S. Dollar and the Delayed J-Curve," *Economic Review of the Federal Reserve Bank of Atlanta,* 73: 4, July/August 1988, pp. 2–12.

Rosenthal, Thomas M., "The Disarray in America's Export Promotion Effort," *Global Trade,* March 1989, pp. 24–28.

Sbrana, Roberto, and Tangheroni, Monica Siena, "Italian Exporting SMFs and Their Use of Support Services," in F. H. Rolf Seringhaus, and Philip J. Rosson, eds., *Export Development and Promotion: The Role of Public Organizations* (Boston: Kluwer Academic Publishing, 1991), pp. 146–160.

Schares, Gail E., Templeman, John, Neff, Robert, Hostein, William J., and Roberts, Stanley, "Think Small: The Export Lessons to Be Learned from Germany's Midsize Companies," *Business Week,* November 4, 1991, pp. 58–65.

Seringhaus, F. H. Rolf, and Rosson, Philip J., "Export Promotion and Public Organizations: State-of-the-Art," in *Export Development and Promotion: The Role of Public Organizations* (Boston: Kluwer Academic Publishing, 1991) pp. 8–11.

Stiglitz, Joseph E., "On the Economic Role of the State," in Arnold Heertje, ed., *The Economic Role of the State* (Oxford, U.K.: Basil Blackwell, 1989), pp. 9–81.

Thompson, Roger, "Business Plans: Myth and Reality," *Nation's Business,* 76: 8 (1988): 17–23.

U.S. Foreign and Commercial Service, United States Dept. of Commerce, *A Basic Guide to Exporting* (Washington: U.S. Govt. Printing Office, 1986).

U.S. Foreign and Commercial Service, United States Dept. of Commerce, *A Short Course in Export Marketing,* Detroit: U.S. Dept. of Commerce District Office Memo, May 9, 1989.

van Mesdag, Martin, "Winging It in Foreign Markets," *Harvard Business Review,* 65: 1 (1987): 71–74.

Webster, Elaine, Mathis, Edward J., and Zech, Charles E., "The Case for State-Level Export Promotion Assistance: A Comparison of Foreign and Domestic Export Employment Multipliers," *Economic Development Quarterly,* 4: 3 (1990): 203–210.

Chapter 7

Patterns of Technological Capability and International Trade Performance: An Empirical Analysis

Paolo Guerrieri

Abstract *The new international trade environment and technological opportunities have affected all the major countries and increased the pressure to adjust their productive systems. This essay analyzes trade performances and specialization patterns of all major countries over the past two decades, using an original data base for trade flows. It shows that each major country is characterized by a distinct trade specialization pattern and that national differences have increased over the past decade. The result has been profound changes in the competitive positions of individual countries which have been deeply influenced by "technology factors".*

INTRODUCTION

Technological capabilities and innovative activities are widely recognized as key factors driving international trade performance and the competitiveness of single countries (Krugman, 1987; Soete, 1987; Dosi, Pavitt, and Soete, 1990). According to recent innovation theory,[1] innovative activity is a cumulative process that is both country- and firm-specific because it is differentiated in both its technical characteristics and its market application (Teece, 1986; Pavitt, 1988; Cantwell, 1989). Processes of technological change tend to assume varying sectoral features in terms of differences in technological opportunities, sources, and appropriability conditions (Levin et al., 1984; Scherer, 1986). In this respect, the links between various industrial sectors assume great importance in terms of innovation user-producer relationships (Schmookler, 1966; Scherer, 1982; Pavitt, 1984; Lundvall, 1988). Technological change also affects these structural links and, through them, affects competitiveness of each sector, and hence of the industrial system as a whole (Rosenberg, 1982; Chesnais, 1986).

Pavitt (1984, 1988) presents a taxonomy of industrial sectors referring to these features of technology. It identifies four different types of industries according to a combination of sources, user requirements, and means of appropriation of technology: science-based, scale-intensive, specialized-suppliers and supplier-dominated or traditionals.

This essay uses Pavitt's taxonomy[2] in a comparative analysis of the trade performances and specialization of all the major countries (the United States, Japan, the European Community, and the Asian NICs) over the last two decades (1970–1989). The aim is also to provide empirical evidence for the differences in technological and innovative capabilities of single countries. To this end all traded industrial products are classified into Pavitt's four categories plus the group of the food industries, which is considered separately. All other nonindustrial products are grouped into three broad economic categories, for a total of nine product groups (see the Appendix for sectors within each group).[3] The analysis relies on a new and original trade data base (SIE - World Trade) comprising UN and OECD statistical sources (400 product classes, 98 sectors, and 25 commodity groups) for more than 80 countries (OECDs, NICs, ex-CMEA, and LDCs).[4]

THE CHANGING COMPETITIVE POSITIONS
OF JAPAN AND THE ASIAN NICs

Over the past two decades trade patterns of the major countries have been dominated by the impressively rapid advance of Japan and, to a lesser extent, of the Asian NICs (Hong Kong, Singapore, South Korea, and Taiwan).

In trade of manufactured products, both Japan's share in world exports and standardized trade balances[5] increased significantly over the period considered here (tables 1 and 2). With regard to single sectoral groups, both indicators show a huge rise of the Japanese industry in science-based sectors (electronics) and in specialized-suppliers (mechanical engineering), whereas in traditional sectors (e.g., textiles, clothing, leather, and footwear) the growing deficits in the late 1980s show a relative disengagement of the Japanese industry from these products.

This sharp strengthening of the competitiveness of Japanese products may be related to the profound changes in the patterns of Japan's trade specialization in the past two decades. An indicator measuring the relative contributions to a country's trade balance (ICTB) by the various groups of sectors considered here[6] (CEPII, 1983) is used to evaluate Japan's specialization patterns (figure 1). In the early 1970s, the scale-intensive and traditional sectors represented the strong points (comparative advantages) of the Japanese specialization patterns. Since then the latter has been characterized by a dynamic reallocation of productive resources, oriented toward a sharp strengthening of the special-supplier and science-based sectors in the 1980s. In contrast, scale-intensive sector contributions to the trade balance have been decreasing, and the traditional sectors have greatly changed their role.

Many analyses suggest that a highly innovative capability has been an important ingredient in Japan's impressive performance.[7] Japan has adapted its spe-

Table 1

Shares of Selected Countries and Areas in World Trade of Single Product Groups*

	Manufactures 1970-74†; 1985-89		Traditional 1970-74; 1985-89		Scale intensive 1970-74; 1985-89		Specialized suppliers 1970-74; 1985-89		Science based 1970-74; 1985-89	
United States	13:4	11:0	7:0	5:1	11:4	9:1	20:6	12:8	26:9	21:2
Japan	9:2	12:1	7:8	4:5	12:1	14:7	7:2	15:3	8:7	16:2
EEC (12)	48:4	43:7	50:2	42:8	46:3	43:2	56:5	50:2	46:3	37:9
Germany	15:1	13:9	21:1	10:6	15:1	14:7	25:1	21:1	16:4	12:4
France	7:4	6:6	7:2	5:3	7:3	6:7	7:1	6:1	7:1	6:8
United Kingdom	7:5	5:6	8:1	4:3	6:5	5:1	9:7	6:8	9:8	7:2
Italy	5:5	5:7	8:5	10:4	4:7	4:1	6:7	8:2	4:4	3:5
Asian NICs	2:7	7:6	7:3	15:4	1:6	5:2	1:2	3:7	1:7	8:8

*Ratio of a country or area's exports to world exports; in percentages.
† Average value in each subperiod.
Source: SIE-World Trade data base.

Table 2
Trade Balance of Selected Countries and Areas in Single Product Groups

	Manufactures 1970–74[†]; 1985–89		Traditional (1970–74; 1985–89)		Scale intensive (1970–74; 1985–89)		Specialized suppliers (1970–74; 1985–89)		Science based (1970–74; 1985–89)	
United States	−0.88	−8.08	−8.01	−16.07	−5.35	−11.39	12.75	−2.94	15.95	1.88
Japan	5.53	7.72	4.32	−0.41	8.74	10.14	4.42	12.82	4.33	12.41
EEC (12)	7.41	4.13	5.21	1.57	7.89	3.93	19.11	14.55	6.04	0.19
Germany	5.49	4.51	−0.02	−0.02	5.75	5.61	18.25	13.41	8.19	3.02
France	0.82	−0.11	0.88	−1.72	1.19	0.21	−0.31	−0.59	−0.45	0.31
United Kingdom	0.57	−1.19	−0.34	−3.04	0.82	−1.33	4.15	0.47	3.42	−0.23
Italy	1.09	0.91	5.09	6.58	0.41	−1.16	2.29	4.23	−0.06	−0.95
Asian NICs	−0.51	1.08	3.49	8.42	−1.04	−0.02	−2.76	−3.44	−2.23	−0.31

Standardized trade balances expressed as percentage of total trade in single product groups. For methods and formula see note 5.
[†] Average value in each subperiod.
Source: SIE-World Trade data base.

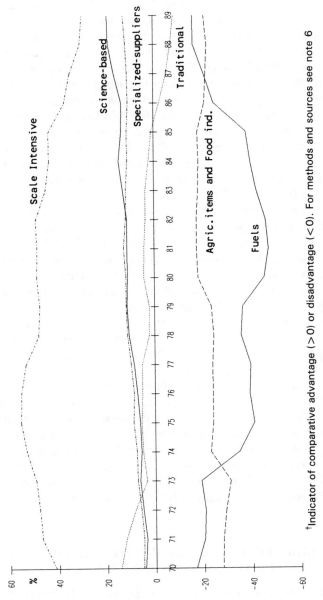

Figure 1 Patterns of trade specialization of Japan.*

†Indicator of comparative advantage (>0) or disadvantage (<0). For methods and sources see note 6

cialization patterns to the changing dynamic and commodity composition of world demand much better than have the other major countries. The data presented here indicate that technological factors deeply influenced these changes in Japan's competitive position in the world market, mostly through a strengthening of R&D intensive sectors (science based) and an effective intersectoral network for diffusion of innovation, as in the case of specialized suppliers.

In addition to Japan, it is important to note the remarkable performances of Southeast Asian countries (Asian NICs) over the entire period (1970–1989), in terms of rapidly increasing market shares (see tables 1 and 2). This improvement may be connected with the export-led growth strategies followed by the Asian NICs since the end of the 1960s. The industrial development of these countries was initially supported by the production and export of consumer goods requiring large amounts of unskilled labor, for which they benefited by the highest comparative advantages. To this end either state interventions or incentive and subsidy policies were used on a large scale and in different forms (Bradford and Branson, 1987).

The specialization pattern clearly shows that traditional industrial sectors played and continue to play a key role in the export growth of Asian NICs (figure 2); after increasing consistently until the end of the 1970s, however, the contribution of traditional goods to the trade balance decreased significantly throughout the 1980s. This trend stems from the diversification process of manufacturing output since the second half of the 1970s. Consequently the import dependence of Asian NICs on science-based and scale-intensive sectors has greatly decreased, as shown by substantial improvements in the trade balance contribution indicators of these two sectoral groups. Conversely, in specialized-suppliers sectors, the Asian NICs still registered notable comparative disadvantages in the 1980s[8] (figure 2).

Further evidence of these trends can be drawn from the competitive patterns of the Southeast Asian countries in single product groups (tables 1 and 2). They confirm that the development strategies of the Asian NICs were initially based on competitiveness "clusters," including labor-intensive consumer good exports, and have gradually carried out a diversification of industrial structure through a strengthening of capital-intensive productions, and particularly of technology-intensive industries. Within the latter group, the significant achievements of the Asian NICs in many electronic sectors is emblematic (Guerrieri, 1991).

TRADE SPECIALIZATION AND COMPETITIVENESS OF THE UNITED STATES AND THE EUROPEAN COMMUNITY

The upsurge of Japan and the Asian NICs deeply affected both the United States and the European countries, but in different ways. The U.S. share in world manufactures exports experienced a sharp decline from 1970 to 1989, concentrated in the first half of the 1980s; since the mid-1970s the U.S. trade balance

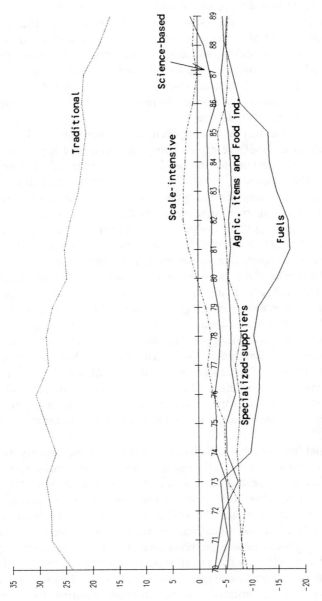

Figure 2 Patterns of trade specialization of the Asian NICs.

has registered a persistent deficit (tables 1 and 2). This overall deterioration is further evidenced by the evolution of U.S. competitiveness in single sectoral groups. The most negative results have been those in specialized-supplier sectors (mechanical engineering, i.e., machine tools), in which the U.S. industry declined sharply either in the 1970s or in the 1980s. In traditional sectors the U.S. economy also had a declining market share and a growing trade deficit, primarily in the past decade, whereas in scale-intensive industries the major losses have been in growing trade deficits over the 1980s. Only in science-based sectors did the U.S. industry maintain a positive trade balance even in the 1980s, but it too manifested a sharp decrease in its market share (electronics sectors) over the past two decades.

It is certainly true that the adverse cyclical evolution of the U.S. economy in the first half of the 1980s (e.g., the strong and prolonged appreciation of the dollar) may partly account for the rise in the U.S. trade deficit in this period (Lawrence, 1984; Bergsten, 1988). But it is also true that the indicators reveal negative trends in many sectoral groups dating from the second half of the 1970s. They show that the relative decline of the U.S. competitive position also derives from structural disadvantages that would not be easy to neutralize (Dertouzos, Lester, and Solow, 1989), even in the presence of a significant reversal of trends in the exchange rate, as was the case in the second half of the 1980s.

Indirect evidence of the above lies in the evolution of the trade specialization pattern of U.S. industry (figure 3). The comparative advantages of the United States have been and are increasingly concentrated in R&D-intensive product groups, which are science based. In scale-intensive (particularly automobiles) and traditional industries (especially textiles and clothing), on the other hand, the comparative disadvantages of the United States have been consolidated over the past two decades. The new element in the evolution of the U.S. pattern of specialization is the sharp decrease in the positive contribution to trade balance (ICTB) of the specialized-supplier sectors such as mechanical engineering, although they maintained a slight comparative advantage by the mid-1980s (see figure 3).

This trend indicates that U.S. industry is finding it increasingly difficult to transform its high-level scientific research capability into innovative products with significant commercial value in the other manufacturing sectors. An inverse correlation exists between the strengthening of U.S. specialization in R&D-intensive products and the overall negative trade (industrial) performance. It indirectly demonstrates that the availability of sources of "primary" innovation (high-tech or science-based sectors) does not necessarily generate broad spill-over effects in the overall production system. Intersectoral technological links play an increasing role in the process of development and diffusion of "primary" innovation throughout the economy, ensuring the technological progress of a country's industry as a whole (Rosenberg, 1982; Scherer, 1982). In the case of the United States, unlike Japan, these links did not function

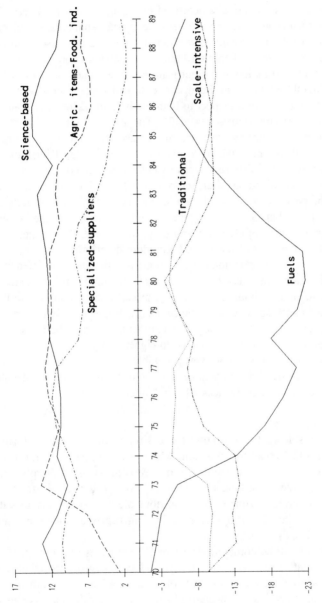

Figure 3 Patterns of trade specialization of the United States.

properly, impeding a positive technological adjustment in many innovation "user sectors," such as the specialized suppliers.

Patterns of trade performance and specialization in the EC do not provide clearcut indications and are characterized by strengths and weaknesses distributed across sectors and member states. The market shares in world manufactures exports of the EC countries registered a relative decrease from the early 1970s to the late 1980s. Although their trade balances for manufactures also decreased, they still maintained significant positive values (see tables 1 and 2).

This general evolution in European competitiveness, however, has been sharply differentiated with respect to both the individual member countries and single sectoral groups (tables 1 and 2). The positive trade performances of Germany and Italy contrast with the more uncertain outcomes in France and particularly with the negative trade patterns of the United Kingdom (tables 1 and 2). With regard to different types of industries, the competitiveness of EC countries in specialized-supplier sectors (mechanical engineering) was very strong in the past and maintained high levels in the 1980s, particularly in terms of positive trade balances (see figures 5 and 6). This was the result of the positive performances of Germany and Italy; in contrast, the competitiveness of France and particularly of the United Kingdom deteriorated sharply.

The EC competitive position has also remained firm in scale-intensive industries. Once again, this may be attributed to the highly differentiated performances of major EC countries. Germany, in particular, continued to be highly competitive in such sectors, and France also maintained a trade surplus during much of the period considered here; the competitiveness of the United Kingdom and Italy, on the other hand, deteriorated significantly.

In traditional products, there was a notable decrease in EC competitiveness in the 1980s, mostly to the advantage of the Asian NICs. This may be attributed to the declining competitiveness of the United Kingdom, France, and, to a lesser extent, Germany, whereas Italy strengthened its competitive position in traditional industries.

Finally, in science-based sectors the EC registered a more uniform performance. The EC competitive position, which was relatively strong in the early 1970s, experienced a huge decline in the 1980s in terms of sharply decreasing market shares and trade balances. This negative performance affected all EC countries, including Germany, and is attributable almost entirely to a dramatic deterioration in the EC competitive position in nearly all electronic sectors of the science-based group.[9]

These trends in the competitiveness of EC countries are fully confirmed by their specialization patterns over the period considered here (figure 4). The European industry maintained sound comparative advantages in many chemical and mechanical sectors of specialized-supplier and scale-intensive groups. In contrast to these areas of relative strength, EC specialization patterns reveal a declining trend in science-based (electronic) industries and in traditional sectors.

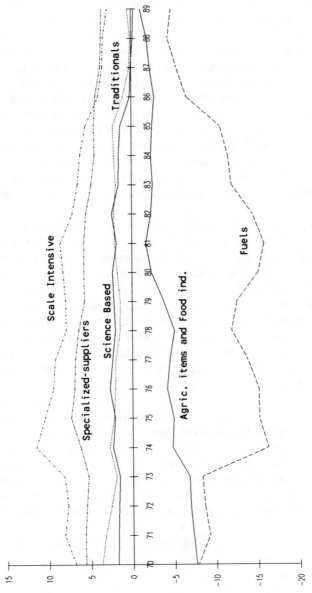

Figure 4 Patterns of trade specialization of the EC (12).

93

These overall trends, however, as we have already noted, mask the sharp differences that have characterized the trade specialization patterns of individual EC countries. The most interesting cases are those of Germany and Italy.

The positive German performance (tables 1 and 2) may be attributed to a relatively stable pattern of specialization, which continues to be based on comparative advantages in the scale-intensive industries (especially automobiles, chemicals, and pharmaceuticals) and specialized-suppliers (particularly machine tools and mechanical components) (figure 5). This consolidated consistency of the German trade specialization has also favored a widespread diffusion of innovations into the whole system of production through a strong and positive interaction between innovation producer and user sectors in the mechanical and chemical industries. The evolution of Germany's competitiveness thus reveals a renewed strength of German industry with respect to those of its EC partners. The German competitive position, however, does not appear as sound when compared to that of Japan because of its relative weakness in many science-based sectors (tables 1 and 2; figures 1 to 5), such as electronics (Guerrieri, 1991).

Italy has been characterized by a distinct trade specialization pattern with respect to those of the other major EC countries (figure 6). The trade performance of Italian industry has been decidedly positive over the past two decades (Tables 1 and 2). This is attributable not only to the strong competitive position of Italian firms in traditional sectors, but also to the strengthening of Italian specialization in capital goods in mechanical engineering (specialized suppliers), such as machinery for specialized industries. This is the result of the process of extensive restructuring in Italian industry beginning in the mid-1970s, based largely on the application and diffusion of mostly imported technology. This process also allowed some so-called mature sectors to be revitalized through positive interaction between mechanical engineering and traditional sectors of innovation user-producer type. In this respect, the case of Italy shows that the concept of maturity of sectors should be treated with extreme caution because technological change may remove the aging symptoms of the more traditional industries. These Italian comparative advantages are, however, countered by a significant decline in Italy's competitive position in many science-based and scale-intensive sectors. Such deterioration has been a side effect of the process of restructuring in the past decade (Guerrieri and Milana, 1990) and has disturbing implications for the future competitive position of Italian industry.

In summary, the data presented above indicates complex trends in the EC that cannot be interpreted unambiguously. Two points, however, should be stressed. The first is the severe loss of competitiveness suffered in the last decade by the EC countries as a group in science-based sectors, and especially in electronics technologies. The second point relates to the growing heterogeneity and differences within the EC. Both trends are bound to be of particular importance once the European internal market is completed.

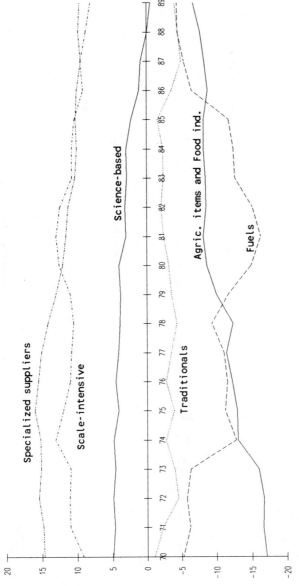

Figure 5 Patterns of trade specialization of Germany.

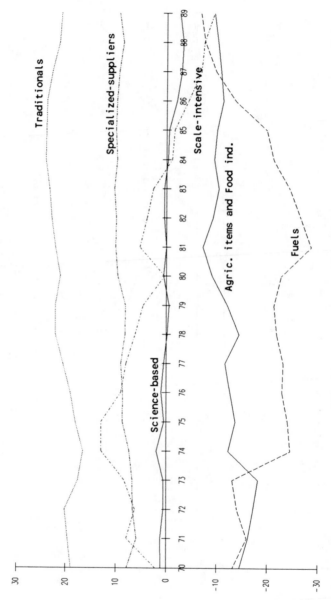

Figure 6 Patterns of trade specialization of Italy.

CONCLUSION

In this essay we have analyzed the trade performances and specialization patterns of all major countries and areas over the past two decades. Using an original data base for trade flows and a sectoral taxonomy that classifies different types of industries according to their distinct role in the process of innovation, we focused mainly on the relationship between the technological capabilities and trade performances of individual countries.

As demonstrated by the case of Japan, structural adaptability to a changing international trade environment appears to be a key element in a country's trade performance. The varying levels of adaptation of single countries seem to be linked to factors related to the long-term features of the pattern of technological and trade specialization. Although technology factors have proved to be fundamental, it does not necessarily follow that success in high-technology (science-based) industries is crucial to a country's trade performance; this is highlighted by the cases of the United States on the one hand, and Germany and Italy on the other hand.

Furthermore, despite increasing "intra-industry" trade, the patterns of trade in manufactures of the most advanced countries did not converge. The process of trade (industrial) adjustment followed different patterns in the major economies and achieved very different levels of success. Each major country presents a different structure of trade specialization and comparative advantages, and these national differences increased rather than diminished in the last two decades, bringing about major changes in the relative competitive positions of individual countries.

NOTES

1. Extensive surveys of this literature on innovation and technical change can be found in Freeman (1982), Rosenberg (1982), Scherer (1986), and Dosi et al. (1988), among others.

2. In this regard more traditional taxonomies that divide the different types of industries into high, medium and low technology-intensity product groups, such as those used in OECD (1985), Kremp and Larroumets (1985), and Koekkoek (1987), tend to ignore the prominent differences between the industrial sectors in terms of mechanisms for producing and diffusing technologies.

3. The three broad economic categories are (1) food items and agricultural raw materials, (2) fuels, and (3) other raw materials. The nine classes of products are drawn from the 400 product groups included in the data base SIE-World Trade.

4. For a detailed presentation of the data base SIE-World Trade used in this study, see Guerrieri and Milana, 1990.

5. The standardized trade balance (indicator of relative competitive position, IRCP) highlights the international distribution over time of trade surpluses and deficits among countries in each group of products. Trade balances are normalized by total world trade in the same group of products (CEPII, 1983; CEPII, 1989). The evolution of trade

balance distribution permits us to highlight competitiveness patterns of single countries in a certain group of products. For each country (j) the indicator is given by:

$$IRCP = \frac{Xi - Mi}{WTi}$$

where Xi equals the total exports of country (j) in the product group (i); Mi equals the total imports of country (j) in the product group (i); and WTi equals the total world exports (imports) in the product group (i).

6. The indicator of the contribution to trade balance (ICTB) of a country (j) with respect to a given group of products (i) is the following:

$$ICTBi = \frac{(Xi - Mi)}{(X + M) / 2} * 100 - \frac{(X - M)}{(X + M) / 2} * \frac{(Xi - Mi)}{(X + M)} * 100$$

where Xi equals the total exports of country (j) in the product group (i); Mi equals the total imports of country (j) in the product group (i); X equals the total exports of country (j); and M equals the total imports of country (j). Positive ICTB values indicate those product groups whose positive contribution to trade balance is greater than their weight in total trade (import plus export). Therefore, they represent comparative advantage sectors in trade specialization of a given country. Opposite considerations are associated with negative ICTB values. The sum of the indicators with respect to the various product groups (i) is equal to zero (see CEPII, 1983). This indicator was calculated for each of the nine groups of products in which total trade has been disaggregated for each country.

7. See Freeman (1987); Saucier (1987).

8. For a more in-depth analysis of the evolution of trade specialization of the Asian NICs, see Guerrieri and Milana (1990), Guerrieri (1991).

9. In electronic products the EC registered huge and increasing trade deficits with respect to both Japan and the United States. By the mid-1980s even the Asian NICs had accumulated significant surpluses with respect to the EC countries in all major electronics sectors (see Guerrieri, 1991). With the exception of electronics, however, the sectoral indicators reveal a positive evolution and a maintenance of the competitive position of European industry in many science-based (R&D-intensity) product groups over the 1980s, such as chemical-pharmaceuticals, electrical machinery, engineering instruments, and more recently aerospace—see Guerrieri and Milana (1990) and Pavitt and Patel (1991).

REFERENCES

Bergsten, C. F., *America in the World Economy: A Strategy for the 1990s,* Institute for International Economics (Washington, D.C., 1988).

Bradford, C., and Branson, W. H., *Trade and Structural Change in Pacific Asia* (Chicago: University of Chicago Press, 1987).

Cantwell, J. A., *Technological Innovations and Multinational Corporations* (Oxford: Basil Blackwell, 1989).

CEPII, *Economie mondiale: la montée des tensions* (Paris: Economica, 1983).

CEPII, *Commerce international: la fin des avantages acquis* (Paris: Economica, 1989).

Chesnais, F., "Science, Technology and Competitiveness," *OCSE STI Review,* n. 1, (1986), pp. 85–129.

Dertouzos, M. L., Lester, R. K., and Solow, R., *Made in America* (New York: Harper Collins, 1989).

Dosi, G., Pavitt, K., and Soete, L. *The Economics of Technical Change and International Trade* (Brighton: Wheatsheaf, 1990).

Dosi, G., et al., *Technical Change and Economic Theory* (London: Frances Pinter, 1988).

Freeman, C., *The Economics of Industrial Innovation* (London: Frances Pinter, 1982).

Freeman, C., *Technology Policy and Economic Performance: Lessons from Japan* (London: Frances Pinter, 1987).

Guerrieri, P., Technology and International Trade Performance of the Most Advanced Countries, *BRIE Working Paper* (Berkeley: University of California, 1991).

Guerrieri, P., and Milana, C. *L'Italia e il commercio mondiale* (Bologna; Il Mulino, 1990).

Koekkoek, A., "The Competitive Position of the EC in Hi-Tech," *Weltwirtschaftliches Archiv,* n. 1 (1987).

Krugman, P., "The Narrow Moving Band, the Dutch Disease, and the Competitive Consequences of Mrs. Thatcher: Notes on Trade in the Presence of Scale Dynamic Economies," *Journal of Development Economics* 27 (1987): pp. 41–55.

Lawrence, R., *Can America Compete?* (Washington, D.C.: The Brookings Institution, 1984).

Levin, R. et al., *Survey Research on R&D Appropriability and Technological Opportunity* (New Haven: Yale University Press, 1984).

Lundvall, B. A., "Innovation as an interactive process: from user-producer interaction to the national system of innovation" in *Technical Change and Economic Theory,* G. Dosi et al. (eds.) (London: Frances Pinter, 1988).

OECD, *Trade in High Technology Products* (Paris: Directorate for Science, Technology and Industry, 1985).

Pavitt, K., "Sectoral Patterns of Technical Change: Towards a Taxonomy and a Theory," *Research Policy,* 13 (1984): 343–373.

Pavitt, K., "International Patterns of Technological Accumulation," in *Strategies in Global Competition,* Hood, N., and Vahlne, J. E. (eds.) (London: Croom Helm, 1988).

Rosenberg, N., *Inside the Black Box* (Cambridge: Cambridge University Press, 1982).

Saucier, P., *Specialisation Internationale et Competitivité de l'Economie Japonaise* (Paris: Economica, 1987).

Scherer, F. M., Inter-industry technology flows in the United States, *Research Policy,* 11 (1982): 227–245.

Scherer, F. M., *Innovation and Growth. Schumpeterian Perspectives* (Cambridge, Mass.: MIT Press, 1986).

Schmookler, J. *Invention and Economic Growth* (Harvard: Harvard University Press, 1966).

Soete, L. "The impact of technological innovation on international trade patterns: the evidence reconsidered," *Research Policy,* 16 (1987): 101–30.

Teece, D. J. "Profiting from technological innovation," *Research Policy,* 15(6) (1986): 285–306.

APPENDIX

SIE-World Trade Data Base

The world foreign trade statistics used for the analysis in this chapter stem from the SIE-World Trade data base. The network of trade data worked out by the SIE (Servizi Informativi per l'Estero) provides detailed information on exports and imports for 83 countries with respect to 400 product groups, 98 sectors, 25 broad commodity groups, and 5 main product categories.

The data base includes trade statistics with respect to the 24 OECD countries, the newly industrializing countries (NICs), the other developing countries, and the former CMEA countries, and makes it possible to examine and analyze the entire world trade matrix. The source for the basic trade statistics of the SIE-World Trade is the publications of the OECD and the United Nations provided on magnetic tapes. The SIE data base is organized in different product group classification at various levels of disaggregation (400 product groups, 98 sectors, 25 categories, 5 branches) according to the three Standard International Trade Classifications (SITC), *Revised, Revision 2*, and *Revision 3*, defined by the Statistical Office of the UN (1961, 1975, 1986) as to the periods 1961–1975, 1978–1987, and 1988 on.

The nine product groups classification used in this chapter is based on the 400 product groups of the SIE-World Trade. A summary list of the product groups included in each of the nine classes of products is provided below:

1. *Food items and agricultural raw materials* (41 product groups): Food—Live animals, animal oil and fats, natural rubber, vegetable and animal textile fibers, cork and wood, and skins.
2. *Fuels* (4 product groups): Coal, petroleum oil, and gas.
3. *Other raw materials* (17 product groups): Iron ore, ores of base metals, and other crude minerals.
4. *Food industry* (36 product groups): Meat and meat preparations, dairy products, vegetables and fruit preparations, cereal preparations, sugar preparations, and other edible products.
5. *Science based* (59 product groups): Synthetic organic dyestuffs, radioactive and associated materials, polymerization and co-polymerization products, antibiotics and other pharmaceutical products, nuclear reactors, automatic data processing machines and units, telecommunications equipment, semiconductor devices, electronic microcircuits, electronic measuring instruments, electric power machinery and apparatus, internal combustion piston engines, aircraft and associated equipment, medical instruments, optical instruments, and photographic apparatus and equipment.

6. *Scale Intensive* (106 product groups): Paper and paperboard, organic chemicals, inorganic chemical products, other chemical materials and products, medicinal and pharmaceutical products, petroleum products, rubber manufactures, nonmetallic mineral manufactures, iron and steel, nonferrous metal products, television, radio, other image-sound recorders and reproducers, household-type electrical equipment, ships and boats, railway vehicles and equipment, and road vehicles.

7. *Specialized Suppliers* (43 product groups): Agricultural machinery, machine tools for working metals, metal working machinery, other machine tools for particular specialized industries, construction and mining machinery, textile and leather machinery, paper and paperboard machinery, other machinery for particular specialized industries, other general industrial machinery and equipment, electrical equipment and components, measuring, checking, analyzing instruments, optical goods, and other miscellaneous products.

8. *Traditionals or Supplier dominated* (76 product groups): Textile products, articles of apparel and clothing accessories, leather manufactures, footwear, wood manufactures, furniture, paper and printed products, articles of ceramic materials, glass products, miscellaneous manufactures of metal (structures, tools, cutlery, and other articles), jewelry, gold products, imitation jewelry, musical instruments, sporting goods, toys and games, and other miscellaneous products.

9. *Residuals* (18 product groups): Other product groups n.e.s.

Chapter 8

Why Firms Countertrade in Overseas and Domestic Markets

C. W. Neale and P. Sercu

Abstract *The motivations to countertrade (CT) commonly include a desire to circumvent credit and foreign exchange problems, to surmount barriers to otherwise closed markets, to hide price cuts or simply to remain competitive. CT arrangements essentially constitute packages of buying, selling and financing contracts. Accounting for CT requires an explanation of why such package deals should be preferred to a set of component contracts. Examination of domestic CT stripped of "international ramifications" suggests that the inherent rationales are desired to hide price cuts and a need to overcome cash shortages, motivations consistent with data collected from UK and Canadian firms, who also stress problems of contracting complexity and of finding uses for countertraded goods.*

INTRODUCTION

During the past decade, the phenomenon of countertrade (CT hereafter), the modern equivalent of barter, has received considerable attention. Initially reported as a highly undesirable, even quasi-illegal practice, it is now regarded as a fact of business life that could expand even more as trading restrictions with eastern Europe continue to loosen. Over this period, understanding of the internal mechanics of CT deals and of the motivations of CT partners has escalated. The label CT has become a generic term that is applied to any set of cross-border contracts linking a seller's exports to imports from the buyer, covering practices ranging from direct exchange (barter) to long-term buyback contracts.

All CT deals have a common characteristic—*reciprocity*. In each case, a seller provides a buyer with goods (or services) and undertakes in return to purchase goods (or services) from the buyer. To some, tying sales to purchases represents a throwback to a moneyless age, when a hungry blacksmith had to find a farmer whose horse needed a new shoe. Money and markets evolved to avoid this! CT is thus often presented as an inefficient alternative to trading via cash or credit, although this assessment is somewhat superficial.

Another common feature of CT deals is their complexity, as the following examples illustrate. ICL, the British computer manufacturer, provided components to Poland for building portable televisions to western European standards and then acted as a sales agent for the TVs in the West. The Poles then purchased ICL personal computers in kit form with the hard currency received for the TV sets. These machines were customized for the Polish market and sold locally for zlotys, which were then used to subsidize production of more televisions that ICL sold in the West. 3M Corporation set up a Swiss subsidiary to negotiate deals with Eastern Bloc countries. The proceeds from selling 1 million dollars' worth of Polish nails were deposited in a Western bank and the Polish government drew on the account to buy 3M healthcare products.

However, it would be misleading to present CT as an exclusively international phenomenon—reciprocal trading even occurs within the borders of highly developed economies. Domestic CT is most developed in the United States: Naisbitt (1991) reports that more than 400 barter exchanges assist their 175,000 members to trade products and services. A typical domestic barter operator is Andriana Furs Inc. of Chicago, which in 1990 bartered $100,000 in furs for computers, telephones, and advertising spots on a local radio station. In a deal with a cash-short airline, 3M traded space on outdoor billboards for air-freight credits. Nor are all barter exponents traditional businesses. In the run-up to the 1984 Olympics, the Los Angeles organizing committee traded licensing rights of the Olympic logo and mascot for free transport from United Airlines, 500 Buicks from General Motors, and 250,000 rolls of film from Fuji.

In this chapter, we briefly examine various forms of CT and attempt to identify the fundamental reasons why firms engage in these practices in *both* overseas and domestic markets; we then present some evidence on this issue.

FORMS OF COUNTERTRADE

The simplest type of CT is "barter," or direct goods-for-goods exchange— exports are traded for goods (or services) from the importing market, without a cash transfer. Recently, Greece exchanged 200,000 tons of wheat for 600,000 tons of Algerian crude oil. The computer manufacturer ICL has accepted eggs, furniture, jewelry, and plastics to sell computers into Eastern Europe.

"Compensation" is a derivative of barter and is probably more prevalent. This also involves direct exchange of goods but each leg of the transaction is valued in monetary units and reflected in a counterflow of finance. Figure 1 illustrates a compensation deal between a Western exporting firm and a state import agency. "Financial flows" may consist of the clearing of claims, and do not necessarily require foreign exchange transfers. Indeed, most such deals are arranged to avoid currency transfers. Payment for the primary delivery is al-

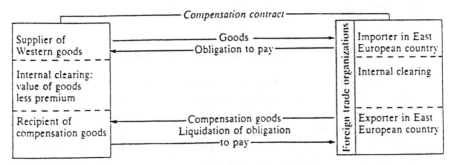

Source: C. Raemy-Dirks (1986)

Figure 1 Compensation with assignment. *Exhibit from 'Trade Financing' published by Euromoney Books, London.*

lowed on credit by the supplier, whose claim for payment is registered in a clearing account and is liquidated by the counterdelivery.

"Counterpurchase" is the commonest form of CT. As a condition of securing a sale, the exporter undertakes to purchase goods and services selected from a "shopping list" of available goods. A recent example was Iran's purchase of $24.5 million of Indonesian tea, plywood, rubber, and other goods in return for Indonesian purchases of Iranian crude oil. Counterpurchase differs from barter and compensation by the existence of an option to take delivery of the countertraded goods at any time within a specified time period. In this respect, it resembles a futures contract.

Imbalances in long-term bilateral trade, often between Eastern European countries and developing nations, may lead to the accumulation of uncleared credit surpluses. For example, Brazil once had a large credit surplus with Poland. Such surpluses can be tapped by third countries, so that UK exports to Brazil might be financed from the sale of Polish goods to the United Kingdom or elsewhere; this is called "switch-trading." Switch deals typically involve swapping the documentation (and destination) of goods on the high seas, thus making the forward contract and delivery option transferable.

In a "buyback," suppliers of plant or equipment agree to take payment in the form of the future output of the investment. For example, Italy sold a $90 million synthetic fiber plant to the former Soviet Union in return for deliveries of acrylic fiber. In effect, a single forward deal is replaced by a long-term subcontracting arrangement, essentially a series of forward contracts.

Sercu (1990) argues that all CT techniques involve combinations of standard contracts (import, import financing, and forward export). A CT contract is not merely a device for trading without cash—it is a deal in which imports, secured loan, and exports form part of a "bundled package" of trade and financing contracts. But this bundling is costly and complex—why do such deals occur?

We must look for specific advantages of packages to explain the incentive to tie several interlocking contracts into one complex deal.

EXPLANATIONS FOR COUNTERTRADE

The resurgence of CT is attributed to numerous factors. It occurs in cases of international credit or hard currency shortage and when governments wish to access Western marketing channels, avoid balance of payments problems, mask dumping, unload poor quality goods, or move produce in global excess supply (Kaikati, 1981; Yoffie, 1984). Western exporters prefer hard currency or Letters of Credit to payment in goods because currency is more liquid, more certain, and less troublesome, despite the greater exchange rate volatility of recent times. If, however, Western exporters face problems like general spare capacity and strongly competitive rivals, they may accept customer demands for CT to meet their own volume objectives and achieve contributions to their fixed costs.

CT is often regarded as a "second-best" alternative, reluctantly adopted only when orthodox approaches appear unworkable. However, experience breeds expertise, a "global countertrade service industry" (Palia, 1990) has arisen to handle CT risks, and many firms now operate specialist units to manage their CT operations. Why do they use CT rather than orthodox trading channels?

Some overseas customers who possess little or no export marketing expertise may be anxious to gain access to Western marketing channels, offering in return especially favorable exchange terms, as well as "ready-made" local distribution outlets (Zurawicki, 1988). CT can thus be more efficient than orthodox trade if it reduces search and transactions costs, such as agents' commission. It may avoid the bureaucratic delays in a currency rationing process under an exchange control regime, advancing the receipt of traded goods. CT thus resembles selling accounts receivable (Mirus and Yeung, 1986).

Bundling may be a response to imperfections in less developed economies, with only embryonic market systems, unreliable legal systems, and paucity of information (Mirus and Yeung, 1991). In some transactions, the quality of goods and services is only fully observable to suppliers, encouraging sellers to undersupply the unobservable characteristics. Conversely, property rights over information-based goods and services are difficult to protect. With CT, the agency problems are reduced as the exporter finds that the value of the contract depends on his own efforts to identify and sell exportable local goods. Moreover, he can withdraw marketing services if his property rights are threatened.

CT packages, despite serious drafting and implementation costs, may thus be preferable under certain conditions to sets of independent contracts. However, CT arrangements between firms in developed economies require separate examination.

THE RATIONALE FOR DOMESTIC COUNTERTRADE

Domestic CT is most highly developed in the United States, where a network of specialist "barter brokers" has arisen to match clients. Using extensive computer data bases, these brokers can quickly and cheaply locate potential exchange partners, largely eliminating the transactions costs that traditional barter involves. The resulting deals may be multilateral, locking several companies into linked transactions.

Where matches are difficult to find, barter brokers may stock goods for which they have no immediate buyers in return for trade credits ("barter dollars"). The recipient can use these credits to buy goods from the broker's stocks at a later date or goods offered by another of the broker's clients. In a formalized barter exchange, members sell to the broker, who credits their accounts with trade dollars that can then be used to purchase goods from the broker's ever-changing "catalogue." A barter broker charges a commission of about 10% of the value of the deal arranged. For participants, this represents the value of avoiding more conventional marketing techniques.

In principle, domestic barter is no different from international barter. It operates where buyers and sellers are widely dispersed, as a response to the market's inefficiency in disseminating information about exchange opportunities, and is most commonly found among companies with surplus stocks. These may fetch a better "price" (albeit discounted) if placed with a carefully chosen barter partner than if sold via regular marketing channels. Barter in the United States is most commonly offered by airlines (surplus seats), television companies (surplus advertising time) and hotel groups (surplus accommodation). Naisbitt (1991) is emphatic: "Look for the greatest growth among small, cash-poor businesses in sluggish industries."

International CT is often driven by shortage of foreign exchange reserves—the domestic analogue is liquidity difficulties among traders. For example, a cash-short newspaper or broadcasting company might prefer to "sell" advertising slots in exchange for vital inputs like printing paper or video equipment. The advantage of CT is speed. A standard, open-account sale of the same advertising space to a third party should always be possible if a sufficient discount is offered, but settlement requires time, whereas with CT the transaction is "immediate." The preference for CT stems from financial distress so it is perhaps not applicable under normal trading conditions.

A second possible rationale for CT is the desire to camouflage part of a business agreement. In CT, prices need not be made explicit in the contract. Firms might prefer to conceal a discount that, if known, might set a precedent to be invoked by other customers, violate antidumping or fair trading practices legislation, or trigger a price war. There may also be a mutual desire to inflate sales.

In summary, the rationales for domestic CT (besides the standard advantages of trading on credit) are, firstly, desire to inflate sales or to hide price cuts (by one or both parties), and secondly, the appeal of a relatively simple and quick credit fix under financial distress. The main drawbacks, beyond those inherent in forward contracts or subcontracting deals, are cost and complexity.

EVIDENCE

Evidence on domestic CT practices and attitudes is sparse and the established United States' "barter exchanges" have not been extensively researched. However, two surveys of countertrading activity conducted by Neale and Shipley (1988) in the United Kingdom and by Neale, Shipley, and Dodds (1991) in Canada derived data from both overseas and domestic countertraders. Information from the second group on the perceived benefits and drawbacks of CT in the domestic arena may allow us to cast some light on our suggested reasons for domestic CT.

Response rates and respondents' participation in different forms of CT showed a high degree of comparability. Tables 1, 2, and 3 respectively show how respondents engaged in various types of CT, and their perceptions of benefits and drawbacks.

CT Participation

The participation data in table 1 indicate that some firms engage in several CT media. It is surprising to encounter the buy-back and switch-trade variants, these usually being associated with overseas trading, but direct exchange and counterpurchase combined occupy the major proportion of CT activity, 79% for the United Kingdom and 83% for Canada. Direct exchange is more prevalent among Canadian respondents.

Table 1
Participation in Forms of CT*

	UK (22 firms)		Canada (15 firms)		Pooled data (37 firms)	
	N	%	N	%	N	%
Counterpurchase	15	68	9	60	24	65
Buy-back	4	18	1	6	5	14
Switch-Trade	2	9	3	20	5	14
Direct Exchange	7	32	10	66	17	46
Totals	28	127	23	152	51	139

*The percentages express proportions of the relevant sample that had undertaken the indicated practice. These exceed 100 due to participation in more than one form of CT.

Table 2
Benefits from Domestic CT

	UK (N = 22)		Canada (N = 15)		All (N = 37)	
	Mean	Rank	Mean	Rank	Mean	Rank
Increases competitiveness	2.82	1	3.06	3	2.92	2
Increases sales volume	2.77	2	3.40	2	3.03	1
Allows fuller use of capacity	2.36	3	3.60	1	2.86	3
Overcomes credit difficulties	2.32	4	1.87	7	2.14	6
Allows entry into difficult markets	2.14	5	2.66	5	2.35	5
Source of attractive inputs	2.13	6	2.74	4	2.38	4
Disposal of declining products	1.96	7	2.13	6	2.00	7

Means are based on responses to questions based on a 5-point Likert scale with a range of 1 = "no benefit" to 5 = "utmost benefit." Rank correlation coefficient between samples = +0.54.

Benefits of CT

Table 2 is based on relative scores awarded to the benefits from engaging in domestic CT. Results are presented by respondents' domicile and in pooled form, a procedure justified by the broad comparability of financial and commercial environments facing firms in each country. The benefits claimed from CT were comparable across both samples, with the same three benefits—competitiveness, desire to expand volume, and desire to increase capacity utilization–heading each subsample and also the pooled sample. These benefits could reflect the merits of simply doing business, in which case they would not

Table 3
Problems Experienced in Domestic CT

	UK (N = 22)		Canada (N = 15)		All (N = 37)	
	Mean	Rank	Mean	Rank	Mean	Rank
No "in-house use" for goods offered	2.59	1	1.86	6	2.30	1 =
Complex negotiations	2.32	2	2.27	2 =	2.30	1 =
Difficult to resell goods offered by customers	2.27	3	1.80	7 =	2.08	6
Customers' negotiating strength	2.22	4	2.00	4 =	2.14	5
Time-consuming negotiations	2.18	5	2.27	2 =	2.22	4
Problems with "pricing"	2.04	6	2.60	1	2.27	3
Increases costs	1.86	7	1.80	7 =	1.84	7
Customer becomes potential competitor	1.77	8	1.54	9	1.68	9
General increase in uncertainty	1.68	9	1.53	10	1.62	10
Need for costly brokerage	1.50	10	2.00	4 =	1.70	8

Rank correlation coefficient between samples = +0.39.

signify any advantage peculiar to CT. We must revert to the original issue: why would these sales have been impossible without CT?

One interpretation is that CT offers a way to expand sales via a hidden price cut. If this is true, then the responses appear consistent with our analysis. Consider the low rank of "allows disposal of declining products." If sellers aimed to rid inventories of obsolete (rather than struggling) goods, they would not fear starting price wars or setting precedents for other customers and could cut prices openly.

Another suggested explanation for domestic CT is "overcoming credit difficulties," and ranks highly in the UK but not the Canadian subsample. This may be a surprising result for a sample of major UK companies taken in 1985 when credit problems were rare, yet it is consistent with our earlier analysis.

Problems with CT

Table 3 shows the ten menu items offered regarding perceived difficulties with domestic CT.

UK firms experience greatest difficulties in dealing with possibly suspect countertraded goods. This appears less of a problem in Canada where the prime difficulty is how to price CT goods.

The prominence of "complex negotiations" confirms the inherent drawbacks of bundling several contracts into one package deal, implying that CT incorporates advantages that cannot otherwise be obtained. In the pooled sample, the pricing problem ranks third (although only sixth in the United Kingdom), lending some support to the diagnosis of attempts to camouflage part of the contract as a motive for CT.

The low rank of "increase in uncertainty" also fits the risk reduction offered by forward CT contracts or subcontracting arrangements, but this is not a benefit specific to CT. Creating potential competition is not important, which probably reflects the rarity of buy-back deals (where this problem would most likely occur) in domestic CT.

SUMMARY AND CONCLUSION

This chapter considers why firms may prefer CT "package deals," which typically require complex contractual arrangements, to a set of independent selling, purchasing, and finance contracts. Much CT can be explained by imperfections in international markets. This obscures the essential motives for CT, which can be isolated by eliminating international politico-economic factors and studying CT in a domestic context. This analysis suggests that firms undertake CT for two basic reasons: to hide volume-boosting price cuts, and to circumvent short-term credit-financing problems. Evidence from UK and Canadian firms is consistent with the first motive, although only UK firms seem to engage in domestic CT for the second reason.

This analysis is also significant at a global level, especially in the context of the recent liberalization of the economies in eastern Europe, a traditional stronghold of countertrade. It is often argued that international CT will disappear once certain currencies become fully convertible, and when other market imperfections, like bureaucratic restrictions on trade, are removed. However, our analysis suggests that there will be a role for CT so long as traders want to make hidden price cuts and suffer from liquidity and credit problems.

REFERENCES

Kaikati, J., "The International Barter Boom: Perspective and Challenges," *Journal of International Marketing* 1: 8 (1981).

Mirus, R., and Yeung, B., "Economic Incentives for Countertrade." *Journal of International Business Studies* 27: 3 (1986).

Mirus, R., and Yeung, B., "Countertrade: What Have We Learnt? *International Trade and Finance Association* (Marseilles, 1991).

Naisbitt, J., "Business by Barter: Hotter than Ever," *Inside Guide* June (1991).

Neale, C. W., and Shipley, D. D., "Effects of Countertrade: Divergent Perceptions Between Practitioners and Non-Participants," *Journal of Management Studies* 25: 1 (1988): 57–71.

Neale, C. W., Shipley, D. D., and Dodds, J. C., "Aspects of Countertrade Involvement by British and Canadian Exporters: A Comparative Study," *Management International Review* 31: 1 (1991).

Palia, A. P., "Worldwide Network of Countertrade Services," *Industrial Marketing Management* 19: 1 (1990).

Raemy-Dirks, C., "Countertrade: Linked Purchases in International Trade." In *Trade Financing,* Gmür, C. J., ed. (London: Euromoney Publications, 1986).

Sercu, P., "Pros and Cons of Countertrade: A Critical Note," *European Institute for Advanced Studies in Management Working Paper* 90–07.

Yoffie, D. B., "Profiting from Countertrade," *Harvard Business Review* May-June (1984).

Zurawicki, L., "Marketing Rationale for Countertrade," *European Management Journal* 6: 3 Autumn (1988).

Part Two

Regional Integration

Chapter 9

Economic Integration, the European Economic Community, and the Future of the International Trade System

Dominick Salvatore

Abstract *This chapter reviews briefly the development of customs union theory and examines some recent estimates of the static and dynamic effects resulting from the full integration of the European Economic Community by 1992. Then, it examines the relationship among the rise of the new protectionism, strategic trade theory, the formation of trading blocks, and the future of the international trading system.*

INTRODUCTION

Traditional trade theory postulates that free trade leads to the most efficient utilization of world resources and thus maximizes world welfare and output. Before 1950, it was widely believed that to the extent that the formation of a customs union does not increase trade barriers against the rest of the world the elimination of trade barriers among union members represents a movement toward freer trade and, as such, it would increase the welfare of member and nonmember nations alike.

However, Viner (1950) showed that a customs union could increase or reduce the welfare of member nations and of the rest of the world, depending on whether the customs union led to trade creation or trade diversion, respectively. This is an example of the theory of the second best (Lipsey and Lancaster, 1956), which postulates that if all the conditions required to maximize welfare or reach Pareto optimum cannot be satisfied, trying to satisfy as many of these conditions as possible does not usually lead to the second-best position. Viner, however, considered only the production effects resulting from the formation of a customs union and assumed that member nations always consumed commodities in a constant proportion regardless of relative commodity prices. Meade (1955) subsequently showed that when substitution in consumption as well as

115

production is considered, even a trade-diverting customs union could lead to increased welfare for member and nonmember nations.

According to Lipsey (1960), a customs union is more likely to lead to increased welfare: the higher the pre-union trade barriers of member countries are, the lower the customs union's barriers are on trade with the rest of the world; the greater the number of countries is which forms the customs union, and the larger their size, the more competitive rather than complementary the economies of member nations are; the closer the members of the customs union are geographically, the greater the preunion trade and economic relationship is among the potential members of the customs union. The reasons for the greater success of the European Economic Community (EEC) than of the European Free Trade Association (EFTA) are that the nations forming the EEC were much more competitive than complementary, were closer geographically, and had greater pre-union intra-area trade than the EFTA nations.

Besides the static welfare effects discussed above, the nations forming a customs union are likely to receive several important dynamic benefits. These result from increased competition, economies of scale, stimulus to investment, and better utilization of economic resources. Increased competition is likely to stimulate the development and utilization of new technology. Economies of scale can result from reducing the range of differentiated products manufactured in each plant and increasing "production runs." Investments are stimulated not only internally but also from abroad to overcome trade barriers on nonunion products. The massive investment made in Europe by U.S. firms during the late 1950s and 1960s, and by U.S. and Japanese firms in the late 1980s and early 1990s can be explained by their desire not to be excluded from the rapidly growing EEC market. These dynamic benefits are believed to be much greater than the static gains. Indeed, the United Kingdom joined the EEC in 1973 primarily on the expectation of significant dynamic benefits.

INTERNAL AND EXTERNAL EFFECTS FROM THE FORMATION AND EXTENSION OF THE EEC

From the numerous studies that attempted to measure the effect of the formation of the EEC on member nations, we can reach the following conclusions (Jacquemin and Sapir, 1988). The static welfare benefit from the formation of the EEC was 1% or less of member nations' GNP. The rapid growth of the EEC and the reduction to very low levels of the average tariff on imports of industrial products as a result of the Kennedy and the Tokyo Rounds of multilateral trade negotiations significantly expanded trade in industrial goods with nonmembers. However, significant trade diversion in agricultural commodities, particularly in temperate products such as grains from the United States, also resulted. The EEC generally sacrificed consumers' interests to those of community farmers by setting relatively high prices for agricultural products. This resulted in huge agricultural surpluses, skyrocketing storage costs, subsidized exports, and sharp trade disputes with the United States. It also led to the collapse of the Uruguay Round in December of 1990.

Despite the elimination of tariffs on trade among EEC members, many nontariff barriers remain. Even more damaging to efficiency are the red tape and delays created by customs formalities, restrictive practices in public procurement, divergent product standards, and conflicting business and tax regulations. All of these are now scheduled to be eliminated as part of the "Programme for the Completion of the Internal Market by 1992." If successful, it will result in substantial efficiency gains and benefits to EEC members.

Table 1 indicates that the growth of the gross domestic product (GDP) of the EEC members as a group is expected to increase by 0.2% because of the removal of nontariff trade barriers, 2.2% because of the removal of production barriers, 1.65% because of economies of scale, and 1.25% because of intensified competition, for an overall one-time total gain of 5.3% of the EEC's GDP in 1988 (Cecchini, 1990, pp. 84 and 98). This is equivalent to about $265 billion. In addition, the overall rate of inflation is expected to fall by 6.1% and 1.8 million additional jobs are expected to be created, thereby reducing the average rate of unemployment in the EEC by 1.5% from the 10% or so that prevailed during the late 1980s.

Table 2 (Congressional Budget Office, 1990) shows estimates of the effect of 1992 on real GDP, short-term interest rates, and net exports (trade balance) of the EEC and the United States in each year from 1990 through 1995 and for the year 2000, with a neutral fiscal policy (i.e., one that keeps the budget deficit of EEC members constant in relation to GDP). These estimates were obtained from simulations of the McKibbin-Sachs Global Model (MSG). We see from Table 2 that the 1992 reform program would raise the GDP in the EEC by about 6% above what it would otherwise be by the year 2000. The effect on real short-term interest rates would be insignificant. The EEC's net exports or trade balance would improve by $35 billion by the year 2000. The effect on U.S. real GDP, real short-term interest rates, and net exports is zero or very small. All of these figures are based on the assumption that the level of protectionism in the

Table 1
Potential Benefits from a Fully Integrated Internal Market
in the EEC by 1992

Gains from:	Percent of GDP
Removal of nontariff trade barriers	0.20
Removal of production barriers	2.20
Economies of scale	1.65
Intensified competition	1.25
Overall total gains	5.30

Table 2
Estimated Effects of 1992 on the EEC and on the U.S.

	1990	1991	1992	1993	1994	1995	2000
EEC							
Real GDP*	0.8	1.6	3.0	4.9	6.9	7.4	6.0
Real short term $i^\dagger$	0.4	1.3	1.4	1.6	0.6	0.0	0.0
Net exports‡	1.4	1.9	8.7	15.8	26.1	30.3	34.5
United States							
Real GDP*	0.0	0.0	0.1	0.2	0.3	0.3	0.0
Real short term $i^\dagger$	0.0	0.0	−0.2	−0.2	0.0	0.1	0.1
Net exports‡	−0.5	−0.5	−2.3	−2.3	−1.8	−1.8	−2.1

*Percentage difference from base line.
$^\dagger i$ = Interest rate as difference from baseline in percentage points.
‡Difference from baseline in billions of 1989 dollars.

EEC will remain the same as in the late 1980s. Outsiders, particularly the United States and Japan, however, fear that as the EEC tears down internal barriers to form a single, unified market it might become protectionistic externally ("fortress Europe"). A fully integrated internal market will certainly confer on the EEC great economic and political strength that could be used to keep competition out. Whether it will actually do so only time will tell.

TRADE PROTECTIONISM, GATT, AND THE FORMATION OF TRADING BLOCS

Despite the unquestionable success of the present trading system under the General Agreement on Tariffs and Trade (GATT), several fundamental weaknesses have become evident during the past decade. The first arises from the increasing tendency of nations to bypass GATT rules and impose many new types of nontariff trade barriers (NTBs) to international trade (Salvatore, 1987a, 1987b, 1988, 1989, 1992). These are collectively referred to as "new protectionism" and include "voluntary" export restrains, orderly marketing arrangements, antidumping measures, countervailing duties, and so on. As much as 50% of world trade is now affected by this new protectionism. Because these new nontariff barriers are applied only against the exports of specific nations (i.e., they are discriminatory), they are pushing the world more and more away from multilateralism and freer trade toward bilateralism and more restricted trade. If this process continues the leading nations may even begin to demand specific shares of each other's market as a condition for allowing foreign products continued access to their own market.

The superiority of an international trading system characterized by greater multilateralism and international specialization over a trading system based on protectionism, bilateralism, and division of the world into major trading blocks is by no means as clearcut today as it was a decade ago. There are two reasons for this. One is that many new nontariff trade barriers are considered part of the arsenal of policies that a nation believes is necessary to achieve some important domestic objectives. An example of this is the protection from foreign competition and the subsidies provided by many leading nations to their national computer and data processing industries. The second is that in recent years the very theoretical foundation of the modern theory of international trade, which for nearly two centuries has been consistently based on the alleged superiority of free trade over a system based on trade restrictions, is being questioned (Krugman, 1986). Thus, on theoretical grounds as well for reasons of political feasibility, the world faces a choice between a more restricted or a more open trading system. The direction chosen in the next few years is crucial in determining the type of international trade order the world will have in the twenty-first century.

Today all the leading countries impose some type of restriction on the importation of automobiles, steel, textiles, consumer electronic products, and agricultural products. Practically all nations provide direct and indirect subsidies to their computer and data processing industry, aircraft industry, and most other high-tech industries. Industrial nations regard these trade restrictions and subsidies as crucial, either to protect employment in large and mature industries (such as automobile, steel, and textile) or to promote the growth of high-tech industries (such as the computer and aircraft industries), which are deemed essential for international competitiveness and future technological progress. These goals are promoted by tax benefits and subsidies for research, education, and investment, and most nations regard these as purely internal matters.

An example of this is Japan's industrial strategy. It is well known that Japan provides protection from foreign competition and a maze of direct and indirect subsidies to an industry targeted for growth. After the industry has grown and is able to meet foreign competition, with the tacit approval and indirect support of the government, the industry begins to dump the product (i.e., to sell the product at below domestic production cost) on the world market on a massive scale until it has driven foreign competitors out of business or rendered them impotent. Then the industry raises prices and proclaims full support for the principle of free trade, pointing to its then-unprotected industry as a model of efficiency. Japan has successfully and systematically applied this policy to steel, automobiles, and computer memory chips, and is now doing this in computers and financial services. Understandably Japan is not ready to abandon an industrial strategy that proved so successful and one that has been instrumental in turning the nation into a first-class economic power in just a few decades.

Although somewhat less aggressively and generally less successfully, the leading European countries have also used some of these same policies (e.g., the Airbus and the Arianne space program) and, to some extent, so has the United States (through the commercial applications of the technological discoveries arising from its military and space research programs). Thus, while the leaders of the major industrial countries pay lip service to the great benefits of and their preference for a free multilateral trading system, they have become more protectionistic since the mid-1970s. Charging interference with national sovereignty, the leading industrial nations are even objecting to having to provide information to GATT on these new indirect forms of trade protection. The attempt at the Tokyo Round (1974–1977) to negotiate rules of behavior to limit the use of these new forms of protectionism and making them more transparent (e.g., by replacing then with equivalent open tariffs) has, in general, not been successful.

The more protectionist trade alternative is also characterized by more bilateral trade deals. This is evidenced by the incessant movement toward the formation of three major trading blocs in the world today: the EC; the United States, Canada, and Mexico; and Japan with the Southeast Asian countries and possibly Australia. The EC is scheduled to remove all remaining barriers to the internal flow of goods and resources by the end of 1992. In 1988, the United States negotiated a free trade agreement with Canada to remove all barriers to trade and is now negotiating to do the same with Mexico. As a result Japan is becoming increasingly concerned about being excluded from these two large trading blocs and may in response set up a free trade area with some other Asian countries and Australia. One could argue along the lines of customs union theory that such free trade areas are second-best trade arrangements if a true worldwide free trade system cannot be achieved under present conditions. The formation of these trade blocs, it is argued, will lead to increased specialization in production and raise world welfare if the net effect is to stimulate trade within each bloc without reducing trade among the blocs. The latter expectation, however, may not materialize and the formation of trading blocs may in fact have a net trade-diverting effect. This will impose efficiency and welfare costs on the world similar to those resulting from the oligopolization of previously near-perfect competitive markets.

Protectionism and bilateralism are also indirectly being encouraged by the recent questioning of the superiority of the time-honored free-trade model of international economics. Ricardo's theory of comparative advantage is attacked as being entirely static in nature and not very relevant to international trade in a world characterized by imperfect competition, technological breakthroughs, product cycles, intra-industry trade, multinational corporations, and integrated capital markets. Some of this criticism is not new but it seems to have gained new force and legitimacy because some leading theoreticians are joining in the criticism of traditional comparative advantage. It is now believed that most of today's international trade is based on comparative advantage that is created by industrial policies (which give rise to new technologies and new industries) rather than by traditional comparative advantage based on inherited international differences in factor endowments across nations.

It is interesting, however, that Paul Krugman (1987), one of the advocates of strategic trade theory, eventually came to the conclusion that interferences with the free flow of international trade, by using industrial policies to create comparative advantage, may lead to even greater market imperfections and inefficiencies. Frankly, I do not think that these recent criticisms of comparative advantage amount to much. Market imperfections and inefficiencies do exist, but as Bhagwati (1971) pointed out two decades ago, these imperfections can be corrected with the appropriate policies in the markets where the imperfections occur. Similarly, the theory of comparative advantage can be extended to include dynamic changes in the form of new products and new technologies. Furthermore, industrial policies intended to create comparative advantage face the serious theoretical criticism that it is often very difficult for the government to pick winners in the technological race. Indeed, for each success story, a counterexample of a major failure could also be cited (e.g., the abandoned synthetic fuel program in the United States, the economic losses of the Anglo-French Concorde, and the still higher cost of electricity generated by atomic power). These recent attacks on traditional trade theory in general and comparative advantage in particular led Paul Samuelson to state that he has looked and found nothing that makes sense in these recent criticisms of comparative advantage: "They wouldn't pass peer review in any economic journal. I am afraid it's a very superficial diagnosis. . . . Competitive advantage is the only competitive theory that there is." (Paul Samuelson, 1987.) This is also the view of Jagdish Bhagwati (1988).

PROTECTIONISM, TRADING BLOCS, AND THE FUTURE OF THE INTERNATIONAL TRADING SYSTEM

Although the outcome of the current round of trade negotiations can certainly affect the international economic order of the twenty-first century, I believe that the world is already locked into a trading system characterized by three major trade blocs. The EC is already a political and economic reality, the United States-Canada-Mexico free trade area seems to be more or less agreed upon, and the only question is the speed with which the agreements are carried out in practice. Least developed is the Asian trade bloc around Japan, but the dynamics of the situation are such that its formation is all but inevitable if the other two trading blocs continue to keep to their implementation schedule.

What the current round of trade negotiations can do is to determine the degree of openness of trade among the three economic blocs. If the Uruguay Round achieves only meager results, commercial relations among the blocs will be seriously restricted and trade frictions will be the order of the day. The total volume of world trade will fail to rise and may even decline, international specialization in production will be limited mostly by the extent of the market within each trade bloc, and the stimulating force that trade can play in the world economy will be seriously constrained. Under these circumstances, the full dynamic benefits associated with a truly free world trading system would be lost. On the other hand, if the Uruguay Round is very successful and either achieves its goals or at least sets the framework for their future achievement, then trade frictions among the trade blocs are likely to diminish over time, and the volume of trade and the international flow of resources will increase. Under these circumstances many of the dynamic benefits resulting from a truly "free-trade" multilateral trade system can be realized. Indeed, the movement toward the formation of trading blocs could conceivably even be reversed.

Speculating about the outcome of the current multilateral trade negotiations, I would say that it is most unlikely that they will succeed in fully reversing the trend toward protectionism and in fully liberalizing trade in services and in agricultural products. What is possible is to negotiate for a reduction of traditional trade barriers and explicit nontariff trade barriers and accept as inevitable the existence of some implicit nontariff trade barriers (such as government aid to sunset and sunrise industries that the nation might be unwilling to give up). Nations could counteract with appropriate domestic policies the most disturbing effects of implicit foreign nontariff trade barriers in a manner that minimizes the resulting trade controversies. Success in these negotiations was made more difficult by the loss of the hegemonic position that the United States enjoyed during the 1950s and 1960s. The most that can reasonably be expected from the Uruguay Round is that it will (1) reassert the principle of an open multilateral trading system, (2) strengthen the dispute settlement procedure of GATT and raise its status to that of the International Monetary Fund and the World Bank, and (3) set up the framework and establish the principle for subsequent trade liberalization in trade in services and agriculture. I believe that there is an even chance of achieving these limited but important results.

REFERENCES

Bhagwati, J., "The Generalized Theory of Distortions and Welfare." In Bhagwati, J., *International Trade: Selected Readings* (Cambridge, Mass.: The MIT Press, 1971), pp. 171–189.

Bhagwati, J., *The World Trading System at Risk* (Princeton, NJ: Princeton University Press, 1998).

Cecchini, P., *The European Challenge: 1992* (Aldershot, England: Wildwood House, 1990).

Congressional Budget Office, Congress of the United States, *How the Economic Transformation in Europe will Affect the United States* (Washington, D.C.: U.S. Government Printing Office, 1990).

Jacquemin, A., and Sapir, A., "European Integration or World Integration?" *Weltwirtschaftliches Archiev* 124: 1 (1988): 127–139.

Krugman, P., "Is Free Trade Passé?" *The Journal of Economic Perspectives* 1: 1 (1987): 131–144.

Krugman, P., ed., *Strategic Trade Policy and the New International Economics* (Cambridge, Mass.: The MIT Press, 1986).

Lipsey, R. G., "The Theory of Customs Unions: A General Survey," *Economic Journal,* 70: 279 (1960): 496–513.

Lipsey, R. G., and Lancaster, K., "The General Theory of the Second Best," *Review of Economic Studies,* 24: 1 (1956): 11–32.

Meade, J., *The Theory of Customs Unions* (Amsterdam: North-Holland, 1955).

Salvatore, D., "Global Imbalances and U.S. Policy Responses," in Saunders, C., and Bertsch, G., *East-West Economic Relations in the 1980s* (London: Macmillan Co., 1989), pp. 37–54.

Salvatore, D., ed., *Handbook of National Trade Policies* (Westport, CT: Greenwood Press, and Amsterdam: North-Holland, 1992).

Salvatore, D., "Import Penetration, Exchange Rates, and Protectionism in the United States," *Journal of Policy Modeling,* 9: 1 (1987a): 125–141.

Salvatore, D., "The New Protectionism with Nontariff Trade Instruments," in Saunders, C., *Macroeconomic Management and the Enterprise in East and West* (London: Macmillan Co., 1988), pp. 155–182.

Salvatore, D., ed., *The New Protectionist Threat to World Welfare* (New York and Amsterdam: North-Holland, 1987b).

Samuelson, Paul, *U.S. News and World Report,* July 13, 1987, p. 46.

"The Economists Take Their Lumps," *U.S. News and World Report,* July 13, 1987, p. 46.

Viner, J., *The Customs Union Issue* (New York: The Carnegie Endowment for International Peace, 1950).

Chapter 10

International Supervision
of Multinational Enterprises:
Lessons from the European Community

Anthony Scaperlanda

Abstract *Recognizing that there is an inherent conflict between the goals of multinational enterprises (MNEs) and the goals of the broader society, some scholars have asserted that an international organization is needed to supervise MNE activity. This chapter examines selected policies associated with the EC's (European Community's) "1992" process and finds that certain provisions of the process promote non-invidious technological transfers among EC MNEs and attempt to control MNE rent-seeking activities. Consequently, the EC can be said to exercise some supervision over MNEs.*

INTRODUCTION

National antitrust laws and other measures designed to control industry bespeak society's fear of large enterprises and their power. Their size and dominance often enable them to amass monopolistic or oligopolistic profits by appropriating the lion's share of productivity gains. If such appropriation is an enterprise goal, it may conflict with a goal of other elements of society to distribute productivity gains more broadly. The explosive growth of multinational enterprises (MNEs) in the last 40 years, introducing new competition into some national markets, has the potential for bringing the goals of enterprises at the national level into line with the goals of the broader society. On the other hand, because MNEs are increasingly dominant, their expansion threatens to cancel the positive effects of the new competition and thus fuel the conflict with society's broader goals and with the attempts of government to protect the social order.

In 1970 Paul Goldberg and Charles Kindleberger recognized that "[r]educed to its simplest terms there is an inherent conflict between the objectives of the international corporation and the nation-states" (1970, p. 296), and called for a GATT-type organization to supervise MNE activity so that the world will be put "on a path towards global efficiency in resource allocation, production and distribution of goods" (1970, p. 323). Although MNEs are monitored by some international agencies, an organization dedicated specifically to adjudicate matters connected with the expansion and conduct of MNEs has yet to be seriously considered, much less created.[1] In the absence of an international agency to supervise MNEs, a question arises: Are any governmental units supervising the activities of MNEs in an attempt to reconcile private profit goals with public goals tailored to serve the best interests of the citizens of nation-states?

Economists can look to the evolving EC (European Community) treatment of intra-EC MNEs to evaluate the extent to which super-governmental organizations can promote a convergence of the goals of MNEs and the goals of society. Brent McClintock's work suggests two criteria for judging whether international governance or supervision of MNEs encourages a convergence of these goals. First, does the supervision "expedite noninvidious technological transfers" so that production more completely meets society's material needs?[2] Second, does the supervision reduce or eliminate MNE rent-seeking activities (1988, pp. 481–82)?[3] This chapter examines selected aspects of the EC's "Europe 92" process to determine if, in addition to MNE efficiency and profits, EC directives both promote noninvidious technological transfers and control MNE rent-seeking.

After establishing the historical perspective within which the inquiry is embedded, I examine the substance of selected "Europe 92" Directives and Regulations intended to promote both greater industrial efficiency and an interfirm transfer of technology within the Community. I then reexamine these developments in order to identify any MNE rent-controlling objectives they may include. If EC policies are found either to promote interfirm technology transfer or reduce rent-seeking activities, the EC *is* exercising supervision over MNEs to bring enterprise objectives into harmony with the objectives of the broader society.

HISTORICAL PERSPECTIVE

Beginning with the signing of the Treaty of Rome in 1957, the EC has been moving toward the single internal market projected for the end of 1992. The White Paper of 1985 together with the Single European Act of 1986, which made major changes in the EC's constitution, set in place the "1992 process." Some aspects of the potential and/or targeted institutional adjustment may not be completed by the end of 1992.[4] Nonetheless, as attested to by the accords reached in December 1991 at Maastricht, which project monetary unification for the EC for no later than 1999, the integration process seems irreversible.[5]

From among all the institutional adjustments made by the EC, this chapter singles out those that shape the operational efficiency and hence the profitability of multinational enterprises. In particular, it focuses on selected aspects of the EC's competition and technology policies aimed at improving efficiency in production and ultimately MNE profits and the potential for EC economic growth. In addition, some consideration is given to the EC's embryonic social policy.

THE PROMOTION OF EFFICIENCY IN THE EC

The EC's competition policy is intended both to foster competition within the Community and to ensure that European firms are not disadvantaged in competition with extra-EC enterprises. The reduction and the eventual elimination of national subsidies for which national firms are given preferential treatment are important avenues for fostering internal competition. To ensure that firms from all member states and of all sizes have greater opportunity to bid on projects that are being subsidized by the governments of the EC's member states, the EC Commission is collecting, categorizing, and publishing information about all new subsidies.

A European firm may be at a disadvantage in international competition if it is prevented from merging with or acquiring a firm located in another member state. In addition to forbidding the blocking of a merger by a firm's managing directors without an affirmative vote of stockholders, the Commission has attempted to facilitate mergers by issuing three directives to ensure that merging firms are not at a tax disadvantage: a mergers directive, a parent companies and subsidiaries directive, and an arbitration procedures directive. These three directives are based on a recognition that the size of many European firms continues to be suboptimal (in both production and distribution) from a cost minimization perspective.[6] They recognize implicitly the advantage that accrues to a MNE that internalizes operating linkages rather than operating at "arm's length" with several other national enterprises in a cooperative venture.[7] They recognize as well that EC-based mergers and acquisitions (M & A) are of growing importance, increasing over 500% (from 29 to 197) between 1983–1984 and 1988–1989 compared to a 150% increase in M & A by extra-EC enterprises initiated during the same period. However, of greatest importance is the fact that the three directives offer insights into EC policy positions that bear on the matter of intra-EC MNE expansion and EC supervision of MNEs.[8]

The "mergers" directive, by delaying the taxation of capital gains that result from transnational, intra-EC mergers until the actual transfer of asset values, effectively establishes the same tax environment for intra-EC MNEs as that faced by firms merging within the borders of one of the EC's member states. In the absence of this directive, the added tax cost of intra-Community, transnational mergers stood effectively to deter them, thereby undercutting much of the opportunity established by the Commission's European company statute of 1989.

The "parent companies and subsidiaries" directive, also a support to the Europeanization of enterprises, aims to eliminate the double taxation of dividends. To accomplish this, a subsidiary's dividends to the parent firm will be excluded from taxable income in the member state in which the subsidiary is located. The member state in which the parent firm has its headquarters is responsible for the appropriate taxation of an MNE's consolidated dividends.[9]

There is, however, another potential tax-based barrier to the Europeanization of enterprises: the absence in some member states of provisions to consolidate all MNE before-tax profits and losses if some of them occurred in another member state. This is potentially a tax-increasing situation. It will be dealt with ideally by member states extending existing bilateral procedures. For cases in which existing procedures prove inadequate, the "arbitration procedure directive" is designed to promote a solution in which the losses of one branch or subsidiary are combined with the profits of other MNE branches or subsidiaries, regardless of location within the EC, in order to guarantee that a MNE pays taxes only on its net income.

The EC's technology policy is closely related to competition policy. The basic aim of the technology policy is to ensure that from a technical perspective European industry is competitive in the international market.[10] The EC is responsible for what are called the "Framework Programmes," within which many R & D initiatives are dealt with supranationally.[11] These programmes, each of which supports collaborative R & D in a specific industrial sector, are patterned after Esprit (European Strategic Programme in Information Technologies). Begun before R & D became politically popular in 1985, Esprit is the model for the EC-sponsored Framework Programmes and remains the largest of them. Esprit's thrust, like that of other Framework Programmes, is to develop basic technologies cooperatively and to develop Europe-wide standards.

An interesting and dynamic "competition" has materialized in the realm of technological developments in Europe. Effectively competing with the efforts of the Framework Programmes there has developed at the intergovernmental level the European Research Cooperation Agency (Eureka), which includes the EFTA nations and Turkey in addition to the EC member states. Eureka promotes interfirm cooperation in the development of strategic components of final products.

Because the technological emphases of both organizations are established by the firms involved and because a firm may participate in both organizations, it is unlikely that the competition between them will be destructive. Further, since both the Framework Programmes and Eureka focus on enhancing the international competitiveness of European MNEs, one can say that both EC technology policy and the work of Eureka at the intergovernmental level are complementary to that part of the EC's competition policy that is directed at reducing tax barriers to intra-EC mergers. Generally EC technology policy promotes the development and noninvidious transfer of technology and, complemented by competition policy, positions European industry for sustained industrial growth.

A compelling example of the benefits to be derived from collaboration in the development of technology is the Eureka-sponsored, European standard for high-definition television (HDTV). Not only will the European standard for HDTV be compatible with European TV production and distribution technology, but producers throughout Europe can develop products that may be sold across the continent. Generally the development of European product standards should spur the production and sales of European firms. The responses to a 1988 EC Commission survey of European industrialists provides evidence that this is recognized. Of those responding, 38% thought it would be necessary to modify their products (increase standardization) in order to compete in the enlarged internal market (Buigues et al., 1990, pp. 54–5). With Japanese and U.S. firms selling standardized products throughout the Community, European firms must be positioned to do likewise.

What can be loosely called the EC's social policy also affects technological transfer and the competitive position of European enterprises.[12] Still in embryonic form, this social policy will be built on the nonbinding Social Charter that all member states except the United Kingdom adopted in December 1989 and reaffirmed at Maastricht in December 1991. Generally, social policy is based on the premise that the maximum benefit can be obtained from economic integration only if the movement of all factors of production, technological and human, encounters minimum resistance. If human expertise cannot move as rapidly and as freely as the new technology embodied in capital, the industrial structure will be distorted and the growth potential of the EC's single, internal market will be diminished.

In recognizing that the free movement of entrepreneurial, managerial, and technical expertise is essential, the 11 EC member states that support the Social Charter acknowledge that social cohesion must accompany economic integration. Without a cohesive social policy people possessing the expertise to use the new technology most fully will be unable to respond optimally to the changing market incentives induced by changing technologies. With this understanding, it follows that to facilitate the free movement of people throughout the Community, nonwage factors such as professional credentials, insurance coverage, and pension plans must be standardized. The Social Charter also recognizes that the standardization of other nonwage factors such as health protection and vacations will further remove impediments to the movement of people with expertise. The Charter, therefore, provides a relatively comprehensive agenda for the completion of an EC social policy that will permit the realization of productivity gains promised by the "Europe 92" initiatives.

RENT-REDUCING SUPERVISION

Have EC policies that promote technological transfer and industrial efficiency also promoted the control of MNE rent-seeking activities? One answer can be found by referring to the Community's technology policy that encourages the cooperative development of new technologies through the Framework Programmes. This policy explicitly encourages technological transfer among participating EC MNEs. The common standards being developed further encourages additional firms to use the new technology.

Another answer can be found by referring to the mergers and acquisitions aspect of the EC's competition policy. It is clear from the three directives to ensure "fair" tax treatment of mergers and acquisitions as well as from the support given to the Framework Programmes that mergers are not being discouraged. Important here is the fact that these EC policies that uniformly encourage a cooperative technological/industrial effort, are complemented by an EC policy of reviewing large intra-EC mergers in an attempt to constrain MNE rent-seeking activities.

The principal EC constraint/oversight was initiated in December 1989 when the Council declared that mergers undertaken by European MNEs with global sales in excess of 5 billion ECU and EC sales of more than 250 million ECU will be reviewed by the Commission. Mergers that would extend or create a dominant market position and thereby impede competition would not be permitted. John Groenewegan (1992) has pointed out that during the first 15 months after this policy was initiated, the Commission reviewed more than 50 merger proposals and objected to only one. These data suggest that technological transfer, greater efficiency, and international competitiveness take precedence over rent-curtailing measures in the EC's efforts to supervise intra-Community MNEs.

This conclusion should be tempered by a recognition that other EC policies also attempt to constrain MNE rents in order to reconcile the goals of MNEs and those of the broader society. Declan Costello has observed, for example, that to provide a counterbalance to the entrepreneurial flair and "deal-making" that may be unleashed by the new mergers and the new technology, the EC Council is considering proposals to ensure that management is supervised on behalf of shareholders, employees, and creditors. One quite controversial proposal would require some form of employee participation in the formulation and implementation of policy in all firms operating in the EC that employ more than 1000 persons (Costello, 1991, p. 102). The presence of such "public" representatives in the "policy-making loops" of MNEs is designed to ensure that the broad goals of various segments of society are introduced into the MNE policymaking process.

In addition to policies that influence MNE policymaking, the Community's social policy will also constrain MNE rent-seeking. Generally, conditions established to regulate pensions, health care, insurance coverage, and vacations seek to secure worker participation in the benefits of productivity increases. Such assurances will diminish rents that MNEs can appropriate. Consequently, the goals of MNEs will tend to be modified to coincide with the goals of the broader society.

CONCLUSION

The policies and principles that are being unveiled as the evolving European Community moves toward the completion of the "Europe 92" process generally promote greater efficiency and profit for European MNEs by encouraging the development and noninvidious transfer of technology. They also aim to control rent-seeking in general, and rent-seeking by expanded intra-EC MNEs in particular. The combination of these EC initiatives, which promote a convergence of MNE goals with those of society, can be viewed as generally "protecting" society from MNE antisocial tendencies; that is, the EC is endorsing cohesive socio-economic policies through six specific channels: the promotion of technological advances and economic growth; the encouragement of the noninvidious transfer or sharing of technological advances; the oversight of large mergers; the willingness to put "people's representatives" on boards of directors of large firms; the publishing of extensive information about national subsidies; and the general tenor of the Social Charter. These EC policies collectively provide for extensive supervision over European multinational enterprises.

NOTES

1. The Organization for Economic Cooperation and Development is an example of an organization that monitors the activities of MNEs. Through their Committee on Competition Law and Policy and their Committee on International Investment and Multinational Enterprises, the OECD records MNE merger and acquisition activity and the trends and implications of FDI.

2. Technology transfers are noninvidious if the firm that is the source of the technology releases it willingly, if that firm is satisfied that its research and development costs are adequately compensated, and if the receiving firm perceives that it obtained the technology for a reasonable price. Jointly developed technology that is available to all participating firms on an unobstructed, nondiscriminatory basis is by definition noninvidiously transferred. Conversely, technology transfers that result from the likes of patent infringement are invidious and are likely to prompt litigation and/or some form of retaliation. In general, noninvidious technology transfers create a residual of good will rather than animosity.

3. A 1988–1989 dialogue between Peter Buckley and Brent McClintock in the *Journal of Economic Issues* suggests that EC treatment of MNEs may serve as a prototype for the international supervision of MNEs.

4. For example, Jørn Henrik Petersen has concluded that a harmonized EC social security system will probably not be established in the near future. He concludes, however, that pluralistic policy may be an advantage, first because it allows multiple political preferences to be expressed, and second because each public and private jurisdiction or agent has a distinct contribution to make toward realizing society's potential. From a theoretical perspective, in interjurisdictional relations, a stronger or superior jurisdiction should not prevent the lower jurisdiction from using its capacities for the good of society. This so-called principle of subsidiarity provides a theoretical basis to justify less than complete harmonization of policy.

5. This evaluation does not assume that the continued evolution of the EC will be devoid of political struggle. Christopher Brewin and Richard McAllister provide insights into the kinds of struggle that lie ahead. Michael Emerson adds the EC's aging population and the economics of global warming to the list of challenges that confront the EC's continued development.

6. Buigues et al. provide several examples of realized and potential gains (1990, pp. 53–54).

7. Neil Kay has observed (a) that in an open EC market it is likely "that firms will be able to compete . . . without the need for local partners," and (b) because "potential collaborators are also potential competitors . . . firms may be increasingly reluctant to enter co-operative agreements that give away their technological knowledge." He goes on to say that "[t]his is a radically different pattern from that predicted by the White Paper . . . " (1991, p. 351).

8. Although these EC Commission directives address the tax treatment of intra-EC mergers, the taxing authority remains at the national level. The "tax authority" becomes a concern for the EC only if a national practice substantially threatens to distort the location of a MNE's branch or subsidiary.

9. Bob Hagerty has noted in the *Wall Street Journal* that the benefits of these two directives to EC MNEs are not yet clear 18 months after their enactment. He is of the opinion that the benefits MNEs may obtain from merging are firm-specific. Therefore, to date, he thinks the only "clear winners" from the implementation of these two directives are "the lawyers and accountants advising those companies" considering an EC merger.

10. See John Peterson (1991) for a description of the evolution of technology policy within the Community, both at the supra-national EC level and at the intergovernmental level.

11. Declan Costello provides summary descriptions of the various Framework Programmes on pages 134–38.

12. Patrick Venturini provides a description of EC social policy in *1992: The European Social Dimension*. On pages 114–117, he provides a comprehensive list of what has been done and what is proposed concerning the social dimension of the internal market.

REFERENCES

Brewin, Christopher, and Richard McAllister, "Annual Review of the Activities of the European Community in 1989," *Journal of Common Market Studies*, 28, 4 (1990), pp. 451–96.

Buckley, Peter J., "The Institutionalist Perspective on Recent Theories of Direct Foreign Investment: A Comment on McClintock," *Journal of Economic Issues*, 23, 3 (1989), pp. 879–885.

Buigues, P., Ilzkovitz, F., and Lebrun, J.-F., "The Impact of the Internal Market by Industrial Sector: The Challenge for the Member States," *European Economy: Social Europe*, special edition (Brussels: Commission of the European Communities, 1990).

Costello, Declan, "The Internal Policies of the Community," in Ludlow, Peter (ed.), *The Annual Review of European Community Affairs 1990* (London: Brassey's Centre for European Policy Studies, Brussels, 1991), pp. 43–139.

Emerson, Michael, "Europe After 1992: Aspects of Economic and Monetary Policy," *Essays in International Finance,* Princeton, N.J.: International Finance Section, 182 (1991), pp. 5–15.

Goldberg, Paul M., and Charles P. Kindleberger, "Toward a GATT for Investment: A Proposal for Supervision of the International Corporation," *Law and Policy in International Business,* 2, 2 (1970), pp. 295–325.

Groenewegen, John, "The United States of Europe," presented at the annual meeting of the Association for Evolutionary Economics, New Orleans, Louisiana, January 2–5, 1992.

Hagerty, Bob, "EC Rules Create Both Tax Havoc and Tax Haven," *The Wall Street Journal,* February 11, 1992.

Kay, Neil, "Industrial Collaborative Activity and the Completion of the Internal Market," *Journal of Common Market Studies,* 29, 4 (1991), pp. 347–62.

McClintock, Brent, "Recent Theories of Direct Foreign Investment: An Institutionalist Perspective," *Journal of Economic Issues,* 22, 2 (1988), pp. 477–84.

McClintock, Brent, "Direct Foreign Investment: A Reply," *Journal of Economic Issues,* 23, 3 (1989), pp. 885–889.

OECD, *International Direct Investment and the New Economic Environment* (Paris: Organization for Economic Co-operation and Development, 1989).

OECD, *International Mergers and Competition Policy* (Paris: Organization for Economic Co-operation and Development, 1988).

Petersen, Jørn Henrik, "Harmonization of Social Security in the EC Revisited," *Journal of Common Market Studies,* 29, 5 (1991), pp. 505–26.

Peterson, John, "Technology Policy in Europe: Explaining the Framework Programme and Eureka in Theory and Practice," *Journal of Common Market Studies,* 29, 3 (1991), pp. 269–290.

Venturini, Patrick, *1992: The European Social Dimension* (Luxembourg: Office for Official Publications of the European Community, 1989).

Chapter 11

U.S. Firms' Acquisitions in Anticipation of Europe-1992 and the Stock Market Reaction

Pochara Theerathorn and Dominique Vacheron

Abstract *This chapter examines 334 major acquisitions of European businesses by U.S.-based multinational corporations from 1981 through 1990. It was found that the trend in such acquisitions was generally upward in the early 1980s; however, the pace quickened in both number and dollar value after 1985 as U.S. companies attempted to establish their European bases of operation in response to Europe-1992, in order to avoid trade diversion and to take advantage of the anticipated removal of internal trade barriers. The event-study results indicate that the reactions from stock markets to the move of U.S. firms have on average been favorable, and have been significantly more favorable for the post-1985 acquisitions.*

INTRODUCTION

In 1985, the European Commission unveiled a program to revitalize Europe's economy. Titled "Europe 1992," the program's objective is to integrate the European market more fully. Although the 12 member countries had earlier removed all formal tariffs and quotas in trading within the EC, there still remained in 1985 regulatory barriers to the flow of goods and factors of production. Europe-1992 was designed to ensure the complete mobility of goods and factors of production across all internal boundaries of the EC, thus transforming it into a true common market.

For European firms, the beneficial results of Europe-1992 were anticipated to be immediate cost savings as a result of the disappearance of regulatory impediments, plus long-term benefits from economies of scale. When barriers are dismantled, trade among the EC countries is certain to increase and the most efficient producers within the common market will benefit, both from a higher level of sales and from the economies of scale resulting from the increased production to satisfy the increased sales (trade creation). On the other hand, if the most efficient producers happen to be from outside, they will face new external barriers, and may lose market share to higher-cost producers within the EC (trade diversion), who gain a competitive edge when the internal barriers are removed.

EFFECTS ON U.S. FIRMS

An adverse effect on U.S.-based MNCs could be a substantial loss of sales. The United States exported $160 billion worth of goods and services to the EC in 1989, about 26.4% of all U.S. exports. After 1992 imports from outside the EC have been expected to drop between 7.9% and 10.3% (Emerson et al., 1988). Other possible impediments include greater barriers against external bidders in the area of public procurement, and rising health and safety standards imposed on imports (Bennett and Hakkio, 1989; Hunter, 1991). These measures would invariably translate into higher manufacturing costs.

On the other hand, those U.S. corporations that are already doing business within the EC will reap the same benefits from the elimination of internal barriers as the European companies. Subsidiaries of U.S.-based MNCs will be treated as indigenous companies because of the difficulty in identifying a product's country of origin. Through their European subsidiaries, the U.S. firms can establish bases of operation to distribute their products throughout the EC, enjoying the advantages of lower transportation costs, lower capital costs, and one of the world's largest markets.

It is thus to the advantage of U.S.-based MNCs without direct European investment to obtain control of business organizations in an EC member country before the full integration date. This study examines recent acquisitions of European business organizations by U.S. corporations. It measures the annual total dollar value and number of acquisitions to ascertain whether the pace of such acquisitions has in fact quickened as 1992 approaches. In addition, this chapter studies the response of financial markets to those anticipatory acquisitions to see whether investors agree with the MNCs' assessment on the impact of Europe-1992.

DATA AND METHODOLOGY

A sample of acquisitions of European business enterprises was collected from the "U.S. Investments Abroad" roster of *Mergers and Acquisitions* with effective dates from the first quarter of 1981 through the fourth quarter of 1990. This roster lists all transactions valued at $1 million or more, where the acquirer is a U.S.-based corporation, or the European subsidiary of a U.S.-based firm, and the target is a company or a business unit located in a European country that was a member of the EC on the effective date. *Mergers and Acquisitions* also provides the identity and country of the target, plus the amount of the transactions (if disclosed).

For this study, the acquisition of a business organization means one of the following: a merger, acquisition of majority interest, a takeover, a tender offer, or an acquisition of a unit. Majority interest is defined as control over 50% of equity. To be included in the sample, the acquiring company must not undertake any other acquisition within the 120-day period surrounding the current one.

On inspection of the sample it was found that acquisitions of British firms number more than the acquisitions of firms in all other 11 EC countries combined. Because the British and American systems are very similar economically and culturally, and because British firms have the highest level of direct investment in the Untied States and vice versa, it was thought that British acquisitions may represent a normal growth movement rather than an attempt to beat the 1992 deadline. To prevent the results for a single member from dominating those for the remaining eleven, the data of British acquisitions were excluded from analysis.

To gauge the effect of unanticipated announcement of acquisition on the market, the event-study technique, described in full detail by Brown and Warner (1980), was applied to the acquirers' stock price. The event date (t = 0) was defined as the day prior to an appearance for the first time in the *Wall Street Journal* of an announcement of the offer by the bidder. If the announcement was not published in the *Wall Street Journal,* the effective date reported in *Mergers and Acquisitions* was designated as the event date.

Daily returns of the acquiring firms' common stock for 120 days prior to and 60 days subsequent to the event date were obtained from the CRSP database. For firm i to day t, the "Market Model" excess return was defined as:

$$E_{it} = R_{it} - (A_i + B_i R_{mt}) \qquad (1)$$

where R_{mt} is the daily return from the S&P 500 index, A_i and B_i are the coefficients obtained from regressing firm i's return (R_{it}) on the market return during the time $(-120, -61)$ relative to the event date (the estimation period). The expression in parentheses on the right side of (1) represents "normal" return for stock i; R_{it} is the actual return; and E_{it} is therefore the excess or abnormal return for stock i on day t.

Around the announcement date, E_{it} measures the market response to the acquisition. Normally, E_{it} fluctuates randomly around 0. A statistically significant E_{it} indicates a measurable impact, positive or negative, of the unexpected announcement of the acquisition. Given N, the number of firms in the study, two measures of abnormal return were computed:

$$MAR_t = \sum_{i=1}^{N} E_{it}/N; \qquad \text{for } t = -60 \text{ to } +60 \qquad (2)$$

and

$$MCAR_T = \sum_{t=-60}^{T} MAR_t \qquad (3)$$

MAR_t may be interpreted as the excess return on day t from an equally weighted portfolio comprising stocks of acquiring companies in the sample. $MCAR_T$ is the cumulative sum of these abnormal returns over the period (-60, T). To assess the statistical significance of these abnormal return measures, a Z score was also calculated for each MAR_t. The critical values for the Z score at the 5% and 1% significance level are 1.96 and 2.58, respectively. Finally, the daily ratio of firms with a positive abnormal return to firms with a negative abnormal return was also computed.

PRELIMINARY ANALYSIS

Table 1 lists, for each of the 10 years, the number of acquisitions, and the total and average value (in $ million) of the acquisitions of business enterprises in each of the 10 EC countries. Of the 12 current members, the United Kingdom has already been excluded, and Greece provides only one year of usable data. Spain and Portugal joined the EC on January 1, 1986, and only those acquisitions taking place in 1986 and later were included. Germany registers the highest number (111) of acquisitions overall, but France and the Netherlands claim higher values—both total and average—of acquisition amounts. In all, 334 acquisitions were recorded. Of these, however, only 61 (18%) disclosed the transaction value.

Figure 1 plots the annual number of acquisitions, together with the regression line. The trend is clearly upward, but the slope becomes steeper after 1985. This is confirmed by the significantly large difference between the rates of growth of acquisitions for the two periods: 10.67% during 1981 to 1985 and 19.40% for 1986 to 1990.

The annual total and average values of acquisitions are plotted in figures 2 and 3 respectively. The annual value exhibits a slightly downward trend between 1981 and 1983, rises in 1984, and then grows at an increasing rate in the next 3 years to pass the $1 billion mark in 1987. The acquisition value drops to $576 million in 1988, probably because the October 1987 stock market crash caused uncertainty about the prospect of a possible recession in the United States. When the downturn did not materialize, the value exploded to almost $2.6 billion in 1989, partly because the planned acquisitions for 1988 were resumed, and partly because the talk about Europe-1992 and its consequences became much louder. The single-year disclosed value of 1989 is five times that of 1988 and exceeds the combined values of the previous 8 years. This is a good indication of the quickened pace of "Europeanization" of U.S. MNCs as 1992 drew closer.

Table 1
Acquisitions of EC Business Enterprises by U.S. Firms*

	1981	1982	1983	1984	1985	1986	1987	1988	1989	1990
Germany	8	9	7	10	11	12	10	9	14	21
	54	9	—	7	41	172	408	55	64	148
	13	3	—	7	14	86	204	55	32	49
France	5	4	2	6	8	7	13	8	11	18
	2	43	—	—	4	145	10	—	2187	162
	2	22	—	—	4	48	10	—	364	54
Italy	1	2	3	1	7	1	8	6	13	5
	—	4	14	—	18	—	5	8	31	93
	—	4	14	—	18	—	5	8	16	48
Holland	5	2	2	3	2	2	4	3	9	6
	26	—	—	31	165	—	719	513	262	—
	13	—	—	31	165	—	360	513	131	—
Belgium	0	2	0	2	1	1	0	2	1	4
Luxembourg	0	1	0	0	1	0	1	1	0	0
Denmark	1	0	1	2	0	3	0	0	1	2
Ireland	0	1	0	3	0	0	0	0	1	2
	—	—	—	7	—	—	—	—	—	8
	—	—	—	7	—	—	—	—	—	8
Greece						0	0	0	0	2
Spain						5	4	3	2	2
						—	8	—	41	—
						—	8	—	41	—
Portugal						0	0	0	1	1
						—	—	—	—	15
N	20	21	15	27	30	31	40	32	53	63
Total $	82	56	14	45	228	317	1150	576	2585	426
Average $	12	9	14	15	38	63	164	192	199	43

*Each cell contains number of acquisitions, acquisition value ($ million), and average value per acquisition.

The average acquisition value increased every year from 1982 to 1989. The rate of increase was quite small during 1982 to 1984, became very steep between 1984 and 1987, and then moderated in 1988 to 1989. The abrupt drop in 1990 of the total and average acquisition value is due primarily to unavailability of data: the majority of the announcements did not disclose the acquisition value. Nevertheless, the plots appear to be consistent with the conclusion that the average acquisition value shifted to a new and much higher level after the 1985 announcement of Europe-1992. Because not all acquisition values were disclosed, this graph may not represent the full extent of anticipatory acquisitions. But the rising trend is generally very visible from 1985 onward.

EVENT STUDY RESULTS

Of the 334 acquisitions accounted for in table 1, the price data of only 252 were available on the CRSP tape. Table 2 lists the average abnormal return (MAR), cumulative abnormal return (MCAR), and the ratio of positive to negative abnormal returns over the $(-15, +15)$ period. Positive abnormal returns appear

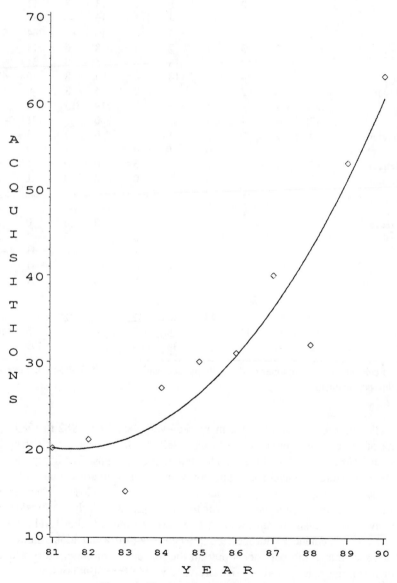

Figure 1 Number of acquisitions per year.

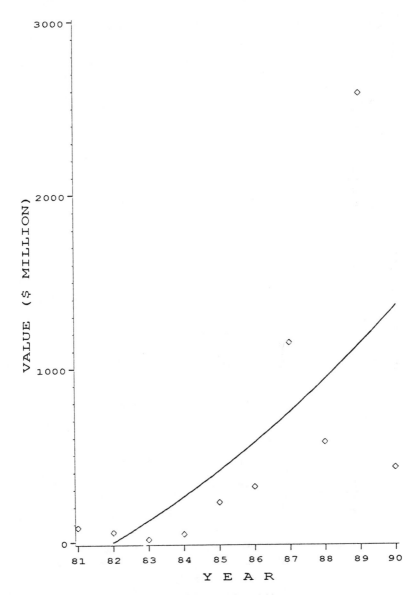

Figure 2 Total value of acquisitions.

to be more numerous than the negative ones, indicating a generally positive response to the acquisitions from the market.

MAR and MCAR are plotted in figures 4 and 5, respectively. The average abnormal return fluctuates randomly around 0 until about 10 days before the announcement date, when initial information about the impending acquisition probably arrives. Table 2 reveals that 6 days before the announcement the

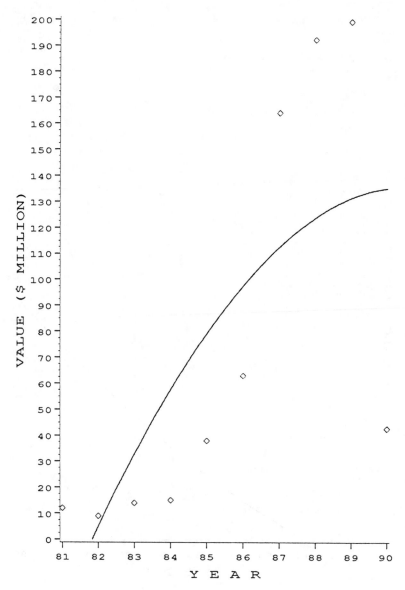

Figure 3 Average value of acquisitions.

excess return becomes significantly positive and remains so until the day following the announcement, when it turns negative for 20 days in succession
(MAR for days 16 through 20 are not shown in table 2). The abnormal return
becomes random again on the ninth day subsequent to the event date. A possible explanation for this pattern of return behavior is that, although speculation

Table 2

Daily Abnormal Returns and Cumulative Returns for 1981–1990 and the Two Subperiods

Day	1981–1990			1981–1985		1986–1990	
	MAR	MCAR	Ratio	MAR	MCAR	MAR	MCAR
−15	0.274[†]	3.509	138 : 114	0.333	3.572	0.229*	3.462
−14	0.039	3.548	127 : 125	0.220	3.791	−0.099	3.363
−13	0.089	3.637	120 : 132	−0.159	3.633	0.277*	3.640
−12	0.062	3.699	129 : 123	0.083	3.715	0.046	3.686
−11	0.265*	3.964	137 : 115	0.115	3.830	0.379*	4.065
−10	0.516[†]	4.479	145 : 107	0.301*	4.132	0.679[†]	4.744
−9	0.234	4.713	126 : 126	0.240	4.372	0.229	4.973
−8	0.060	4.773	119 : 133	0.295*	4.667	−0.119	4.855
−7	−0.001	4.772	131 : 121	0.158	4.825	−0.122	4.732
−6	0.409[†]	5.181	132 : 120	0.222	5.047	0.552[†]	5.284
−5	0.239[†]	5.420	140 : 112	0.340*	5.387	0.162*	5.446
−4	0.486[†]	5.906	152 : 100	0.468[†]	5.854	0.499[†]	5.946
−3	0.317[†]	6.223	142 : 110	0.444*	6.298	0.220*	6.165
−2	0.715[†]	6.938	166 : 86	0.857[†]	7.156	0.606[†]	6.772
−1	0.729[†]	7.667	173 : 79	0.564[†]	7.720	0.855[†]	7.627
0	1.759[†]	9.426	224 : 28	1.934[†]	9.654	1.626[†]	9.253
1	−1.347[†]	8.080	29 : 223	−1.318[†]	8.336	−1.369[†]	7.884
2	−0.745[†]	7.335	75 : 177	−0.898[†]	7.438	−0.628[†]	7.256
3	−0.461[†]	6.873	96 : 156	−0.527[†]	6.911	−0.411[†]	6.845
4	−0.290[†]	6.583	99 : 153	−0.340*	6.571	−0.252*	6.593
5	−0.445[†]	6.138	106 : 146	−0.673[†]	5.897	−0.272	6.321
6	−0.136	6.001	119 : 133	−0.204	5.694	−0.085	6.236
7	−0.232*	5.769	105 : 147	−0.484[†]	5.210	−0.041	6.195
8	−0.468[†]	5.301	97 : 155	−0.291*	4.919	−0.603[†]	5.593
9	−0.299	5.002	112 : 140	−0.383	4.536	−0.235	5.358
10	−0.187	4.815	119 : 133	−0.129	4.407	−0.232	5.126
11	−0.054	4.761	119 : 133	0.202	4.609	−0.249	4.876
12	−0.071	4.690	120 : 132	−0.169	4.440	0.003	4.880
13	−0.134	4.556	128 : 124	−0.106	4.334	−0.155	4.725
14	−0.175	4.381	118 : 134	−0.333	4.001	−0.054	4.671
15	−0.017	4.364	116 : 136	0.250	4.250	−0.221	4.451

*Significant at the .05 level.

[†]Significant at the .01 level.

$N = 252$ acquisitions.

about a European acquisition might have started as early as 6 days before it was made public, the actual announcement was unanticipated by the majority of the market participants and it took an average of 2 weeks for the market to assimilate this new information.

From figure 4 the announcement effect was significantly positive (1.76%

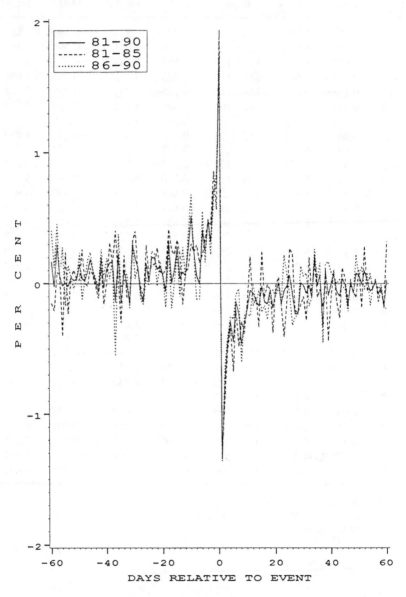

Figure 4 Mean abnormal return.

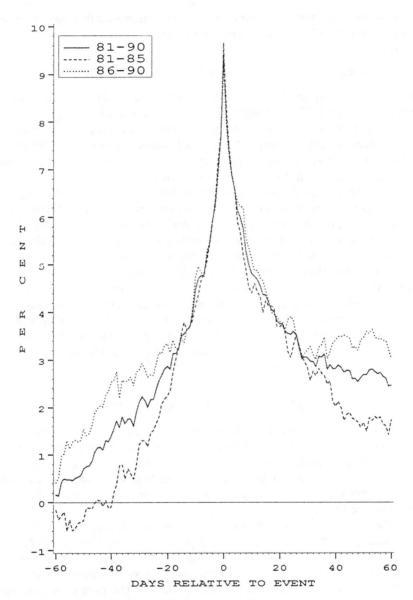

Figure 5 Cumulative abnormal return.

excess return) on the announcement date (day 0). But profit taking on the
following day causes a 1.35% drop. The plot of cumulative return in figure 5
shows that, after the first wave of reactions, the excess return settles to a new
level about 2.5% higher than that of the pre-announcement period. This supports the conclusion that, on average, the financial markets value positively the

acquisition of EC business enterprises, and the premium for this type of investment is about 2.5% over any normal-risk projects.

PRE- AND POSTANNOUNCEMENT OF EUROPE-1992

In order to account for the effect of the 1985 European Commission announcement of Europe-1992, the sample was divided into two time periods: 1981 to 1985 and 1986 to 1990. The event-study technique was applied to each of the two subsamples and their results are reported in columns 5 through 9 of table 2. The plots of average abnormal return and cumulative return for these two subperiods also appear in figures 4 and 5, respectively.

From these tables and plots, it is evident that the market reaction during the post-1985 period is much more positive than that before Europe-1992 was proclaimed. The post-1985 excess return registers a significant number as early as day -6 and does not become random until day $+5$. Although the abnormal return fluctuates randomly around 0 before an acquisition becomes public in both cases, the 1981 to 1985 portfolio exhibits more negative returns subsequent to the event date than the post-1985 portfolio. In fact, for the 1981 to 1985 portfolio, these negative numbers bring its cumulative return steadily back toward 0 around day $+10$ on. The cumulative return of the post-1985 portfolio, in contrast, remains between 3% and 4% from day $+20$ to day $+60$, significantly shifting to a higher permanent level and indicating a premium for direct investments in the EC countries during 1986 to 1990.

SUMMARY AND CONCLUSION

A multinational corporation may be motivated to invest in a particular locality if the host country (1) offers additional markets in case a direct investment is made; (2) has natural resources, labor, or capital that are less costly or in addition to those already under the control of the firm; or (3) offers an advantageous regulatory framework (e.g., reduced taxes, protection from competition, etc.) for the firm.

When the European Community set 1992 as the "full integration" date, it was anticipated that such a preferential regulatory framework would benefit "European" businesses even more. It was also anticipated that multinational corporations would, in turn, try to offset such moves by obtaining control of business organizations in an EC member country. The pace of acquisitions (e.g., total dollar value, number of acquisition in a year) was expected to quicken as 1992 approached.

This chapter attempts to ascertain whether this expectation has been realized and to measure the stock market reactions to such anticipatory acquisition of businesses in the European Community by U.S.-based firms. From 1981 through 1990, 334 acquiring companies were identified from announcements in *Mergers and Acquisitions*. An acquiring firm must have control of more than

50% of the target's equity, and the acquisition value has to be at least $1 million. The event-study technique was applied in order to gauge the effects of an acquisition. Daily returns of the acquiring firms' common stock for 120 days surrounding the event date were obtained from the CRSP database. An equally weighted portfolio of the acquiring companies' stock was formed in event time. Average portfolio daily returns, adjusted for market movements, and cumulative average returns centered on the event date, were calculated and analyzed.

It was found that the trend in acquisition of EC business enterprises by U.S. firms was generally upward from 1981 to 1989. The post-1985 growth rate in number of acquisitions was almost double that from 1981 to 1985. The annual dollar value of acquisitions, although disclosed by only 18% of the sample firms, shows a similar pattern: slow growth during 1981 to 1985, exponential growth from 1986 onward. Finally, the average value per acquisition, relatively stable during 1981 to 1984, started to grow in 1985, and only slowed down in 1989. It can be concluded that the American companies took measures in anticipation of 1992.

The event-study results indicate that, on average, the market value of the acquiring U.S. firms increases as a result of the unexpected announcement of the acquisition of an EC firm, reflecting a favorable perception by investors of the proposed investment.

REFERENCES

Bennett, Thomas, and Hakkio, Craig, "Europe 1992: Implications for U.S. Firms," Federal Reserve Bank of Kansas City *Economic Review*, April (1989): 3–17.

Brown, Stephen J., and Warner, Jerold B., "Measuring Security Price Performance," *Journal of Financial Economics*, 8 (1980): 205–258.

Emerson, Michael et al., *The Economics of 1992* (Oxford: Oxford University Press, 1988), 238–241.

Hunter, Linda C., "Europe 1992: An Overview," Federal Reserve Bank of Dallas *Economic Review* January (1991): 17–27.

Chapter 12

EC-92 and East Asian Trade

David Robertson

Abstract *During the 1980s the East Asian economies contributed strongly to growth in world trade. They were the main reason why inter-regional trade increased faster than intra-regional trade during the decade, even though trade within the regions was being liberalized while inter-regional trade became subject to increasing frictions. A breakdown of the Uruguay Round negotiations in conjunction with an inward-looking EC-92 and increasing U.S. regionalism could reduce access to OECD markets for the dynamic East Asian economies, with far-reaching consequences for world trade and development.*

INTRODUCTION

As difficulties in the Uruguay Round negotiations multiplied in the closing months of 1990, talk about regional trade blocs took a more serious tone. In the late stages of previous GATT rounds, the U.S. authorities had resorted to threats of discriminatory or "conditional" trade agreements as an incentive to persuade the EC and other negotiators to be more forthcoming. But this time the U.S. authorities took action by signing the long-discussed free trade agreement with Canada and opening discussions with Mexico. Safe within their own regional common market and its many preferential trade arrangements, EC governments were unmoved by these developments towards increasing bilateralism. Preoccupied with the EC-92 processes and new opportunities in Eastern Europe, the EC seemed to disregard the consequences of failure in the Uruguay Round.

This chapter assesses the effects that EC-92 and U.S. regional trade arrangements might have on the East Asian economies[1] in a post-Uruguay Round trade regime. The drift into regionalism has intensified with the latest U.S. initiatives in bilateral trade arrangements, following the earlier free trade arrangement with Israel and the Caribbean Basin initiative. The East Asian region played a major role in the recovery of world trade growth in the 1980s (GATT, 1990), but if discrimination against that region increases, a more inward-looking strategy may evolve.

Merchandise trade growth in the 1980s favored inter-regional rather than intra-regional trade (GATT, 1990, p. 27). This was caused by the remarkable rate of increase in East Asia's trade (exports and imports), including that of China. The three fastest growing trade flows were Asia-North America, Asia-Western Europe and intra-Asia[2]; intra-North America and intra-Western Europe trade grew more slowly, and trade with developing countries recorded little growth.

In the 1980s, economic integration among the East Asian economies (as measured by trade flows) showed some conflicting trends. At first glance, the interdependence through trade appears significant (table 1); the three country groups transact between one quarter and half their trade with each other. But during the decade, the share of NIE4 exports to, and imports originating in East Asia recorded little change, as did the share of intra-ASEAN4 trade (table 1); falling oil prices reduced sharply the value of Japan's imports from ASEAN4, because of Indonesia's dependence on oil exports to Japan. The share of Japan's trade with NIE4 increased during the 1980s (table 1), but trade with the EC grew at an even faster rate (table 2).

The U.S. market increased in importance for East Asian exports in the 1980s (table 1). Japan's exports to the United States reached a peak of around 38% in 1987. Japan's weight in the region meant that the U.S. market was more important for East Asia as a whole than intraregional trade.

East Asian exports to and imports from the EC countries increased faster than total exports and imports. Nevertheless, in 1990 only around 15% of the region's trade was transacted with the EC12. This suggests that new U.S. bilateral trade agreements that discriminate against the East Asian economies would have more adverse effects on the region's growth prospects than the effects of EC-92. On the other hand, there is probably more potential for new exports to undeveloped EC markets for manufactures, if access could be assured.

TRADE EFFECTS OF REGIONALISM

Nonparticipating countries have three major concerns about the intensification of regional integration, whether in the form of EC-92 or setting up new discriminatory trade arrangements according to article XXIV of the GATT, like the North American free trade agreement.

(i) Trade diversion—where production from member countries displaces lower cost supplies from third countries—may reduce imports from nonmembers, if the degree of preference provided by trade protection (tariff and nontariff) against nonmembers is high and the barriers between members before regional liberalization were high. Removal of mutual trade barriers also increases internal competition and raises efficiency, leading to trade creation—where imports from member countries displace domestic production that had survived behind protection

Table 1
East Asian Trade, 1980–1990 (in percent)

Partner	ASEAN4	NIE4	Japan	East Asia	EC12	United States
Reporter:						
Export shares 1980						
ASEAN4	3.2	17.1	34.5	54.8	13.6	18.7
NIE4	10.6	9.1	10.1	29.8	16.4	24.7
Japan	7.0	14.8	—	21.8	14.0	24.5
EC12	0.7	1.2	1.0	2.9	55.7	5.6
United States	2.8	6.6	9.4	18.8	26.7	—
Export shares 1990						
ASEAN4	4.2	22.1	24.4	50.7	15.8	19.3
NIE4	8.5	11.0	12.0	31.4	15.1	28.2
Japan	7.7	19.8	—	27.5	18.8	31.7
EC12	0.9	2.1	2.1	5.2	60.5	7.0
United States	2.7	10.4	12.4	25.5	24.9	—
Import shares 1980						
ASEAN4	4.0	13.7	24.2	41.9	13.5	16.2
NIE4	10.6	7.0	22.6	40.3	9.5	17.1
Japan	14.0	5.3	—	19.3	5.9	17.4
EC12	1.0	1.7	2.6	5.3	49.4	8.6
United States	4.3	7.3	12.8	24.4	15.6	—
Import shares 1990						
ASEAN4	4.0	18.2	25.4	47.6	15.7	14.4
NIE4	8.0	10.3	22.6	40.9	11.4	17.0
Japan	10.4	11.2	—	21.6	15.0	22.4
EC12	1.1	2.4	4.3	7.8	58.0	7.4
United States	3.6	12.1	18.0	33.7	18.5	—

Source: IMF, *Direction of Trade*, June 1991.

walls—and "dynamic" gains as incomes rise. These changes have opposing effects on nonmembers' trade; the efficiency gains increase potential trade diversion, while as incomes rise new trade opportunities are provided for all suppliers. The net effects on imports from nonmembers depend on their access to the regional market, which depends on trade policies against third countries.

(ii) More regionalism could divert attention away from multilateral trade liberalization and strengthening GATT rules. This has particular relevance for developing countries that are not integrated fully into the GATT system, and for the dynamic East Asian economies that are using

Table 2
East Asian Trade Growth, 1980–1990 (in percent per annum)

Partner	ASEAN4	NIE4	Japan	East Asia	EC12	United States	World
Reporter:							
Exports							
ASEAN4	7.1	7.3	1.2	3.9	9.0	6.8	5.4
NIE4	7.7	16.3	16.8	13.7	14.5	16.0	13.8
Japan	6.0	13.3	—	11.2	13.2	12.7	8.9
EC12	6.6	15.5	17.5	14.3	9.5	10.4	8.1
United States	4.0	11.5	9.0	9.4	5.4	—	5.9
Imports							
ASEAN4	7.2	8.8	7.0	7.6	7.9	5.5	6.5
NIE4	7.1	16.4	12.5	12.1	14.1	11.2	11.3
Japan	1.5	15.9	—	7.3	16.6	8.2	5.1
EC12	8.7	13.1	14.0	13.9	8.4	5.2	4.2
United States	4.6	14.5	12.6	12.3	9.3	—	8.2

Source: IMF, *Direction of Trade*, June 1991.

their GATT commitments as a reason to liberalize their trade regimes. If multilateral trade liberalization is neglected in favor of regional preferences, the "most-favored-nation" (MFN) treatment provided by the GATT will lose its meaning. Moreover, as preferential systems spread, the value of "special and differential" treatment to developing countries (GATT, 1979), including the generalized system of preferences (GSP), will be undermined.

(iii) As regionalism spreads it will create vested interests in preferences, which have to be defended against inroads from new preferences once MFN is relinquished. Reciprocity takes on new importance and the scope for multilateral trade liberalization diminishes (Bhagwati and Irwin, 1987). These developments disable GATT rules and make market size and bargaining power the main determinants of trade flows.

The dynamic economies of East Asia have become integrated into the global economy during the 1980s through extensive trade and investment flows. They are in a position to take advantage of new trade opportunities. But this also places them at risk of being shut out of important markets by protection increases and by trade diversion. Already some of those countries have suffered from discriminatory nontariff measures in specific sectors, such as textiles and clothing, and consumer electronics. With EC-92 leading to a new common external trade policy against third countries, these countries have a good reason to fear loss of access to the EC market on a broad scale. ("Europe is more likely to become a rampart facing east than a fortress," was Lawrence's comment on Dornbusch, 1989.) On the other hand, they would be in a good position to take advantage of accelerated EC economic growth if they can retain reasonable access for their manufactured exports.

NEW DISCRIMINATION FROM EC-92

The United States' emphasis on bilateral free trade arrangements with its neighbors (Wonnacott, 1990) poses some threats to East Asian exports, but the strongest evidence of increasing regionalism comes from the EC-92 program and the potential extension of EC preferences granted to other regions. EC-92 is important not only in itself but also because of the retaliation it may generate in other regions and the damage that might cause to the multilateral trading system.

Essentially, the Single Market Act (SMA) and its 279 directives to complete the internal market and to allow the free movement of goods, services, capital, and people in the 12 EC countries is an internal EC matter. Several of the instruments to be used to achieve the SMA, however, will affect international trade relations.

- Harmonizing standards and certification (including "mutual recognition") means that suppliers from third countries may have to adapt the goods and services they sell into the present individual national markets of the EC. In the short run this may raise their costs. In the long run, however, the unified standards and certificates for the whole EC market and the elimination of internal border controls will make trading easier and cheaper for indigenous and outside firms.
- Eliminating internal borders is necessary to establish the full common market, but this requires also that a common external trade policy be introduced, in addition to the common external tariff (CXT). EC governments have yet to address this major task.[3] According to recent estimates, 21.7% of EC imports from developing countries were subject to nontariff barriers (NTBs) (World Bank, 1986); most of these were, according to the Multifiber Arrangement (MFA) or sanctioned under article 115 of the Treaty of Rome, national restraints that will have to be rationalized into EC-wide measures after 1992. Negotiating EC-wide restraints is likely to lead to an increase in average levels of protection; where one or more EC members has free access in a tariff-line, the new measures are likely to follow a more restrictive course (e.g., Germany and the Netherlands allow free access for Japanese motor vehicles (subject to the EC tariff) but France and Italy severely restrict imports, using VERs).

EC spokesmen have made much of the benefits that will arise from the single European Market and the advantages that spinoffs will bring to nonmember countries. Several research projects were sponsored by the EC to estimate the expected economic effects of EC-92 (Emerson et al., 1988), and they and other researchers (Baldwin, 1989) have demonstrated that economies of scale, increased competition, improved productivity, and lower transaction costs will raise the annual rate of economic growth of the EC by between 0.25% and 1% during the 1990s. Because the EC12 is the world's largest trading entity (table 1), it is assumed that nonmembers will gain from this faster growth in incomes, according to the income-elasticity of demand for their exports and changes in price relativities (Robertson, 1992). Although some increase in EC imports is to be anticipated, the extent of any gains to outsiders will depend also on their access to the EC market and the sources of the faster EC growth.

The models used to assess the economic effects of EC-92 (Emerson et al., 1988; Baldwin, 1989) show that the increase in growth arises from increased consumption (as productivity gains reduce price inflation) and an improvement in the trade balance brought about by improved international competitiveness (i.e., a favorable movement in the terms of trade) and by trade diversion. Improved productivity and increased competitiveness of EC producers affects third country exporters, both in the EC market and in other markets. So, even within the constraints of EC-sponsored researches (which assume no increase in protection against outsiders), initially nonmember countries will face trade losses, although faster EC growth should increase growth in the EC market and offer new trade opportunities.

In fact, the EC's trade policy against third countries appears to be increasingly discriminatory. First, intra-EC trade continues to increase as a proportion of total EC trade, while the share of trade with non-OECD countries is declining (table 1) (Schott, 1991). Second, the EC has established a pyramid of preferential trade agreements.[4] The EC's common external tariff applies only to a few countries (non-European OECD, Taiwan, Korea, and some political outcasts among the centrally planned economies and South Africa) and only to around 16% of EC imports. This different treatment makes it difficult to judge the effect that EC-92 will have on trade with nonmembers. At the same time that the EC governments have to negotiate the new external trade policy, several of the existing preferential arrangements are under pressure for increased preferences, particularly from countries adjacent to the EC12, such as members of EFTA, the newly independent East European states, and the Mediterranean countries. Once the MFN principle is compromised, the value of preferences granted under competing schemes becomes uncertain and subject to sudden changes that may have serious consequences for investment decisions.

The EC Commission has demonstrated a predilection to "manage" trade, and the new external trade policy offers new scope for discriminatory and more protectionist policies.

- EC agricultural trade is managed under the auspices of the common agricultural policy (CAP), with its complex structure of variable import levies, income supports, and export subsidies. Technically the CAP is not covered by EC-92, but the removal of internal borders will prevent use of so-called "green currencies," which allow agricultural supports to be determined in national currencies. As border controls are removed, agricultural support prices are likely to be raised towards the highest national price level to pacify farmers' complaints about falling prices. The effect will be to increase protection of EC agriculture, unless an agreement to reduce agricultural support is reached in the Uruguay Round.

- Strong competition in manufactures from third countries has been countered largely by using national bilateral trade restraints, for example, against clothing and textiles, motor vehicles, and consumer electronics. In some industries like steel, however, the Commission has a mandate to apply EC-wide trade measures. The Commission also administers antidumping legislation based on the Tokyo Round code. Criticism of EC antidumping practices has been widespread (Hindley, 1988; Nicolaides, 1990), because antidumping duties have been used to curtail import competition rather than to counter "unfair" trade practice, as the antidumping code intends. Moreover, the EC Commission has sought to use antidumping duties against so-called screwdriver factories. These are foreign-owned plants using imported components, some of which are subject to antidumping actions. Local content requirements are beginning to replace the "screwdriver" plant antidumping since an adverse decision by a GATT panel in 1990. Rules of origin are also being expanded; these have been an impediment to CAP countries' exports for many years.

The historical experience with EC-wide trade policies does not suggest that the external trade policy will develop along less protectionist lines than existing national policies, and there must be a fear that the lowest common denominator approach will tend to select the least favorable external policy from among existing national policies.

Economic conditions in the EC after the single market takes effect, in 1993 or later, could produce forces that will augment traditional protectionist biases. In industries where scale economies increase market concentration, threats of plant closure in some locations will invoke calls to limit imports and save jobs. These issues could quickly spill over into the area of the proposed EC "social contract." Harmonization of labor markets, including job security, wage rates, and social security could undermine the new competitiveness expected from EC-92. If EC countries with low wages and productivity are required to raise wages, they will become uncompetitive with outsiders as well as the more advanced EC members, and demands for protection will increase from the southern countries like Spain and Portugal, which are already the most protectionist EC members. Finally, even if EC protectionism should not increase, its mere threat is likely to be enough to attract MNEs to invest in tariff factories in the EC to supply the new integrated market. This will shift production into the

EC and away from the rest of the world, even if the protection does not materialize (Dornbusch, 1989, p. 353).[5]

EC-92 AND EAST ASIA

East Asian countries are well represented among the small group of countries subject to the EC-CXT. The continuing saga of agricultural trade and the unrelenting CAP concern several OECD countries (Canada, United States, Australia, and New Zealand). But it is widely accepted that any tendency for EC-92 to increase industrial protectionism would be directed primarily at the dynamic economies of East Asia. Several of them enjoy access under the GSP, although the value of that is doubtful, and that special access may be withdrawn (Langhammer and Sapir, 1987). The EC-ASEAN economic and commercial cooperation agreement and EC participation in ASEAN ministerial meetings have not established any formal economic links.

Most other countries—developed and developing—are either parties to a preferential trade arrangement with the EC (or are seeking one), or they enjoy GSP access for many of their exports. The East Asian economies, therefore, are the most vulnerable to EC discriminatory treatment on manufactured exports.

Even in the 1950s, when Japan joined the GATT, West European countries applied exceptional measures of protection against Japan's exports (Patterson, 1966, chap. VI). The NIEs received similar treatment in the 1980s, when NTBs were applied increasingly against their competitive manufactured exports, either by national authorities or by the Commission.

Latest data on EC antidumping actions indicate the extent of their use against East Asia. The NIE4 and ASEAN4 experienced increasing exposure to antidumping action in the 1980s, and levels of protection increased sharply, causing up to 25% reductions in export values (Hoekman and Leidy, 1989). (Developing countries enjoying preferential trade agreements with the EC were found to be equally subject to EC antidumping actions.) In the period from 1979 to 1988 the EC initiated 349 antidumping cases and made positive findings in 76% of cases (Nicolaides, 1990, p. 277). Cases against East Asian countries tended to cover several countries, which suggests either massive collusion on their part, or that antidumping is being used for general protection against competition (Hoekman and Leidy, 1989).

This bias in antidumping actions is significant because after 1992 the EC Commission will administer the common external trade policy, comprising VERs, import quotas, and other NTBs. The experience with antidumping administration since the completion of the Tokyo Round does not inspire confidence in a liberal EC trade regime.

Trade between East Asia and the EC increased strongly in the 1980s (table 2), but East Asia's share in EC trade remained small, though rising (table 1).

(Around 15% of East Asia's exports and imports are transacted with the EC, which is much less than the EC's share in world imports.)

REGIONAL INTEGRATION IN EAST ASIA

Trade among the nine East Asian economies grew strongly in the 1980s and it accelerated in the past few years as outside pressures for market-opening measures and deregulation of capital markets altered comparative advantage within the region. Japan's trade with its ASEAN and NIE neighbors has increased strongly since 1987. ASEAN4 exports of manufactures, especially from Malaysia, Thailand, and Indonesia increased rapidly to all destinations, including within East Asia.

Part of the rapid growth in ASEAN4 exports is explained by the relocation of industries from Japan and the NIEs, where rising wages and exchange rates are reducing international competitiveness. Foreign direct investment (FDI) flows increased strongly after 1983 (IMF, 1989) and Japan and the NIE4 participated increasingly in the globalization of world production. Japan's share of FDI outflows rose from 10% of world total in 1983 to over 20%; Southeast Asia received almost half of all FDI going to developing countries, almost 10% of total FDI flows.

The concern about EC-92 leading to a fortress Europe extends to diversion of investment as well as trade. To protect market shares, Japanese and NIE firms could be attracted to invest in manufacturing inside the EC. Already some redirection of investment towards Eastern Europe is seen as a threat. The ASEAN4 would be the most likely to suffer from diversion of investment because these low-cost producers have become a conduit for manufactured exports by Japanese and NIE firms. If EC antidumping legislation and rules of origin are directed at the ASEAN4, the prospect of East Asian investment being diverted towards the EC will increase.

Internal policy changes in East Asia and awakening consumer aspirations in these rapidly growing economies, added to changing patterns of comparative advantage, will intensify their economic integration without the need for discriminatory trade arrangements. But their growth prospects will diminish if access for their exports to the EC and U.S. markets are curtailed by intensification of regional trade arrangements.

REGIONALISM AND THE URUGUAY ROUND

The shadow cast by the Brussels breakdown of the Uruguay Round negotiations does not promote confidence in the GATT system as an alternative to regionalism. EC-92 and U.S. protectionism pose a serious threat to market access for exports from the East Asian countries, which have relied on strong growth in exports for their strong economic performance in the 1980s. East Asian interest in a liberal multilateral trading system was evident in their efforts in the Uruguay Round on issues such as agriculture, import safeguards, antidumping and efforts to strengthen GATT articles. It is also evident in the Asia-Pacific Economic Cooperation (APEC) declarations on multilateral trade.

EC-92 offers scope to increase world welfare by improving efficiency, accelerating economic growth, and increasing competition in Western Europe. Given flexible exchange rates and free movement of capital, these benefits will be dispersed to third countries, although not to all of them. But the EC already discriminates against groups of countries and against trade in specific products (e.g., agriculture, textiles and clothing). The distribution of any gains from the creation of the single market depends on outsider access to EC markets. Liberalization of financial markets proceeded rapidly in the 1980s when trade liberalization became bogged down. An inconclusive outcome to the Uruguay Round, economic recession in parts of the EC, and continuing unrest and slow adjustment in Eastern Europe would increase the temptation for the EC to "manage" its trade relations. The East Asian economies stand to lose most if this trend towards regionalism intensifies.

NOTES

1. In this paper East Asia refers to NIE4 (Korea, Taiwan, Hong Kong, Singapore), ASEAN4 (Indonesia, Malaysia, Philippines, Thailand), and Japan.

2. GATT's definition of Asia does not coincide with the above definition of East Asia; GATT's definition of Western Europe comprises the EC and EFTA.

3. The EC common external tariff was implemented in 1968, but the common commercial policy intended to take effect at the same time remains incomplete. According to article 115 of the Treaty of Rome, national authorities can obtain Commission approval to maintain border measures (VERs, import quotas) against third countries. These require internal border controls to prevent trade deflection through other EC countries. 176 approvals were given under article 115 in 1985, which was reduced to 4.5 in 1991; France, Ireland, and Italy are the main users. Removing internal barriers under the Single Market Act will require either EC-wide restrictions on this trade, or complete liberalization under the common commercial policy.

4. The EC has established the following systems of trade preference: free trade in industrial goods with the EFTA countries to be extended to the European Economic Area; trade preferences with the Mediterranean countries; the Lomé treaty determines trade with the 69 African, Caribbean, and Pacific countries; GSP for manufactures applies to all developing countries not covered by regional preferences; and bilateral trade agreements with former CMEA countries are being renegotiated (GSP now applies to several East European countries). The World Development Report 1986 identified 11 types of EC preferences for developing countries.

5. New Japanese and United States investments in the EC, made necessary by rules of origin and local content rules as well as VERs and antidumping, will largely duplicate existing plants elsewhere (e.g., motor vehicles, consumer electronics, microchip diffusion, etc.). This could create overcapacity and result in new efforts to manage trade (Hufbauer, 1990).

REFERENCES

Baldwin, Richard, "The growth effects of 1992," *Economic Policy* October (9) (1989): 247–281.

Bhagwati, Jagdish N., and Irwin, Douglas A., "The return of the reciprocitarians: U.S. trade policy today," *The World Economy* June 10 (2) (1987): 109–130.

Cecchini, Paolo, *The European Challenge: 1992: The Benefits of a Single Market* (London: Gower, 1988).

Dornbusch, Rudiger, "Europe 1992: macroeconomic implications," *Brookings Papers on Economic Activity* 2 (1989): 341–381.

Emerson, Michael et al., *The Economics of 1992: The EC Commission's Assessment of the Economic Effects of Completing the Internal Market* (Oxford: Oxford University Press, 1988).

GATT, *Agreements Relating to the Framework for the Conduct of International Trade* (Geneva: GATT Secretariat, 1979).

GATT, *International Trade 89–90; Vol. 1* (Geneva: GATT Secretariat, 1990).

Hindley, Brian, "Dumping and the Far East Trade of the European Community," *The World Economy* December 11 (4) (1988): 445–463.

Hoekman, Bernard M., and Leidy, Michael P., "Dumping, anti-dumping and emergency protection," *Journal of World Trade* 23 (5) (1989): 27–44.

Hufbauer, Gary C. (ed.), *Europe 1992: An American Perspective* (Washington, D.C.: The Brookings Institution, 1990), pp. 39–41, 271–279.

IMF, *Balance of Payments Statistics, 1988*, Washington, D.C.: IMF, 1989.

Langhammer, Rolf J., and Sapir, André, *Economic Impact of Generalized Tariff Preferences*, Thames Essay No. 49, Trade Policy Research Centre (London: Gower, 1987).

Nicolaides, Phedon, "Anti-dumping measures as safeguards: the case of the EC," *Intereconomics* November-December 25 (6) (1990): 273–279.

Patterson, Gardner, *Discrimination in International Trade: The Policy Issues 1945–65* (Princeton: Princeton University Press, 1966).

Robertson, David, "The single market and commercial relations for nonmember countries: views from other countries without preferential arrangements with EC," *Journal of Development Planning* 21 (1992): 205–225.

Schott, Jeffrey, J., Trading blocs and the world trading system, *The World Economy,* March 14 (1) (1991): 4.

Wonnacott, Ronald J., *US Hub-and-Spoke Bilaterals and the Multilateral Trading System* (Toronto: C. D. Howe Institute, 1990).

World Bank, *World Development Report, 1986* (Washington, D.C.: IBRD, 1986), p. 23.

Chapter 13

The Impact of EC-1992 on Hungary's Trade and Industrial Structure

Alfred Tovias

Abstract *The impact of EC-1992 on Hungary's economy may go well beyond that of Hungary's exports of goods to the EC. The completion of the EC's Single Market is expected to raise the level of competitiveness of EC-based firms, including those competing in third markets with Hungarian producers. More generally, EC-1992 will affect Hungary's geographical distribution of exports because of the all-pervading effects of a switch from East to West of capital equipment suppliers. Industrial structure and comparative advantage will also be affected by the switch in embodied technology.*

INTRODUCTION

In 1990 the EC became the principal trade partner of Hungary. The share of the 12 countries of the present EC in Hungarian exports increased from 15.9% in 1983 to 35.5% in 1990. Given present dependence levels on Western markets and the new industrial strategies of Hungary, which involve relying on an expansion of exports to the West and particularly to the EC12, what may happen after the completion of the EC's Internal Market by January 1, 1993, is of utmost importance. The impact of the Community's Internal Market program on Hungary may go well beyond that of its exports of goods to the EC (discussed below). Very significant is the large share (37.8%) that the EC had in Hungary's imports of machinery and transport equipment in 1990. For suppliers of intermediate products, machinery and equipment have a large influence in shaping the future economic structure of the purchasing countries by imposing these suppliers' standards, patterns, models, norms, customs, and procedures. This is expected to happen after December 31, 1992, with an all-pervasive effect on Hungary's economy.

What of the controversial dynamic effects? Although there is considerable debate in the EC itself about the impact of EC-1992 on growth rates, the consensus is that some positive impact will occur. But it is extremely speculative to infer from this the effect on Hungary's exports to the EC; in part that would depend on the success of Hungary's own adjustment efforts (these interlinked aspects are also briefly discussed later in this chapter). This chapter does *not* deal with the economic impact of the new association agreement between the EC and Hungary signed in early December 1991. The effects of EC-1992 on Hungary described can be analyzed independently of the consequences of this new treaty (which deals mainly with the abolition of tariffs between the two sides, leaving aside the issue of NTBs).

SHORT-TERM IMPACT OF EC-1992 ON HUNGARY'S EXPORTS[1]

In the EC-1992 program there are many measures that eliminate obstacles to trade (e.g., removal of border controls). Following Tinbergen, these will be labeled "negative integration" measures. Other measures fall under the category of "positive integration," that is, the transfer by member states of instruments of trade regulation to a supranational unit, or the application by member states of instruments of trade regulation adopted in another member state (e.g., mutual recognition of norms and certification procedures). New controls at the entry into the Community to compensate for the elimination of internal controls would fall under "positive integration."

Negative Integration

Trade diversion resulting from a reduction in intra-Community transaction costs. Because Hungary's exports have not been dependent on the EC market, the danger for Hungary of trade diversion resulting from the EC-1992 program is rather limited. Some food products (such as meat preparations or preserved fruit) are outstanding exceptions, because in their case the EC's share in total exports is significant and they will be affected by new EC directives concerning phitosanitary products. The famous Checchini Report shows that in sectors where Hungary displays comparative advantage in the EC (such as textiles or iron and steel products), the expected decrease in extra-EC imports ranges from 5% to 12%.[2] However, agriculture, a very important item in Hungary's export basket to the West, was excluded from the estimations.

In fact, there are only minor problems arising from the discriminatory abolition of NTBs within the EC, particularly regarding changes in the regulatory environment concerning norms, standards, and certification. Although Hungary is not a member of European standards organizations such as CEN or CENELEC, adjusting to EC norms should not be a problem for key export products because Hungary has adopted German norms, for example, in the domain of electrical equipment. This is not, however, true for many other sectors, where firms have been producing according to CMEA, Soviet, or homemade standards; in those cases switching to EC standards may be more difficult. Also, there are currently some problems with health standards in food products that must be overcome.

Trade diversion resulting from greater EC competitiveness. The general deregulation entailed by the EC-1992 program is already translating into greater intra-EC competition, a wave of mergers, and a better exploitation of scale economies. This will intensify the competition from EC firms faced by Hungarian firms in third markets. A typical example is railroad equipment currently exported by Hungary to the Third World.

Positive Integration: Harmonization, Coordination, and Mutual Recognition of Some of the Individual Members' Policies

The adoption of one EC-wide norm in some cases means that there will be a reduction in the number of standards (from 12 to 1) with which Hungarian producers will have to comply. The application of the principle of mutual recognition of tests and certification among EC member states will also reduce drastically the number of tests and certification procedures that Hungary's products will have to pass. This is very important for the country's food and machinery sectors, which may be able to achieve some scale economies thanks to the dismantling of the EC's internal technical barriers. The main beneficiaries in Hungary would be food, chemical, pharmaceutical, and equipment industries.

EC-1992 AND CHANGES IN HUNGARY'S INDUSTRIAL STRUCTURE

In 1990, 37.8% of the machinery and equipment imported by Hungary originated in the EC. This share should increase in coming years as a result of the trade and cooperation agreement between the EC and Hungary, as well as Hungary's trade liberalization and its new modernization strategy. To the extent that FDI will originate predominantly in Western Europe, machinery is also likely to originate from there. Importing machinery implies importing embodied technology; consequently, Hungary will have to switch progressively toward German or EC-wide technical norms and standards and away from the ex-Soviet or East European (mainly ex-GDR) ones. This will be a painful process in some cases, but should offer a substantial advantage in the long run: goods produced under the new norms are most likely to be accepted everywhere, not only in Western Europe. In fact, it is in Hungary's interest to make the switch as soon as possible because it will help in the modernization of its industrial base and allow Hungary to choose its potential clients carefully. It is unlikely that Hungarian producers would have difficulty in penetrating the ex-USSR or other East European countries after the switch, because the latter will themselves convert sooner or later to Western technology, and because the EC-wide norms are usually set at levels beyond those that were adopted in the former CMEA or USSR.

Such a forecast is consistent with the view of Findlay (1978). He assumes that the rate of technological progress in a relatively backward economy (e.g., Eastern Europe) is an increasing function of the gap between its own level of technology and that of the advanced region (e.g., Western Europe), and the degree to which the former is open to FDI. The basic idea is that development occurs by "contagion," the carrier of which is the transnational corporation or TNC, whose higher efficiency inspires those in the backward economy to demand more of themselves. Therefore, the extent to which the activities of TNCs pervade the local economy is very important.

A similar view is implicit in Vernon's (1966) product-cycle theory, which postulates that when a good produced by a TNC is debugged by local firms, a standardization process takes place in the developing economy. The local firms can, in principle, compete in world markets because some domestic factors (e.g., labor or land) used intensively in production of the standardized product are very cheap. However, once TNCs are replaced by local firms, developed countries may well restrict imports with tariffs or NTBs. It is for this reason that Hungary has an interest in becoming integrated in the EC or at least in the European Economic Area.

Indeed, according to Finger (1975), there is a misconception as to what a standardized product really is. It certainly need not be a product that is technologically old: production of plate glass or footwear is fairly standardized, despite continual improvements in the production process. Products with these characteristics should, therefore, be produced in semi-industrialized economies (such as Hungary) for export to developed countries.

It is sometimes argued that some NICs have been able to sell to other developing countries products or technologies that, while not wholly indigenous, are also not mere carbon copies of whatever was initially imported from developed countries. Here, developing economies hold a comparative advantage based on small improvements in up-to-date technologies on the one hand and on demand factors on the other (such as similarity of tastes in neighboring markets and natural or artificial protection). There is a series of case studies documenting this phenomenon in Korea, India, and Argentina and other South American countries (see Amsden, 1980, 1983; Kim, 1980; Stewart and James, 1982; Katz, 1984; Lall, 1984; Teitel, 1984). A similar process could take place in Hungary, as the combined result of a relatively abundant skilled labor force and the adoption by Hungary of European (especially German) technology after 1992. Hungary would then be able to sell in the East some nonstandardized manufactured products, using EC norms but adapted to the needs of East European or CIS markets. There are machinery sectors that are well adapted to "niche" markets, and there is ample room for product variety. Modern information technology allows as well for flexible manufacturing, ideally suited for a country with the factor endowments of Hungary.

But on the other hand, Hungary could no longer rely on preferential access to these markets, since the former CMEA has not been replaced by a new preferential arrangement among East European countries. This is a new handicap, and one that will force Hungary to look toward the West. Moreover, the idea of adapting technology to local conditions is partially at variance with the principle that technology should meet international quality standards and specifications. Exports to regional, less developed markets are, in such a context, merely a spillover or side effect of the development of local sales.

There are at least two other reasons why, as a result of EC-1992, Hungary will turn to Western Europe in order to modernize its economy. Recent experience shows that in those rare cases in which geography makes developing and developed countries neighbors, proximity will actually limit communication problems between supplier and consumer. This applies in particular to final consumption goods, which are bulky, such as heavy transport equipment. Mexico and Spain, for example, are considered to be ideal export platforms to the United States or the EC respectively for production processes, where communication between supplier and consumer plays a key role.[3] Hungary, with its relative abundance of skills, is in the same relative position. It is fortunate that many of its regional trade partners are in the most developed part of the world.

In turn, concentrating exports to the EC (and more generally to the European Economic Area) may stimulate the transfer of technology. For instance, it is well documented that foreign customers, whether willingly or unwillingly, in time become agents that transfer some elements of the technologies required, because they are obliged to specify in their ongoing contacts with the supplier what they really expect from the latter. Thus, in attempting to explain Korea's competitive edge, it was found that technical assistance from foreign buyers of Korean products and technical assistance from foreign suppliers of capital equipment and raw materials were an important source of technology acquisition by 10% of exporting firms surveyed (Pursell, Ross-Larson, and Whee-Ree, 1984). The more traditional the sectors considered, the more important was this source of assistance. The same is reported by Morawetz (1980) with respect to Colombia's clothing industry. The literature on subcontracting (e.g., Asian Productivity Organization, 1978; Germidis, 1980) underlines the same point: technical advice and assistance for the training of workers received by the supplier in the developing country is considered by the customer to be part and parcel of the deal, since production is supposed to comply with the norms and standards of his country. Clearly, the progressive penetration of Hungary by West European capital equipment would make local firms working for European clients or parent firms aware of the importance of quality control and of working according to international standards and qualifications. This is particularly important for Hungary because the accumulated experience shows that foreign influence is particularly strong in traditional sectors, such as food and clothing, where Hungary has shown comparative advantage.

To sum up, Hungary is more likely to adopt the Spanish model of modernizing its economy than the South American or Indian model. First, traditional sectors would be modernized in terms of quality control, hygiene, and so on. Second, Hungary may develop comparative advantages in products using technologies that have been standardized fairly recently (such as popular cars) and are suited to nearby markets in the European Economic Area (particularly united Germany, Austria, and Switzerland). Thirdly, there is a vast area for production of specialized capital goods to supply "niche" markets in the West but later on also in the East, when the financial situation in the latter improves. The role of joint ventures between Western European and Hungarian firms could be non-negligible in the domain of specialized capital goods production.

EC GROWTH PATTERNS AFTER 1992 AND HUNGARY'S EXPORTS AND INVESTMENT LEVELS

In focusing on Hungary, two very different subjects must be distinguished. The first is the direct or indirect impact that changes in the level and composition of the EC's GDP, deriving from the completion of the Single Market, will have on Hungary's exports. The second is the impact that changes in the EC's business environment will have on investment flows to Hungary.

Concerning the first issue, a positive impact can be expected on industries producing goods or services with high income elasticities of final demand in the EC. Typical examples are all services connected to tourism (including passenger transport). But for most other Hungarian exports, namely, primary products (including food), textiles, clothing, some chemicals, and middle-level machinery, income elasticities are low.

One of the expectations of the Commission is that as an outcome of EC-1992, more resources will shift from low-tech to high-tech industries and services. Thus a larger GDP does not mean that the demand for inputs in all sectors will grow in the same proportion. High-tech industries and services are generally less resource-intensive than low-tech ones. Since many Hungarian exports serve EC industries in the latter category (e.g., textiles, leather, chemicals), the favorable effect of EC-1992 is likely to be limited. An exception may be the electrical and electronic industries.

Some EC experts have argued that pollution-intensive industries will be abandoned progressively in favor of "clean" industries. How this would affect Hungary is highly speculative. On the one hand, EC demand for intermediate or final products that are polluting (e.g., some chemicals imported from Hungary) would diminish. On the other hand, some pollution-intensive production units (e.g., chemical or leather tanning production) might be shifted to countries with fewer environmental constraints, including Hungary.

Finally, Sapir (1989) anticipates a favorable "political economy" effect of EC-1992 on nonmembers' exports, which is also linked to the growth issue discussed here. He argues that growth deriving from the completion of the Internal Market will reduce demands for more protectionism in the EC, which in turn will result in increasing imports. However, this argument is only valid in the long term; in the short run, the argument works in the opposite direction. Should there be adjustment problems and new unemployment created by EC-1992, particularly in weaker countries such as Portugal or Greece, the demand for protectionism would increase rather than decrease.[4] The two arguments are quite relevant to Hungary. In the short run, Portugal and Greece, and even Spain or Germany (on behalf of the ex-GDR), may lobby within the EC in favor of introducing new NTBs against countries on the EC's periphery with overlapping production features. Alternatively, weaker EC member countries may ask for protective measures on nonmembers' exports competing in their own markets with exports of other EC member countries, particularly in the realm of services, such as banking and insurance. This would be of no concern to Hungary. Moreover, Germany, the United Kingdom, and Italy (but not France, Spain, Greece, or Portugal) will probably try to exempt Hungary, when feasible, from new or tougher NTBs generally applied to developing countries, for their own geopolitical and strategic reasons. A proof of the EC's intentions was its willingness to sign a comprehensive association agreement with Hungary in December 1991 as an intermediate step toward the full integration of Hungary in the European Economic Area and later on in the Community itself.

In light of these arguments and counterarguments, apart from a few exceptions (e.g., tourism), it is difficult to assess the net impact new EC growth will have on Hungary's exports to the EC.

With respect to investment, it is now conventional wisdom that the unified EC market is likely to attract new investment from inside and outside the Community. This argument has gained more validity now that the ex-GDR is in the EC and that negotiations for the creation of a European Economic Area have been completed. By investing within the Community, a firm gains access (for its output) to a market of 341 million consumers, whereas if it tried to penetrate the EC from an outside location, such as Hungary, it would face a variety of trade restrictions. In that respect, the completion of the Single Market is bound to influence location decisions made by prospective investors that focus on a product (good or service) that can be produced competitively both in the EC (or the wider EEA) and Hungary, and that faces before 1993, serious intra-EEA NTBs, which are bound to disappear afterward. There are many products in Hungary's export basket that meet these two conditions (e.g., all foodstuffs), whereas the first condition applies to clothing, specific chemicals, and electrical machinery and its spare parts.

Because in most cases the overlap in comparative advantage is between Hungary on the one hand and Spain and Portugal on the other, some experts attribute investment diversion in favor of the latter (e.g., in agro-industry projects) to their entry into the EC. There is also a counterargument that predicts a rapid rise in labor costs in the Iberian Peninsula as a result of the completion of a single labor market for EC nationals, thereby increasing the labor cost differential in favor of Hungary. But this ignores the facts that the level of unemployment in Spain is the highest in the OECD and that Spain may be prepared to import workers from North Africa, at least on a temporary basis. The experience of the 1960s and 1970s shows as well that the freedom of movement of workers stipulated by the Treaty of Rome did not lead to massive migrations from Italy to the other five EC members, which in turn retarded labor cost convergence that might have been expected.

Thus it still makes sense for Hungary to liberalize further its foreign investment laws in the perspective of EC-1992 and do all that is feasible to promote joint ventures. Second, in some cases the amount of investment in the EC that a Hungarian firm (whether local- or foreign-owned) may need to overcome the problem of market access may be small, ranging from opening a marketing office in the EC to establishing a joint venture with EC firms. Even capital-poor countries, like Hungary, can try this route, although it would require a further relaxation of exchange controls. There is, however, a logistical problem in that there is no time to establish viable subsidiaries or branches until January 1, 1993.[5] It is also difficult to envisage outward investment by Hungarian firms, not only because capital is not the abundant factor but also because of the tremendous balance of payment and foreign debt problems Hungary currently faces,[6] which may lead to even tighter exchange controls.

NOTES

1. This section draws from Tovias (1991).

2. A version of the so-called Checcini Report, which analyzes the quantitative and qualitative effects of the completion of the EC's Domestic Market, can be found in Commission of the European Communities (1988). The impact on extra-EC imports is dealt with on p. 183.

3. Spain participates, e.g., in the Airbus program.

4. Estimates are that jobs will decline in the EC by between 25,000 and 50,000 before they begin to rise again sometime around 1994 and 1995.

5. The value of outward investment by Hungarian companies is about $80 million, mostly devoted to the marketing of export products. See GATT (1991), vol. 1, p. 84.

6. Foreign debt stood at $19.9 billion in June 1991. See Economist Intelligence Unit (1991).

REFERENCES

Amsden, A., "The Industry Characteristics of Intra-Third World Trade in Manufactures," *Economic Development and Cultural Change,* 29: 1 (1980): 1–19.

Amsden, A., "De-skilling," Skilled Commodities and the NICs' Emerging Comparative Advantage, *American Economic Review,* May (1983), pp. 333–37.

Asian Productivity Organization, *International Subcontracting: A Tool of Technology Transfer* (Tokyo: 1978).

Commission of the European Communities, Fifth Report of the Commission to the Council and the European Parliament concerning the Implementation of the White Paper on the Completion of the Internal Market, COM(90)90 final, Brussels, March, 1990.

Commission of the European Communities, The Economics of 1992 ("The Checchini Report"), Directorate General for Economic and Financial Affairs, *European Economy*, No. 35, March (1988).

Economist Intelligence Unit *Hungary*, Country Reports (1991).

Findlay, R., "Relative Backwardness, Direct Foreign Investment and the Transfer of Technology: A Dynamic Model," *Quarterly Journal of Economics*, 92 (1978): 1–16.

Finger, J. M., "A New View of the Product Cycle Theory," *Weltwirtschaftliches Archiv*, 111 (1975): 79–99.

GATT, *Trade Policy Review: Hungary*, vols. 1 and 2.

Germidis, D., ed. *International Sub-contracting* (Paris: OECD, 1980).

Katz, J., "Domestic Technological Innovations and Dynamic Comparative Advantages: Further Reflections on a Comparative Case-Study Program," *Journal of Development Economics*, 16: 1–2 (1984): 13–37.

Kim, L., "Stages of Development of Industrial Technology in a Developing Country: A Model," *Research Policy*, 9 (1980): 254–77.

Lall, S., "Exports of Technology by Newly Industrializing Countries: An overview," *World Development*, 12: 5/6 (1984): 471–80.

Morawetz, D., "Why the Emperor's New Clothes Are Not Made in Colombia," World Bank, Staff Working Papers No. 368, Washington, January, 1980.

Pursell, E., Ross-Larson, B., and Whee-Ree, Y., *Korea's Competitive Edge* (Baltimore: John Hopkins University Press, 1984).

Sapir, A., "Does 1992 Come Before or After 1990?" In Jones, R., and Krueger, A., eds., *The Political Economy of International Trade* (Oxford: Basil Blackwell, 1989), pp. 197–222.

Stewart, F., and James, J., *The Economics of New Technology in Developing Countries* (London: Frances Pinter, 1982).

Teitel, S., "Technology Creation in Semi-Industrial Economies," *Journal of Development Economics*, 16: 1–2 (1984): 39–61.

Tovias, A., "EC-Eastern Europe: A Case Study of Hungary," *Journal of Common Market Studies*, 29: 3 (1991): 291–315.

Vernon, R., "International Investment and International Trade in the Product Cycle," *Quarterly Journal of Economics*, 80 (1966): 190–207.

Westphal, L. et al., "Republic of Korea," *World Development*, 12: 5/6 (1984): 505–33.

Chapter 14

The Impact
of the Canada-U.S. Free Trade Agreement
on the Household Furniture Industry
in Canada

Hamdi F. Ali*

Abstract *With respect to the furniture industry, the Canada-U.S. Free Trade Agreement calls for the elimination of tariffs between the two countries in five equal annual steps. However, for some furniture inputs imported into Canada from the U.S., the transitional period will last for ten years. The Canadian industry is expected to pass through a difficult period of adjustment in the face of increased U.S. competition. Medium-sized firms are the most severely affected by the agreement; some plants will shut down while others will meet the competition by investing in modern computerized technology or by emphasizing a market niche in which design and quality are seen as more important than price.*

INTRODUCTION

During the past 15 years the Canadian economy has grown faster than that of all other major industrial countries except Japan. The economy is further characterized by a high reliance on international trade. However, most of Canada's trade (76% of exports and 69% of imports in 1987) is with the United States, which is over 10 times larger than Canada. The Canada-U.S. Free Trade Agreement (hereafter referred to as FTA) is believed to be a landmark in trade relations between the two countries, and is aimed at establishing more secure and open trade.

Accounting for 1.8% of the GDP in 1990, the Canadian furniture industry

---

*The writer would like to acknowledge the contribution of the studies conducted by the Aktrin Research Institute, Oakville, Ontario, to the contents of this paper. In addition, thanks are also due to Dr. Stefan Wille, Director of the Institute, for his help and cooperation.

171

ranks sixteenth in terms of output, and fourteenth in terms of employment (3.5% of total employment). It comprises three sectors: household (40% of output), office (27% of output), and other furniture including bed springs, mattresses, institutional furniture, and frames (33% of output). This chapter examines the impact of the FTA on the household furniture industry in Canada. It is organized into three sections: industry characteristics and growth, present competitive position, and the impact of the FTA on future industry growth.

INDUSTRY'S CHARACTERISTICS AND GROWTH

The household furniture industry is characterized by a relatively small but heterogeneous market. It is serviced by small, labor intensive enterprises that are oriented to the domestic market and have low profit and investment levels.

The market size of the industry, estimated at CDN $2.98 billion, is small relative to that of the United States or the EC. Between the years 1980 and 1989, real growth in the domestic market averaged 2.5% yearly. The inflation factor accounts for another 5.4%, resulting in a nominal increase of 7.9% per annum. In terms of regional distribution, Ontario (41%) and Quebec (29%) account for 70% of the entire domestic market.

In addition to being functional, furniture is considered to provide decorative and status appeal. On the average, Canadian families are estimated to spend approximately 1.1% of their pre-tax income on furniture. This percentage is higher in low- and middle-income families and lower in families with earnings above CDN $100,000 per year. In addition to income, other criteria such as the size and age of the family, the size of the living community, and the ethnic group determine the demand for furniture.

Furniture products may be classified as low-, medium-, and high-priced; the manufacturers gear themselves to a wide variety of styles and designs in each of the three price ranges. Variations in consumer taste make it a heterogeneous product.

On the supply side, the industry is dominated by small firms. Wood furniture accounts for 50% of industrial shipments, upholstered furniture for 35%, and metal and plastic products account for 15%. In 1985, the industry consisted of 994 firms located mainly in Quebec (45%), Ontario (35%), and Western Canada (17%), distributed equally between Manitoba, Alberta, and British Columbia.

Table 1 shows the employment structure of the industry. Of the nearly 1000 firms, 56 large firms (with 100 or more employees) account for 46.9% of total shipments. In contrast, 719 small institutions (with 20 or fewer employees) account for only 13.1% of total shipments. Thus, the industry is dominated by a small number of large firms despite the existence of numerous medium and small companies.

Table 2 shows the industry's domestic shipments, imports, and exports between 1973 and 1989. Share of domestic output in the Canadian market de-

Table 1
Industrial Structure of Canadian Household Furniture Industry*

	Number of firms	Number of employees	Shipments in CDN $ million
Very large firms (over 200 employees)	17	5,392	332
Large firms (100 to 200 employees)	39	5,681	361
Medium firms (50 to 100 employees)	77	5,218	330
Small firms (20 to 50 employees)	142	4,464	260
Very small firms (fewer than 20 employees)	719	5,631	194
Total	994	24,386	1,477

*Source: Statistics Canada

clined from 88% in 1973 to 62.5% in 1989. During the same period, the origin of imports shifted from the United States (total Canadian imports declined from 66% to 55%) to Asia (total Canadian imports increased from 5% to 19%), and Western Europe (total Canadian imports increased from 20% to 25%).

Total Canadian exports rose from CDN $22 million (3.7% of industrial shipments) in 1973 to CDN $300 million (15% of shipments) in 1989. Their main destination is the United States, which receives between 90% and 98% of total Canadian exports.

Materials are the most important item in total costs (46%), followed by wages and salaries (30%). A variety of raw materials, components, and parts are bought from domestic and foreign sources. Purchases include lumber- and wood-based components, particle board, textile products, hardware, and finishing materials. A comparison of shipments per employee between small firms (CDN $53,000) and large firms (CDN $62,000) suggests that even large firms are not fully realizing potential economies of scale.

Table 2
Imports and Domestic Shipments of Canadian Household Furniture Industry*
(in CDN $ millions)

	1973	1980	1982	1984	1986	1989
Exports	22	46	66	132	220	300
Domestic shipments	569	1164	1046	1245	1363	1769
Imports	79	200	176	276	400	775
Canadian market	648	1318	1222	1521	1763	2069
Exports (% of market)	3.7	3.5	5.9	9.6	13.9	14.5
Imports (% of market)	12.2	15.2	14.4	18.1	22.7	37.5

*Source: Statistics Canada

Although profits have been reported regularly in the industry, after-tax profit margins have been low (between 2% and 3% of sales); this may account for the low investment levels in the industry, estimated at 2% of shipments, compared to 6% for total manufacturing.

THE COMPETITIVE POSITION

The Canadian household furniture industry is not considered cost competitive with either the United States or other foreign countries in the low- to medium-priced categories. This is generally because of three factors: the nature of the market, the structure of the industry, and the technology. The market factor refers to the small but heterogeneous Canadian market that forces producers to fall short of optimum levels of production. Shorter production runs induce frequent changeovers, idle capital, and costly inventory. By contrast, the U.S. industry has attained a high level of product specialization and standardization by virtue of its much larger market.

The emergence of knock-down or ready-to-assemble furniture in the medium- and lower-priced category has favored Asian producers in both Canada and the United States. In several instances, Canadian manufacturers are importing full sets, partial sets, or some component parts to assemble in their own plants and/or to complete their product line. In addition, some West European countries are particularly competitive in the small but high-priced market segments featuring modern designs.

Structural factors include establishment size, and the lower profit margins and investment levels observed in the Canadian industry. Table 3 shows that in the United States the percentage of large enterprises is higher (12% vs. 5.6% in Canada), with higher output per firm for almost all sizes of firms. The average output per U.S. enterprise is 67% higher than that for a Canadian firm.

Table 3
Industrial Structure of U.S. Household Furniture Industry*

	Number of firms	Number of employees	Shipments in U.S. $ million
Very large firms (over 200 employees)	195	111,400	4895
Large firms (100 to 200 employees)	353	56,000	2764
Medium firms (50 to 100 employees)	422	29,900	1400
Small firms (20 to 50 employees)	747	24,400	1072
Very small firms (fewer than 20 employees)	833	16,000	709
Total	2550	237,700	10,840

Source: Statistics Canada

Canadian profit margins have been lower than those in the U.S. industry. Dun and Bradstreet reports average after-tax profits of 3% to 4.8% of sales in the United States compared to 2.5% in Canada. The end result of an industry characterized by smaller firms with lower profit margins is low investment in capital goods and reduced technological developments.

The technology factor refers to the potential for adoption of advanced computerized machinery in the production process. Until recently, advances in production technology were mainly in machine and tool precision and speed, with managers emphasizing product standardization and longer production runs. Newer computer-based manufacturing technologies such as computer-integrated manufacturing (CIM), flexible manufacturing systems (FMS), and computer-assisted design and manufacturing systems (CAD-CAM) are lengthening production runs and making the benefits of economies of scale possible in smaller firms. American companies have, however, maintained the lead in technological advancements and in the integration of computer technology into the production process.

IMPACT OF THE FTA

An examination of the tariff structure reveals that the elimination of duties under the FTA is not favorable to the Canadian household furniture industry. First, duties imposed by Canada on finished products are generally much higher than those in the United States. In Canada, these duties range between 12.5% for metal furniture and 15% for wooden furniture. By contrast, U.S. duties incurred by Canadian exports range from 2.5% for wooden furniture to 7% for upholstered furniture. Second, upholstery fabric imports to Canada are subject to a very high import duty (25%) compared with the United States (15%). In addition, the tariff elimination period for fabric imports will be 10 years (as compared with 5 years for finished products).

These factors are not favorable to the Canadian furniture industry. It stands to lose a great deal from tariff elimination on finished products, especially in the upholstery sector, in which duties will be paid on its fabric imports from the United States for an additional 5 years after the elimination of duties on finished products. Given that Canadian manufacturers import up to 50% of their upholstery fabrics from the United States, whereas American producers obtain their fabrics duty free from local sources, it is inevitable that the Canadian upholstery manufacturers will be at a severe cost disadvantage. In recognition of this problem a recent agreement was reached to accelerate tariff elimination on 50% of upholstery fabric imports. This will only partially relieve the pressure felt by the Canadian upholstery manufacturers.

Despite the fact that manufacturers will have free access to the U.S. market under the FTA, accessing this market will require considerable adjustment, and investment would be necessary in order to meet competition from U.S. manufacturers who possess more advanced technology and lower production costs.

Besides that, annual tariff reduction on Canadian imports is 3% whereas the corresponding reduction on U.S. imports is about 0.5%. As a result, American manufacturers will reap more benefits from the tariff elimination scheme than the Canadians.

Imports from the United States have increased drastically since the implementation of the FTA to reach a record high of 47% of total imports in the wooden household sector, 60% in the upholstered furniture sector, and 45% in the other household furniture sector. Some authorities estimate that imports from the U.S. will surpass 60% of total Canadian imports by the end of 1993, and others assert that they will surpass domestic shipments by the turn of the century.

Table 4 shows estimates of a study commissioned by the Canadian Council of Furniture Manufacturers, predicting a considerable loss of employment and domestic market share by 1993, coupled with only a small increase in exports.

Increased U.S. imports into Canada will not reduce the growth in imports from the EC or Southeast Asia, except in relative terms. Imports from EC countries, of which 90% are in the household furniture industry, will continue to grow but at a lower rate than U.S. imports. Asian exports to Canada will continue to enjoy a higher rate of growth parallel to the U.S. rate, especially in the wooden household furniture sector. In addition, with the prospects of a North American FTA, imports from Mexico are likely to increase from U.S. plants based in Mexico because it will be difficult to compete against the low wage rates prevailing in Mexico.

The impact of the FTA on the Canadian household furniture industry will vary according to the industry's sector, quality, and price category of the product, size of the manufacturer, and geographical location. As noted, the Canadian upholstery manufacturers stand to suffer the most negative consequences. These will be felt most by manufacturers of high-priced products where the imported fabric component represents a higher relative cost than it does for medium- and low-priced products.

Table 4
Expected Impact of FTA on Canadian Furniture Industry*

	1986	1993	Change
Shipments	1638	1419	−219
Imports	417	698	+281
Exports	220	218	+61
Employment (number)	26,970	23,470	−3500

*Dollar figures are in millions, constant 1986 dollars.

Source: Canadian Council of Furniture Manufacturers, The Samson Bélair Study, and Aktrin Research Institute.

The wooden household furniture sector will also be negatively affected, but to a lesser degree. In contrast to the upholstery sector, the medium- and low-priced wooden domestic manufacturers will suffer more negative consequences than the producers of high-quality furniture. Due to the larger production runs in the United States, Canadian manufacturers are at a natural disadvantage with respect to computerized and mass-produced budget furniture. Manufacturers of high quality and design products are unlikely to be affected by tariff elimination due to the low price sensitivity of such products.

Other household furniture sectors will witness increasing levels of U.S. imports, especially indoor metal furniture, TV and radio cabinets, and wooden and metal frames, of which the United States is the major supplier. Exports from this industrial segment to the United States will also increase but, in view of the small base of domestic production (48% in 1990), imports from the U.S. will dominate the Canadian market.

Medium-sized firms that offer a narrower product line to a broader market base will be more negatively affected by the FTA because they lack the investment capabilities to update to the most modern technology. According to the study sponsored by the Canadian Furniture Manufacturing Association, firms with between 20 and 200 employees are expected to decrease in number from 258 to 198 (23.3%). Small firms, with fewer than 20 employees, are expected to continue serving their specialized domestic markets. Many large producers are unlikely to be negatively affected, because they have already exploited their marketing niches in the United States by targeting a specific market segment. This fact may well account for the projected increase in Canadian furniture exports (20% of shipments) by the year 1993 as stated by the study.

On the provincial level, Ontario is particularly vulnerable to the FTA. Seventy percent of the shipments in the upholstered furniture sector, which is the most negatively affected by the FTA, originate in Ontario. Another 39% of total shipments in the wooden household sector are produced in this province. Most of these firms, which specialize in medium-, low-priced, and mass-produced budget furniture, will be negatively affected. Above all, more than two thirds of the U.S. imports into Canada are destined for the province of Ontario. Quebec, producing 55% of the wooden household shipments and 26% of upholstered household shipments, will be less affected by the FTA implementation. The wooden household furniture sector in Quebec is known for its relatively small plants on the one hand and for its high-quality products on the other. The upholstered household manufacturers will suffer, however, from the negative consequences of the tariff elimination.

In the long run, many Canadian firms will adjust to the new environment created by the FTA in one of two forms. First, intensive investment programs will be implemented by some manufacturers to upgrade to modern computerized manufacturing. This will establish the potential for cost minimization through longer production runs and the use of standard parts. Furthermore, labor productivity, presently estimated at 80% of the U.S. level, will increase between 10% and 20% as a result of these investment programs. Second, other manufacturers will seek to develop a specialized high-priced market niche in which design and quality are more important than prices.

CONCLUSION

The Canadian household furniture industry will suffer as a result of the implementation of the FTA. The upholstery furniture sector, located mainly in Ontario, will suffer the most as a result of high duties on imported fabrics from the United States; these duties will be eliminated only after 10 years. Firms most affected are medium-sized producers of low- to medium-priced budget furniture that serves the domestic market. Long-term consequences of the FTA will be an increase in computerization, improved labor productivity, and development of a product-niche strategy that focuses on quality and design.

REFERENCES

Aktrin Research Institute, *The Canadian Handbook of Furniture Manufacturing, Wholesaling, and Retailing* (Ottawa: April 1990).

Bond, David E., and Wonnacott, Ronald J., *Trade Liberalization and the Canadian Furniture Industry* (Toronto: University of Toronto Press, 1968).

Department of External Affairs, *Studies in Canadian Export Opportunities in the US Market: Furniture* (Ottawa: Ministry of Supply and Services Canada, 1988).

Department of External Affairs, Services and General Trade Policy Division, *The Canada-US Free Trade Agreement and Services: An Assessment* (Ottawa: Ministry of Supply and Services Canada, 1988).

Department of External Affairs, The International Trade Communications Group (DMTN), *The Canada-US Free Trade Agreement* (Ottawa: Ministry of Supply and Services Canada, 1988).

Department of Finance, Fiscal Policy and Economic Analysis Branch, *The Canada-US Free Trade Agreement: An Economic Assessment* (Ottawa: Ministry of Supply and Services Canada, 1988).

Industry, Science and Technology Canada, *Industry Profile: Household Furniture* (Ottawa: ISTCC, 1988).

Industry, Science and Technology Canada, *Industry Profile: Office Furniture* (Ottawa: ISTCC, 1988).

Industry, Science and Technology Canada, *International Trends in Furniture Manufacturing* (Ottawa: ISTCC, Furniture Division, 1989).

Knoop, Robert, and Sanders, Alexander, *Furniture Industry: Attitudes Towards Exporting* (Montreal: Concordia University, 1978).

Portis, Bernard, and White, John M., *Marketing Household Furniture in Ontario* (Ottawa: University of Western Ontario, 1979).

Quebec Furniture Association, *Menaces et Occasions du Libre-Echange pour l'Industrie du Meuble: Impact de l'Accord du Janvier 1988* (Montreal: February 1988).

Trade Policy Directorate, Department of Regional Industrial Expansion, *The Canada-US Free Trade Agreement and Industry* (Ottawa: Ministry of Supply and Services Canada, 1988).

Part Three

Foreign Direct Investment and the MNC

Chapter 15

The Importance of Intra-Firm Trade

H. Peter Gray and Sarianna Lundan*

Abstract *This chapter suggests that the greater efficiency of hierarchical flexibility of policy and coordination within multinational corporations allows intra-firm trade to increase the efficiency of the global economy and that these efficiency gains will derive importantly but not exclusively from linking marketing-and-distribution units in industrialized countries with production units in developing countries. These gains could be offset, in whole or in part, by the development of global market power on the part of the multinational corporations.*

INTRODUCTION

The orthodox theory of international trade assumes, *inter alia,* that transactions between pairs of production units, between a supplier and a consumer or between a supplier and a distributing organization, take place at arm's length among unrelated economic units. One of the features of modern international trade deriving directly from the existence of multinational corporations (MNCs) is international trade within units of the same firm—so-called *intra-firm trade* (IFT). The importance of IFT for the United States is shown in table 1. Clearly, a specific type of trade of this importance requires explicit recognition in any basic paradigm of international trade. This chapter presents, in the following section, a brief theory of IFT, which draws on the work of contributors to the theory of the MNC. The next section considers IFT's contribution to allocative efficiency[1] and the importance of its role of linking production units with marketing outlets in host nations. The conclusions are discussed at the end of this chapter.

---

*The authors are, respectively, Professor Emeritus of International Business, and graduate student at the Graduate School of Management, Rutgers University, Newark, N.J.

Table 1
Intra-firm Trade in the United States, 1977 and 1982
(Billions of US dollars: trade shares in percent)

	1977	1982
Trade in manufactured goods		
Value of intra-firm exports	32.9 bn	49.3 bn
Value of intra-firm imports	38.8 bn	65.2 bn
Share of exports	40.1 %	34.3 %
Share of imports	50.3 %	45.2 %
Trade in nonmanufactured goods		
Value of intra-firm exports	14.0 bn	18.1 bn
Value of intra-firm imports	25.4 bn	28.2 bn
Share of exports	36.7 %	26.5 %
Share of imports	36.5 %	28.2 %

Source: Hipple (1990).

THEORY

The theory of IFT must allow for the international mobility of factors of production and for the existence of MNCs, and it must be contrasted with a theory
of trade applying to a world in which all trade takes place among independent
economic units. Intra-firm trade takes place because MNCs have in the past
created foreign production capacity and now perceive the existence of a private
gain from international trade by integrating chains of value-added activities
involving two or more countries. These potential private gains from trade may
or may not have been foreseen when the international productive capacity was
created. Where the benefits of intra-firm integration were perceived *ex ante,* it
was what Drucker (1986) called "production sharing."

In principle, a good can be produced in as many countries as there are
separable processes in its production. Each process would combine a particular
set of inputs and would be located in the country in which that set could be
obtained most cheaply. The essential principle here is comparative advantage
defined in terms of an activity instead of the traditional final good. The greater
the disparity in relative factor endowments in different countries, the greater is
the potential cost saving associated with production sharing.

The gains from IFT, in addition to those obtainable by independent firms,
derive from the greater efficiency of hierarchical flexibility of policy and coordination and of intra-firm communications. Williamson (1979) distinguishes
five conditions that contribute to internalization efficiency gains (economies of
common governance) when:

1. The volume of trade between units is large and recurrent;
2. Uncertainties exist with respect to price, quantity, and design of the product traded;
3. Product-specific equipment will reduce costs but will expose both parties in the arm's length relationship to an unequal share of losses or gains when product design and process technologies change within the life of the activity-idiosyncratic capital equipment;
4. Stringent quality standards are imposed by the purchaser (the assumption here is that quality control costs are for both firms or units, an increasing function of the quality standards required for both firms);
5. The parent corporation (or major corporation in a joint venture) owns product-relevant proprietary know-how so that the appropriability is increased by an internal transfer.

The first three items offer hierarchical efficiencies that reduce costs of production relative to those obtainable under an arm's-length or independent contract. The third efficiency is a special case whereby a reduction in uncertainty increases the probability of use of product- or activity-specific equipment. They are therefore more likely to influence the decision to establish the foreign affiliate, and thereby to facilitate international trade, than to affect the pattern of trade directly. The fourth is a straightforward example of an operating (cost-reducing) efficiency deriving from vertical integration, and the fifth makes international production more probable. Hierarchies substantially reduce the costs of negotiation and enforcement of agreements; they can eliminate duplication in quality control activities; they can recognize the desirability of using product-specific equipment where it will generate quasi-rents and can circumvent problems of their allocation; and, finally, they can better coordinate investment in equipment so that inter-unit compatibility is achieved.

Given some extant distribution of parents and affiliates, intra-firm international trade will take place when the gains from differences in costs of production in units located in different countries exceed the costs of transportation and any tariffs (impediments to trade) in effect between those units. Any reduction in transportation and tariff costs will lead to the establishment of foreign affiliates and a greater volume of intra-firm trade subject to the potential gains being seen as exceeding any additional costs of oversight and coordination. Thus, the economies of common governance are likely to be trade-creating (i.e., to result in a larger volume of international trade than would be generated by a system of arm's-length firms), and to enhance global gains from the international production and complementary international trade.[2] Such trade creation is the more likely to occur:

1. The greater the disparity in relative factor costs among countries and the smaller the sacrifice of any economies of scale;

2. The smaller the proportionate costs of transportation and tariffs and the additional oversight costs;
3. The greater the intra-firm efficiencies of vertical integration (Williamson's points 1, 2, and 4);
4. The more easily foreign direct investment (FDI) leading to intra-firm trade creation is permitted to take place by the host government.

The ability to combine low-wage labor, which can be trained to perform production work reliably given the transfer of internationally mobile technology and coupled with the existence of the Williamson features, suggests that there will be a tendency for much of the trade created in manufactures to be North-South in character (although much trade creation within the bloc of industrialized countries can be expected to be brought about by economies of scale).[3]

Major economies of common governance are also likely to arise from the improved quality of communications within a hierarchy. These simple gains in efficiency of operation are caused by frequent interchange among a group of people using a common language (with a firm-specific vocabulary) and having common goals.[4] A hierarchy creates a homology that facilitates closer interaction than would be obtainable between units with separate identities and allegiances.

It is worth noting that the better quality of communication within a hierarchy helps to fulfill one of the basic tenets of international trade theory. Traditional theory assumes that all information is universally available (or that information will not seep through to new places with time: This is implicit in a stationary general equilibrium framework). In practice, the knowledge of decision-makers is severely geographically constrained and is much greater for executives of MNCs who have internal sources of intelligence in each country in which the MNC is located.

Intrafirm trade has different characteristics from arm's-length trade but it cannot be expected to run counter to the principle that the low-cost country will be the exporter (i.e., to the generally expected pattern of trade). MNCs will be attempting to minimize total cost given the distribution of their international productive capacity and will have been attempting to minimize costs in their creation of subsidiaries that were designed to be trade-creating.

In what is probably the most constructive attempt so far to develop a formal theory of IFT, Cho (1988) identifies four groups of factors that will affect the pattern and quantitative importance of intra-firm trade.[5] Two of these groups (government and regional arrangements) can be collapsed into the location-specific category of Dunning's eclectic paradigm (1988): they deal essentially with national policies, institutions, tastes, and endowments. The two remaining categories identify product-specific and firm-specific factors. They include the specificity of product design; uncertainties regarding quality, quantity, and price; the degree of use of proprietary technology; excess capacity in some subsidiaries; and economies of joint operations and of vertical integration. Cho

(1990) also offers some empirical evidence on the effect of product-specific factors on the propensity of U.S. manufacturing MNCs to engage in intra-firm trade. Out of the four factors examined, the technology intensity of the product was found to have a statistically significant positive effect on the volume of intra-firm trade for the product. This is consistent with the hypothesized effects of firm-specific factors in Cho's (1988) model, as well as with Williamson's second condition (1979), as mentioned earlier, regarding uncertainties with respect to price, quantity, and design of product.

The approach proposed by Cho (1988) can be generalized by considering the phenomena that contribute to intra-firm trade as a combination of the elements that generate arm's-length trade (location-specific factors) *together with the features that come from economies of common governance;* these vary, in turn, with the characteristics of the product. The factors that stimulate intra-firm as opposed to arm's-length trade (although long-term contracts can generate some of the cost efficiencies) will derive simply from the reduced costs of operation within a transnational network. Markets and information are not costless and some types of transaction are more efficiently (i.e., cheaply) carried out within different divisions of the same entity: credit risks are eliminated, the level of communication (the flow of information) is much higher, and economies of vertical integration are achieved. Relative to a market consisting solely of arm's length transactions, there is a substantial reduction in costs to be achieved through the exploitation of economies of common governance.

TRADE CREATION

Economies of common governance promote international trade within the hierarchy by lowering the costs of operating at arm's length through the market. The increase in the volume of trade that results from IFT (through the economies of common governance) must then enhance the efficiency of the world economy. These gains are created by the existence of MNCs, and they operate in the same dimension as transportation costs and government-imposed impediments to trade (tariffs and nontariff barriers) and therefore offset the loss of gains from trade due to these impediments. Economies of common governance provide improved allocative efficiency.

Lipsey and Weiss (1981) offer empirical evidence of the trade creation resulting from production sharing in a study on foreign production and exports in manufacturing industries. Using cross-sectional correlations of 44 foreign destinations, they found no evidence that a country's production abroad would substitute for domestic production and employment, but on the contrary concluded that quite consistently the level of activity of U.S. foreign affiliates was related positively to exports from the United States to the same area. In a later study on the foreign production and exports of individual firms, Lipsey and Weiss (1984) found the strongest correlations between output in a foreign area and U.S. exports to that area to exist, not surprisingly, in vertically integrated production processes, that is, processes where intermediate goods were exported from the United States for further processing abroad.

Unfortunately, an atomistic market and economies of common governance are mutually incompatible. The gains from international trade and the corresponding increase in world allocative efficiency that derive from the economies of common governance are inevitably offset (to greater or lesser degree) by the inefficiencies deriving from the existence of market power. However, it is reasonable to assume that competition among large firms will be almost as fierce as competition among atomistic firms so that quasi-rents deriving from negative market imperfections may be expected to be offset or more than offset by quasi-rents deriving from the economies of common governance.[6]

MARKETING AND DISTRIBUTION GAINS

These gains from the unifying influence of an MNC, the homology that an MNC creates among units located in different countries, are likely to assume greatest relative effect where cultural and national distinctions are predominant, that is, in marketing and distribution (m & d) activities. The benefits of an "own" m & d unit are probably strongest when comparative cost advantage for a good has shifted from an industrial to a developing country. The locational shift in the site of least-cost production, whether caused by shifts in the North-South terms of trade or by changes in managerial technology or production technology, will be effected most easily if the production unit does not face severe difficulties in the marketing and distribution of the product in the developed/industrialized country. Third World exporters are likely to lack familiarity with and expertise in large and complex m & d activities. An MNC can effectively combine offshore production with ongoing, or even newly created, m & d organizations, and eliminate any potential barriers that impede the production of the good at its least-cost site. Although indigenous Third World firms could slowly penetrate markets in industrialized countries, the process would be very costly and time consuming.

Such gains are likely to increase with the sophistication required in m & d activities and are likely to be largest for "experience goods." Experience goods are defined as those goods whose performance cannot be determined by visual inspection prior to purchase, which require an after-sales service system, including support for a credible warranty. These goods are likely to be the major part of MNCs' manufacturing activities and are also likely to be able to create the other forms of economies of common governance emphasized by Williamson (1979) and Casson et al. (1986). Such goods are very likely to require the close tolerances and tight control over quality that generate efficiencies of vertical integration, the transfer of process and proprietary technology from parent to subsidiary, and are most subject to rapid changes in design and quantity. These gains are reinforced if the product in question has a short product life cycle (i.e., there is likely to be only a short period of time before the existing design is superseded by the next generation of the same product). In such cases it is essential that the firm be able to bring the product to market very quickly. For a good with, for example, a 3-year life cycle, being late to market (behind a major competitor) will definitely reduce revenues by one sixth but is likely to reduce them by much more. When speed to market is essential, a firm needs an extant global m & d network that can launch the product quickly in all markets. Given the efficiencies of internal communications within a hierarchy, there is a strong argument in favor of a network of owned m & d subsidiaries rather than a series of arm's-length distributors in foreign markets (Vernon, 1979). This argument is reinforced if there is concern with the secrecy of product features and with the appropriation of the design features.

The importance of owned m & d subsidiaries in some service industries is likely to exceed that of those for tangible products. Many services, especially knowledge-intensive services, are delivered to their market either through extant communication systems or by embodiment of the service in a good solely for the purpose of delivery. These services are likely to have all the characteristics that generate economies of common governance. The need for a foreign m & d presence is particularly important. Sauvant (1986) distinguishes between the provision of services through a "pure trade," "pure foreign direct investment" in which the whole operation is performed in the country of sale, and "transactions requiring market presence." The latter can take many forms, including partial local production and total production in one country and only m & d activities in the country of sale. Sauvant cites a Canadian study: "This third case (or variations on it) tend to be the most common in practice."

There are three main reasons why a service firm might need to have related presence in the user's country of residence: Local after-sales support systems—particularly for management consulting and software; cultural adaptation of the service produced abroad (by the parent) may be necessary and can require an ongoing presence to allow the MNC to establish a long-term working relationship with local clients; and economies of scale and scope may encourage centralization of some complex operations in the home country and the output of these operations must be combined with local inputs if a culturally sensitive service is to be provided in a foreign market. It is also quite possible that the importance of an ongoing owned local presence in a foreign market will be enhanced if the services rendered require a good knowledge of the client's operations so that they are client-idiosyncratic: here long-term relationships will be vital.

In a study of the petrochemicals industry, which achieves much of its success through the incorporation of economies of vertical integration and production sharing, Gray and Walter (1983) found long-term corporate strategy to play an important role in foreign direct investment (FDI) decisions. This study of 15 investment projects exhibited three separate cases where assured access to the foreign market was the dominant reason for undertaking FDI. Similar results have also been reported by Lipsey and Weiss (1981) in the U.S. manufacturing industries, where FDI was used by oligopolistic firms as a means to compete for market share in the host countries.

To the extent that service exports require a foreign presence, foreign governments can protect their domestic suppliers of competing services by restricting the freedom of establishment and the freedom to connect with local delivery networks. Equally, governments can impede foreign affiliates by refusing to grant them equal treatment with local firms (so-called national treatment). In principle, an exporter of services could rely on a foreign m & d organization with which it has enjoyed a good, long-standing relationship. In practice, this would prove less efficient because international trade in services has grown rapidly and because the services provided are evolving at a rapid rate.

CONCLUSION

Intra-firm trade is quantitatively important and has significant potential for enhancing global allocative efficiency. However, these efficiency gains are offset to a degree by the negative imperfections deriving from the increased market power on the part of the MNCs. The economies of common governance offer considerable scope for MNCs to increase the volume of international trade because they offset in part such inevitable impediments to trade as transportation costs and tariffs. These economies apply to international trade in nonstandardized, market-sensitive goods and services; because of this lack of standardization, the role of the m & d organization and the economies derived from an "own" m & d network in the foreign market assume particular importance.

NOTES

1. The term "allocative efficiency" is deemed superior to (i.e., less misleading than) the more usual term "economic welfare." Neither term allows for income-distributional effects but a measure of "welfare" should consider this dimension.

2. Dunning (1979) identifies the ability of MNCs to combine proprietary knowledge and internationally immobile inputs as the major efficiency contribution of MNCs: *such gains are enhanced by production sharing and trade creation resulting from economies of common governance and intra-firm trade.*

3. In 1988, Thailand, Malaysia, Indonesia, and the Philippines entered into an agreement whereby tariffs on intra-firm trade were lowered within the region. Subsequently, at least Toyota has integrated its Asian subsidiaries so that they can supply each other within this trading region rather than import components from Japan (UNCTC, 1991).

4. Tomlin (1989) has examined the problems inherent in decentralized research and development activities and finds that the greater the cultural differences (and distances) between units, the greater is the need for active promotion of a network of formal and informal relations if information is to be freely transmitted.

5. Cho's article (1988) could be seen as a synthesis of the major writers in the theory of internalization including Buckley and Casson (1976), Coase (1937), Dunning

(1979), and Williamson (1979). Of these, only Dunning confronts international trade and locational factors directly.

    6. Compare Alhadeff (1954).

REFERENCES

Alhadeff, David A., *Monopoly and Competition in Banking* (Berkeley: University of California Press, 1954).

Buckley, Peter J., and Mark C. Casson, *The Future of the Multinational Enterprise* (London: Macmillan Press, 1976).

Casson, Mark C. et al., *Multinationals and World Trade* (London: Allen and Unwin, 1986).

Cho, Kang Rae, "Determinants of Intra-firm Trade: A Search for a Theoretical Framework," *The International Trade Journal* 3 (Winter, 1988), pp. 167–186.

———, "The Role of Product-Specific Factors in Intra-firm Trade of U.S. Manufacturing Multinational Corporations," *Journal of International Business Studies* (Second Quarter, 1990), pp. 319–330.

Coase, Ronald H. "The Nature of the Firm," *Economica* 4 (1937), pp. 386–405.

Drucker, Peter F. "The Changing World Economy," *Foreign Affairs* 64 (Spring, 1986), pp. 768–779.

Dunning, John H. "In Defence of the Eclectic Theory," *Oxford Bulletin of Economics and Statistics* 41 (Nov. 1979), pp. 269–295.

———, *Explaining International Production* (London: Allen and Hyman, 1988).

Gray, H. Peter, and Ingo Walter, "Investment Related Trade Distortions in Petrochemicals," *Journal of World Trade Law* 17 (1983), pp. 283–307.

Hipple, F. S., "Multinational Companies and International Trade: The Impact of Intra-Firm Shipments on U.S. Foreign Trade, 1977–1982," *Journal of International Business Studies* 21 (Fall, 1990), pp. 495–504.

Lipsey, Robert E., and Merle Jahr Weiss, "Foreign Production and Exports in Manufacturing Industries," *Review of Economics and Statistics* 63 (1981), pp. 488–494.

———, "Foreign Production and Exports of Individual Firms," *Review of Economics and Statistics* 66 (1984), pp. 304–308.

Sauvant, Karl P. *Trade and Foreign Direct Investment in Data Services* (Boulder, Col.: Westview Press, 1986), p. 92.

Tomlin, Tomlin, "Coordination of Multinational Laboratories," in Herbert I. Fusfeld, ed., *Changing Global Patterns of Industrial Research and Development: Background Papers* (Troy, N.Y.: Center for Science and Technology Policy, Rensselaer Polytechnic Institute, 1989), pp. 141–156.

UNCTC, *World Investment Report 1991: The Triad in Foreign Direct Investment* (New York: UNCTC, 1991).

U.S. Department of Commerce, *U.S. Direct Investment Abroad, 1982* (Washington, D.C., 1985).

Vernon, Raymond, "The Product Cycle Hypothesis in a New International Environment," *Oxford Bulletin of Economics and Statistics* 41 (1979), pp. 255–267.

Williamson, Oliver, "Transaction Cost Economies: The Governance of Contractual Relations," *Journal of Law and Economics* 22 (1979), pp. 236–261.

Chapter 16

American Companies' Responses
to the Promotion Programs
of Host Countries:
A Statistical Analysis of LDCs

Hormoz Movassaghi and Fahri Unsal

Abstract *Nearly all of the less developed countries (LDCs) have established incentive programs to attract direct foreign investment since early 1960s. This study investigates the effectiveness of these schemes based on a sample of countries that hosted the majority of U.S. companies' investment abroad. Regression results indicate that these incentives have not been influential. Foreign investors, instead, continue to pay more attention to the market size, availability of natural resources and political stability of their host countries.*

INTRODUCTION

Programs designed to regulate and attract foreign direct investment (FDI) emerged for the first time in developing countries in the late 1950s and early 1960s (NICB, 1969). By the late 1970s, nearly all developing countries and many industrialized countries had instituted schemes differing in scope (OECD, 1983). The decade of the 1980s was one of noticeable relaxation in regulation of FDI and active solicitation of foreign capital in many countries irrespective of their political and economic status (Dermisar, 1988; Wain, 1989).

Empirical research in this area has focused either on describing the characteristics of various incentives for FDI and/or requirements imposed by different host countries on foreign companies, or on analyzing the effectiveness of a selected number of incentive schemes, typically tax-related concessions. The main objective of this chapter is to assess the impact of the *major* incentives offered by various developing countries in order to attract foreign investors. The focus of analysis is whether the extensiveness of these programs and the changes that occurred over the period of study had any bearing on the inflow of foreign investment into the countries in question. This is done by using cross-sectional multiple regression analysis, in order to examine variations in the level of FDI across selected countries in relation to the major incentives offered, while controlling for certain economic and political factors that have commonly influenced the location decisions of foreign investors.

INCENTIVE PROGRAMS IN DEVELOPING COUNTRIES: RECENT TRENDS

Several surveys conducted in the last two decades document the various legislations and specific programs that have been instituted in order to regulate and/or promote FDI into different countries (NICB, 1969; USDOC, 1978, 1981b; OECD, 1983; UN, 1979–1986). Much less information is available on how many firms have been the beneficiaries of different types of incentives.

One major source of data in this area affecting the subsidiaries of U.S. companies is the *Benchmark Survey of the U.S. Direct Investment Abroad* (USDOC, 1981, 1985). Two such surveys of U.S. firms with direct investments abroad have been conducted so far, the first in 1977 and the other in 1982. In both surveys, "non-bank affiliates of non-bank U.S. parent" companies were asked about the type(s) of investment incentives that they received and/or any kind of performance requirement(s) to which they were subject. The 1977 survey indicated that 27% of the affiliates in developing countries and 25% of those located in the developed countries received at least one type of incentive. "Tax concessions" have been the most common form of investment incentive in all countries; "tariff incentives" are more often used in developing countries, and "subsidies" are more frequently offered in developed countries (USDOC, 1981b). This was true both in 1977 as well as in 1982. (See Guisinger et al., 1985; and Moran and Pearson, 1987, for more recent evidence in this area.)

As to how the pattern of investment incentives has changed over time, table 1 shows the percentage of U.S. companies that indicated in the two Benchmark Surveys that they received either one or more of the major types of investment incentives from their host countries. Across all countries and for all subsidiaries combined, there was a general increase in the proportion of the subsidiaries of American companies that received tax and tariff incentives and subsidies. The growth in the number of firms receiving subsidies (55.6%) exceeded those receiving tariff concessions (25%) and tax incentives (19.1%).

Tax incentives have been by far the most pervasive type of policy tool used by governments of both kinds of countries in order to attract FDI. This can be seen by comparing the percentage of U.S. firms that received these types of incentives as opposed to other categories of incentives in various host countries in 1977 and 1982. Among the developing countries, the proportion of U.S. firms that received various forms of tax incentives ranged from a low of 6% in Hong Kong to 16% in Chile, 37% in Singapore, 44% in Brazil, and 53% in South Korea.

Tariff incentives are also widely used, although more commonly by develop-

Table 1

Percent of U.S. Companies Receiving Tax and Trade Concessions,
and Subsidies in Selected Less Developed Countries in 1977 and 1982

	Tax 1977	Tax 1982	Trade 1977	Trade 1982	Subsidies 1977	Subsidies 1982
Turkey	*	36	*	32	0	13
Greece	*	44	*	25	*	30
Portugal	*	39	*	21	*	25
Argentina	30	41	12	16	11	19
Brazil	38	44	20	23	13	25
Chile	*	16	*	11	*	12
Colombia	16	23	16	18	10	16
Ecuador	*	25	22	33	*	12
Peru	28	34	26	19	3	7
Venezuela	23	23	24	26	2	6
Mexico	23	28	13	14	7	15
Panama	19	21	13	13	1	4
Bahamas	*	8	3	10	0	0
Bermuda	19	23	*	1	*	0
Jamaica	*	11	*	17	*	1
Trinidad-Tobago	*	14	*	17	*	6
Egypt	*	23	*	25	0	0
Libya	*	10	*	0	0	0
Liberia	20	11	10	7	0	0
Nigeria	14	10	16	15	*	3
Israel	*	29	17	14	30	25
Saudi Arabia	*	38	*	9	*	6
United Arab Emirates	*	10	*	12	*	0
Hong Kong	*	29	*	17	*	6
India	32	44	11	20	10	23
Indonesia	*	16	*	26	4	2
Malaysia	27	41	28	34	3	7
Philippines	13	18	14	21	1	6
Singapore	22	37	7	7	6	10
S. Korea	52	53	27	23	*	3
Taiwan	40	51	24	37	*	9
Thailand	14	21	7	21	4	12

Source: Compiled by the authors from USDOC 1981 and 1985.
*Denotes missing information.

ing countries. In 1982, the percentage of American firms in developing countries receiving various types of customs concessions ranged from none in Libya to 15% in Nigeria, 26% in Indonesia, and 37% in Taiwan. Southeast Asia and the Pacific and South American nations used this type of incentive more than other regions. Subsidies have also been increasingly used by governments of both kinds of countries in order to attract foreign capital inflows.

REVIEW OF EMPIRICAL LITERATURE

Empirical research that has sought to examine the "effectiveness" of host-countries' incentives and requirements programs may be classified into four groups. The first and crudest method has focused on measuring the impact of fiscal incentive schemes by examining whether the relative share of investment in the GNP of countries offering such schemes did in fact rise following the introduction of these programs (Shah and Toye, 1978). Other examples of this approach include studies by Katz on Mexico, and Karunaratne and Abdullah on Malaysia. Second, several studies have focused on various types of tax incentives and have attempted to determine whether those incentives resulted in increased FDI and/or were beneficial from a cost/benefit vantage point. Papers by Chen-Young (1967) for Jamaica, Ross and Christensen (1959) for Mexico, Azhar and Sharif (1974) in Pakistan, Olaloku (1976) on Nigeria, and Billsborrow and Porter (1972) on Colombia suggest this tradition. Third are studies that examined the impact of the incentive programs, in conjunction with other intervening socio-economic and political variables on the overall flows of FDI into a selected group of countries. Works by Root and Ahmed (1978), Agodo (1978), Situmeang (1978), Lim (1983), and Kulchycky and Lipsey (1984) are representative of this approach. Lastly, several scholars have investigated the influence of such schemes by surveying firms that had received some types of incentives or were subject to some form of requirements. They were asked if the presence of those incentives or requirements had influenced their decision to locate their investment in those countries. Studies by Reuber et al. (1973), Robinson (1983), Guisinger et al. (1985), and Wallace (1990) are examples of this tradition.

In general, the evidence is mixed. For example, Guisinger and Wallace find that investment incentives are important variables in the locational decisions of foreign investors, whereas Reuber et al. (1973), Lim (1983), and Agodo (1978) find that they have very little or no significance in influencing the flow of DFI into the countries they studied. Root and Ahmed (1978) and Situmeang (1978) find that only certain incentives are important. Some general methodological problems in these studies include the typical focus on tax incentives to the exclusion of the other incentives that are commonly offered (as shown in table 1), as well as the quantification of these policy instruments using dummy variables or some scaled grading. In contrast, this chapter focuses on the entire range of the major incentives offered and uses the actual number of firms receiving various incentives as the indicator for the prevalence of such programs.

METHODOLOGY

This chapter explores the relationship between the incidence of selected incentives (i.e., the number of foreign firms receiving different types of incentives from their host countries, as listed in table 1) and the level of their investment in those countries. Because of the absence of information for all foreign firms, the coverage is limited to the U.S. companies for whom such statistics are available. The primary source of information in this regard is the Benchmark Surveys of the U.S. Department of Commerce. As stated before, U.S. companies were asked if they had received any of the following incentives:

1. Tax concessions—including tax concessions on corporate income, export profits, capital expenditures, sales, exports, license fees, turnover, and others.
2. Tariff concessions—including exemption from or reduction of duties on imports, additional duties on imports of competing goods, or rebates on duties on imported inputs.
3. Subsidies—wage subsidies, investment grants, or loans at below market interest rates.
4. Other incentives—local financing, waiving environmental or employment safety standards, research and development support, land sales concessions, exchange control concessions, and others.

Because such incentives are offered more by developing than developed countries, this study focuses on the former. The 32 countries selected for this study (see table 1) account for the overwhelming majority of the FDI by the U.S. companies in developing countries.

REGRESSION MODELS AND DATA ANALYSIS

The main focus of the study was the U.S. companies' investment position in 1982 measured in terms of their net investment in property, plants, and equipment, and changes that have occurred between 1977 and 1982. Thus two dependent variables were identified: NET82, which was net investment in property, plant, and equipment in 1982 in millions of U.S. dollars; and CNET, which was changes in net investment between 1977 and 1982 in millions of U.S. dollars.

The independent variables used in the models reflected various forms of incentives, market size and market growth indicators, and the natural resource abundance of the host country and its political risk.

Another import explanatory variable that was considered in the earlier design of this study as a proxy for possible lower production costs in LDCs was wage rate. Due to conflicting evidence on the significance of this proxy in the recent literature (see Agodo, 1978; Agarwal, 1980; Moran and Pearson, 1987; and Wallace, 1990) and to serious methodological difficulties that were encountered in finding comparable data, it was decided to exclude wage rates as an independent variable for further analysis. (The methodological difficulties mentioned were as follows: some countries reported daily wage rates, others hourly; all countries reported in their domestic currencies, and potential distortions were created by using average annual exchange rates between local currency and dollars; the definition of wages was non-uniform in that some reported only wages whereas others included selected fringe benefits, not to mention that many countries did not report any data on wages for the period under investigation.)

Unless stated otherwise, the changes from 1977 to 1982 were established for these variables. The following is a list of independent variables used in the regression runs and their description:

POL79   Political risk index for 1979 as calculated by Business International Corporation.

GDP77   Gross Domestic Product in 1977 (in billions of dollars) as a proxy for the market size.

GROWTH   Market growth, measured by growth in per capita GDP at constant prices during the 1977–81 period.

CNARS   Percentage change in the exports of fuels, minerals, and metals in a country's export mix used as a proxy for investment attraction due to the abundance of natural resources.

CTAX   Change in the proportion of all affiliates receiving tax incentives between 1977 and 1982.

CTARIFF   Change in the proportion of all affiliates receiving tariff incentives between 1977 and 1982.

CSUBSID   Change in the proportion of all affiliates receiving subsidy between 1977 and 1982.

INCIND   Change in the sum of all incentives received, including tax, tariff, and subsidy incentives.

Four models were developed for the purposes of this study using two dependent and two sets of independent variables. These models and the results of the regression runs are discussed below:

MODEL 1: NET82 = f(POL79, GDP77, CNARS, INCIND, GROWTH)

The regression run for this model indicated that GDP77 and CNARS were significant at the 5% level, while POL79 was significant at the 10% level. The INCIND and GROWTH variables were found to be insignificant. The sign for the INCIND variable was negative and hence contrary to the theoretical expectations. The overall explanatory power of this equation was quite high and the coefficient of determination was equal to 0.78. The F-ratio also indicated that the equation as a whole was significant (table 2).

MODEL 2: CNET = f(POL79, GDP77, CNARS, INCIND, GROWTH)

This model used the same independent variables as in Model 1; the dependent variable was changed. In general, the results were similar. However, the POL79 variable that was significant at the 10% level in the first equation turned out to be insignificant in this model although its sign was positive as expected. The R^2 was somewhat lower in this equation (table 2).

MODEL 3: NET82 = f(POL79, GDP77, CNARS, CTAX, CTARIFF, CSUBSID, GROWTH)

In this model, the individual components of the INCIND variable were used to investigate the specific effects of tax, tariff, and subsidy incentives to attract direct foreign investment. The significant variables were the same as in Model 1. None of the specific incentives were found to be significant. Both CTAX and CTARIFF variables had negative signs indicating that they had a negative impact on the net direct investment position of the firms. Of course, this is contrary to the expectations (table 2).

MODEL 4: CNET = f(POL79, GDP77, CNARS, CTAX, CTARIFF, CSUBSID, GROWTH)

This model used the same independent variables as in Model 3. The only change was the introduction of CNET as the dependent variable in place of the NET82 variable. The only significant variables were GDP77 and CNARS. All the signs remained the same as in Model 3 (table 2).

CONCLUSION

Although there was some variation from one model to the next in terms of dependent and independent variables used, and the explanatory powers of the equations estimated, some common themes emerged from the comparison of the four models introduced in this study. These can be summarized as follows:

1. All the variables related to foreign direct investment incentives, when introduced as a combined index or as specific components, were found to be insignificant in all four models. This is probably the most important finding of this study. It is known that the developing countries place a high priority on designing attractive foreign direct investment incentive programs and this study suggests that they do not play an important role

Table 2
Regression Summaries†

Model number	Dependent variable	Constant	POL79	GDP77	CNARS	CINCIND	GROWTH	R^2	F
					Independent Variables				
1	NET82	−3064	45.43** (2.06)	0.05* (6.62)	58.33* (2.83)	−20.78 (−0.77)	58.59 (0.57)	0.78	11.67 n = 22
2	CNET	−1476	24.67 (1.70)	0.02* (3.51)	34.37* (2.46)	−7.94 (−0.44)	44.01 (0.61)	0.61	4.76 n = 22

Model number	Dependent variable	Constant	POL79	GDP77	CNARS	CTAX	CTARIF	CSUBSI	GRWTH	R^2	F
					Independent Variables						
3	NET82	−3093	45.81** (1.87)	0.05* (5.89)	58.61 (2.69)	−52.50 (−0.65)	−43.06 (−0.61)	21.94 (0.30)	90.44 (0.75)	0.79	7.56 n = 21
4	CNET	−1538	25.77 (1.56)	0.02* (3.10)	34.76* (2.32)	−22.64 (−0.42)	−6.77 (−0.14)	2.84 (0.06)	51.83 (0.62)	0.62	2.98 n = 21

*Significant at the 5% level.
**Significant at the 10% level.
†The coefficients reported are beta values and the numbers in parenthesis are t-ratios.

in attracting such investments. The negative signs for CTAX and CTARIFF variables should be especially disturbing since they imply an inverse relationship between foreign direct investment across the sampled countries and these two types of incentive packages. CSUBSID showed the expected positive sign but was not statistically significant.

2. In all four models, GDP77 and CNARS were significant at the 5% level. This suggests that the market size and the existence of natural resources are the prime factors in attracting foreign direct investment to a developing country. This is consistent with the findings of other studies.

3. The political risk factor seems to be relatively important in foreign direct investment decisions. The POL79 variable was found to be significant at the 10% level for the two models that used NET82 as the dependent variable. In the other two models, it was found to be only marginally significant, but had the expected positive sign.

4. The growth rate of the economy was found to be statistically insignificant in all of the four models. However, the signs were positive as expected. The global recession due to the second "Oil Shock" during the study period might be one reason for this variable becoming insignificant. Moreover, the outflow of FDI from the U.S. showed signs of slowing down starting in 1980.

That the incentive programs offered by many LDCs have seemingly been inconsequential to the multinational firms' locational choices is noted by many of the studies cited before such as Agodo (1978), Lim (1983) and Robinson (1983) to name a few (see Agodo, 1978, for evidence from other studies arriving at similar conclusions).

As Root and Ahmed (1978) also conclude, foreign firms are generally reluctant to make investments that depend critically on tax incentives or other concessions for their profitability, fearing that such incentives would be withdrawn or compromised by host government once the investment was made. According to them, the limited duration of incentives as compared to the relative permanence of corporate income statutes, and the competition among host LDCs also leaves foreign investors making their locational choices based on nonpolicy considerations believing that they would receive such incentives almost everywhere. The existence of competition between host countries was also noted in a recent study conducted for the International Finance Corporation (Guisinger et al., 1987).

It seems evident that while certain specific incentives have been influential in attracting some types of investment (see Guisinger et al., 1985, for recent examples), from a policy point of view developing countries are well advised to get their economic house in order to entice foreign investors as opposed to trying to artificially sweeten up the investment climate hoping that it would mitigate hosts' structural deficiencies in the eyes of foreign investors.

REFERENCES

Agarwal, J. P., "Determinants of foreign direct investment: A survey," *Weltwirtschaftliches Archiv,* 1980: 738–773.

Agodo, O., "The determinants of U.S. private manufacturing investments in Africa," *Journal of International Business Studies,* Winter 1978: 95–107.

Azhar, B. A., and S. M. Sharif, "The effect of tax holiday on investment decisions: An empirical analysis," *Pakistan Development Review,* 1974: 409–432.

Billsborrow, R. E., and R. C. Porter., "The effect of tax exemptions on investment by industrial firms in Colombia," *Weltwirtschaftliches Archiv,* 1972: 396–426.

Chen-Young, P. L., "A study of tax incentives in Jamaica," *National Tax Journal,* Sept. 1967, 39–47.

Demirsar, M., "Foreign investors flooding into Turkey," *The Wall Street Journal,* December 20, 1988, p. A10.

Guisinger, Stephen, and Associates, *Investment Incentives and Performance Requirements—Patterns of International Trade, Production, and Investment* (New York: Praeger Publishers, 1985).

Karunaratne, N. D., and M. P. Abdullah, *Investment Schemes and Foreign Investment in the Industrialization of Post-Independent Malaysia,* Mimeograph, 1977.

Katz, B. S., "Mexican fiscal and subsidy incentives for industrial development," *American Journal of Economics and Sociology,* 1972, 353–360.

Kulchycky, K., and R. E. Lipsey, *Host Country Regulation and Other Determinants of Overseas Operations of U.S. Motor Vehicle and Parts Companies,* National Bureau of Economic Research Working Paper No. 1463, Sept. 1984.

Lim, D., "Fiscal incentives and direct foreign investment in less developed countries," *The Journal of Development Studies,* 1983: 207–212.

Lent, G. E., "Tax incentives in developing countries," in Bird and Oldman (eds.), *Readings on Taxation in Developing Countries,* third edition, 1975.

Moran, H. Theodore, and C. Pearson, "Trade related investment performance requirements," a study prepared for the Overseas Private Investment Corporation, Washington, D.C., March 1987.

Olaloku, F. A., "Fiscal Policy Options for Employment Promotion in Nigeria's Modern Manufacturing Sector," *Bulletin for International Fiscal Documentation,* 1976, pp. 318–327.

Organization for Economic Cooperation and Development (OECD), *Investment Incentives and Disincentives and the International Investment Process,* Paris, 1983.

Reuber, G. L., H. Crookell, M. Emerson, and G. Gallais-Pammona, *Private Foreign Investment in Development* (Oxford: Clarendon Press, 1973).

Robinson, R., *Performance Requirements for Foreign Business—U.S. Management Response* (New York: Praeger Publishers, 1983).

Root, F., and A. Ahmed, "The influence of policy instruments on manufacturing direct foreign investment in developing countries," *Journal of International Business Studies,* Winter 1978: 81–94.

Ross, S., and J. Christensen, *Tax Incentives for Industry in Mexico,* Harvard Law School, 1959.

Shah, S. M. S., and J. F. J. Toye, "Fiscal incentives for firms in some developing countries: Survey and critique," in J. F. J. Toye (ed.), *Taxation and Economic Development—Twelve Critical Studies* (London: Frank Cass and Co., 1978).

Situmeang, B., "The Environmental Correlates of Foreign Direct Investment with Reference to Southeast Asia," Ph.D. dissertation, University of Oregon, 1978.

The National Industrial Conference Board, *Obstacles and Incentives to Private Foreign Investment, 1967–68,* Vols. I & II, Studies in Business Policy No. 130, 1969.

United Nations, *National Legislations and Regulations Related to Transnational Corporations,* Vols. 1–5, 1979–1986.

U.S. Department of Commerce, Bureau of Economic Analysis, Office of International Investment, *Incentives and Performance Requirements for Foreign Direct Investment in Selected Countries,* Staff Economic Report, January 1978.

———, *U.S. Direct Investment Abroad, Benchmark Survey—1977.* Washington, D.C., 1981a.

———, *U.S. Direct Investment Abroad, 1982 Benchmark Survey Data,* Washington, D.C., December, 1985.

———, *The Use of Investment Incentives and Performance Requirements by Foreign Governments,* Washington, D.C., October 1981b.

Wain, B., "Vietnam luring hardy foreign investors," *The Wall Street Journal,* July 12, 1989, p. A14.

Wallace, D. Cynthia, "Foreign direct investment in the third world: U.S. corporations and government policy," in C. D. Wallace (ed.), *Foreign Direct Investment in the 1990s: A New Climate in the Third World* (Martinus Nijhoff Publishers, 1990).

Chapter 17

Evidence on Foreign Direct Investment in the United States

Indudeep Chhachhi, Ike Mathur, Nanda Rangan,
and Sridhar Sundaram

Abstract   *Evidence from foreign direct investment through mergers in the U.S. show overall sample returns to target shareholders that are consistent with prior studies on domestic mergers. However, the returns to stockholders of non-U.K. bidders are significantly positive, which is different from results reported in prior studies. The returns to stockholders of U.K. bidders are significantly negative, which may be attributed to overbidding induced by U.K. tax laws allowing the write-off of merger goodwill against reserves rather than against future earning.*

INTRODUCTION

Recent years have seen a large increase in the dollar amount of foreign direct investments (FDI) through mergers in the United States. International mergers in the United States are in excess of 25% of all U.S. mergers, with British firms alone accounting for about 10% of the dollar value of mergers in the United States in 1988 and 1989.

Numerous studies, including those by Ibbotson, Carr, and Robinson (1982) and Hilliard (1979) have shown that the correlations among international asset returns are very low, indicating that intercountry diversification reduces risk. Solnik and Noetzlin (1982) have also shown that international diversification lowers risk more than just industrywide domestic diversification.

If investors could diversify directly as well as by buying shares in firms expanding overseas, there would be little incentive for firms to seek overseas markets. As Mathur and Hanagan (1983) point out, investors face a number of barriers that prevent them from achieving the full benefits of international diversification. First, investors generally trade in low volume, resulting in high transaction costs (Fieleke, 1975). Second, increases in short-term exchange rate volatility result in higher hedging and transactions costs (Cornell, 1977). Third, the asymmetry in accounting regulations and disclosure requirements across countries restricts significantly the investors' ability to process fundamental information. Finally, the barriers to capital flow in many countries lend further credence to the limited opportunities available to investors for direct international diversification. Overall, it is apparent that investors face substantial barriers to direct diversification.

In contrast, firms expanding overseas can hedge more cheaply than individual investors. Not only can they net out their exposures in different currencies, but they also have greater flexibility in determining the magnitude and timing of profits to be repatriated. Additionally, by acquiring firms overseas they can bring under their control information that is created at the R&D, product development, production, and market servicing stages. Overall, firms expanding overseas have advantages unique to them, enabling them to provide their stockholders with diversification benefits that stockholders cannot achieve on their own (Errunza and Senbet, 1984).

Announcements of FDI through mergers should signal the stockholders of the bidder firms the firms' intent to provide diversification benefits, and therefore, should result in positive abnormal returns surrounding the merger announcement. However, negative abnormal returns would be observed if investors believed that the firm had overbid for the target (Roll, 1986; Thaler, 1988).

Despite the previously mentioned high level of activity by non-U.S. bidders in the United States, there are few systematic studies that examine the wealth effects for non-U.S. bidders. The purpose of this study is to examine the abnormal returns to stockholders of non-U.S. bidders when they announce their intent to acquire a target firm in the United States. Additionally, the analyses are performed separately for U.K. and non-U.K. bidders due to a peculiarity in the U.K. tax laws regarding mergers. Whereas in the United States and many other bidders' host countries bidders must charge off goodwill against earnings over a period of years, U.K. bidders are permitted to write off goodwill against reserves; that is, U.K. bidders do not suffer a deterioration in their future reported earnings when they acquire firms in excess of their book values. This particular aspect of U.K. tax laws may result in returns to U.K. bidders that are different from returns to non-U.K. bidders. Therefore, the overall sample is divided into subsamples of U.K. and non-U.K. bidders.

Returns related to mergers as well as the specific objectives of this study are discussed in the following section. The data and methodology are explained in the third section. The results are contained in the fourth section, followed by the concluding section.

PREVIOUS RESEARCH AND HYPOTHESES

Domestic Mergers Within the United States

A number of studies have addressed different issues and have also examined the returns of the merger participants. Studies by Bradley, Desai, and Kim (1982) and Jarrell, Brickley, and Netter (1988) indicate that successful bidders for targets earned significant positive abnormal returns in the range of 0% to 4%, and the successful targets earned significant positive abnormal returns in the range of 20% to 32%. Dodd (1980) and a number of other researchers have examined takeovers classified as mergers rather than tender offers. These studies have concluded that over a 2-day period around the announcement day, the target firms earn significant positive abnormal returns in the range of 6% to 14%, while the acquiring bidders earn returns insignificantly different from 0 or small negative, but statistically different from zero returns.

International Mergers

Doukas and Travlos (1989) examined the wealth effects for U.S. bidders announcing international acquisitions. Their results indicate that bidder shareholders earn positive but statistically insignificant returns of 0.01% on the announcement date. Their study, which was conducted over the 1975 to 1983 time period, however, does not examine returns to target shareholders. Fatemi and Furtado's (1988) investigation of foreign acquisitions by U.S. bidders shows no significant announcement day effects, except when these mergers constitute an initial entry by the U.S. firm into a foreign market. In this case the returns are a significant 1.12% for the $(-1,0)$ window, that is, the day before and the day of the event.

The objectives of this study are to examine the abnormal returns earned by non-U.S. bidders in acquiring U.S. firms, and the abnormal returns earned by shareholders of U.S. targets in international mergers in the United States.

DATA AND METHODOLOGY

Data

The sample of merger firms for this study were compiled from the transactions listed in the "Foreign Investment in the United States" section of *Mergers and Acquisitions*. Acquisitions had to meet the following criteria to be included in the sample: the acquisition resulted in the U.S. target being fully absorbed by a non-U.S. bidder; the stock of the non-U.S. bidder firm was traded and its daily price data were available in either *The Financial Times* (London edition) or *The Wall Street Journal*.

The event date for the purpose of this study was defined as the date of the first public announcement of the acquisition in *The Wall Street Journal*. The daily stock prices of the target firms (when listed) were collected from *The Wall Street Journal*. The daily stock prices of the bidders as well as the data for the market indices for the different countries (including Standard and Poor's 500 stock index for the United States) were compiled from *The Financial Times* and *The Wall Street Journal*.

Sample Characteristics

Seventy-seven acquisitions completed between the first quarter of 1985 and the third quarter of 1988 that met the sampling criteria comprise the sample for this study. Out of the 77 transactions, 23 acquisitions involved a target that was traded on either the NYSE, the ASE, or the OTC. The other 54 targets either were not traded or were wholly owned subsidiaries of other firms. The acquiring companies were domiciled in nine host countries—Australia, Canada, France, Japan, the Netherlands, Sweden, the United Kingdom, Italy, and Germany.

MEASUREMENT OF ABNORMAL RETURNS

The standard event study methodology pioneered by Fama et al. (1969) is used to measure the excess returns (see Brown and Warner, 1985, for a discussion of the methodology).

The market model prediction errors (PE) for firm i on day t are given as:

$$PE_{it} = R_{it} - (\hat{a}_i + \hat{b}_i R_{mt}) \tag{1}$$

where:

PE_{it} = prediction error for firm 1 for day 5;
$1 = 1, \ldots, N$, where N is number of firms in the sample;
$t = -15, +15$;
R_{it} = return for firm i for day t; and
R_m = return on the market index for day t

$\hat{a}_1$, and $\hat{b}_1$ are the parameter estimates of the market model for firm i, obtained by using an estimation period of 100 days ending 15 days prior to the announcement date. The average prediction error for any event day t is calculated by summing PE_{1t} for the N firms and dividing by N. Standardized prediction errors are computed to test the statistical significance of the prediction errors. Cumulative prediction errors (CPEs) over a multiday interval in the event period are calculated by summing over average prediction errors. Appropriate *t*-statistics are calculated for testing the significance of the CPEs.

RESULTS

Returns to Bidders

CPEs for the entire sample for different windows are shown in table 1. The CPEs for the $(-1,0)$ window are negative (not significant) but if day $+1$ is included in the window, the CPEs become significantly negative (-0.263%). The CPEs for the postannouncement windows are negative and significant. Thus, it appears that unlike most of the domestic studies, the adjustment pro-

Table 1
Non-U.S. Bidder CPEs for the Entire Sample (N = 77)

Test window	CPEs (%)	t-statistic
(− 15 to − 2)	− 0.841	− 0.711
(− 6 to − 2)	− 0.227	− 0.712
(− 1,0)	− 0.082	− 1.451
(− 1 to + 1)	− 0.263	− 1.738**
(+ 2 to + 6)	− 1.429	− 2.269*
(+ 1 to + 15)	− 1.797	− 1.835**
(− 15 to + 15)	− 2.720	− 2.123*

*Significant at 5% level.
**Significant at 10% level.

cess to an international merger announcement is relatively slow. CPEs for the pre-announcement period, however, are insignificant, showing no signs of any leakage or anticipation by the market.

Returns to Targets

Twenty-three acquisitions involved a target that was traded on either the NYSE, the ASE, or the OTC. The CPEs for the targets for the (− 1,0) and (+ 1,0) windows are 27.14% (t = 48.22) and 27.32% (t = 35.48), respectively. The CPEs for the postannouncement windows are insignificant, indicating that all of the effect is captured either on or before the announcement day with no significant effects visible in the postannouncement subperiods.

Table 2
U.K. Bidder CPEs (N = 43)

Test window	CPEs (%)	t-statistic
(− 15 to − 2)	− 0.978	− 1.063
(− 6 to − 2)	− 1.017	− 4.396*
(− 1,0)	− 1.053	− 4.505*
(− 1 to + 1)	− 1.414	− 4.361*
(+ 2 to + 6)	− 2.042	− 2.762*
(+ 1 to + 15)	− 3.778	− 3.186*
(− 15 to + 15)	− 5.808	− 4.074

*Significant at 1% level.

Table 3
Non-U.K. Bidder CPEs ($N = 34$)

Test window	CPEs (%)	t-statistic
(-15 to -2)	-0.608	0.211
(-6 to -2)	-0.296	-0.527
($-1,0$)	1.094	2.866*
(-1 to $+1$)	1.119	2.282**
($+2$ to $+6$)	-0.587	-0.232
($+1$ to $+15$)	0.739	0.919
(-15 to $+15$)	1.225	1.509

*Significant at 1% level.
**Significant at 5% level.

Analysis of U.K. and Non-U.K. Bidders

United Kingdom firms have been active participants in the U.S. market and therefore need to be studied separately. Table 2 reports the CPEs for the 43 U.K. bidders. The CPEs for most of the intervals are negative and statistically significant. The postannouncement results for this subsample are similar to those reported for the entire sample (Table 1)—negative and statistically significant. In addition, the CPEs for the (-6 to -2) period are also significant. These results indicate that not only is there a fairly long adjustment process after the announcement, but there is probably some leakage or anticipation of the merger as well.

The CPEs for the 34 non-U.K. bidders are reported in table 3. In contrast with the results reported for the U.K. bidders, as well as for any other domestic (U.S. or U.K.) study done using data from the 1980s, the CPEs for both the periods surrounding the announcement date—($-1,0$) and (-1 to $+1$) are positive and statistically significant. Moreover, unlike the results reported earlier, the CPEs for both the postannouncement windows ($+2$ to $+6$) and ($+1$ to $+15$) are insignificantly different from 0. The CPEs for the pre-announcement windows are also insignificantly different from zero.

CONCLUSION

At first glance the overall results reported here seem consistent with studies using domestic data. The returns to bidders for the overall sample are negative but insignificantly different from zero and the returns to targets are positive and significantly different from zero. However, when the results for the subsamples of U.K. and non-U.K. bidders are examined, a different pattern emerges, with

U.K. bidders showing significantly negative and non-U.K. bidders showing significantly positive returns.

Within the context of the previously mentioned perspectives on international diversification, the results confirm the hypothesis that target shareholders receive abnormal positive returns. That can be explained by the bidders' willingness to pay a premium over existing market prices for targets so as to capture the advantages associated with the perceived benefits of diversification for the bidders. However, the hypothesis that returns to bidder stockholders should be positive abnormal due to the capture effects of perceived diversification benefits is not borne out, except in the case of non-U.K. bidders. It may be that U.K. stockholders do not price those factors positively, although a more logical conclusion would be that the merger valuation effects associated with hubris and the winner's curse may, in the mind of the bidder's stockholders, outweigh the positive effects of international diversification.

REFERENCES

Bradley, M., Desai, A., and Kim, E. H. "The Rationale Behind Interfirm Tender Offers: Information or Synergy?" *Journal of Financial Economics,* 11, 1, April 1983, 183–206.

Brown, S. J., and Warner, J. B. "Using Daily Stock Returns: The Case of Event Studies," *Journal of Financial Economics,* 14, 1, March 1985, 3–31.

Cornell, B. "Spot Rates, Forward Rates, and Exchange Market Efficiency," *Journal of Financial Economics,* 5, 1, 1977, 55–65.

Dodd, P. R. "Merger Proposals, Management Discretion and Stockholder Wealth," *Journal of Financial Economics,* 8, 2, June 1980, 105–138.

Dodd, P. R., and Ruback, R., "Tender Offers and Stockholder Returns: An Empirical Analysis," *Journal of Financial Economics,* 5, 3, December 1977, 351–373.

Doukas, J., and Travlos, N. G., "The Effect of Corporate Multinationalism on Shareholders' Wealth: Evidence From International Acquisitions," *Journal of Finance,* 43, 5, December 1988, 1161–1175.

Errunza, V. R., and Senbet, L. W., "International Corporate Diversification, Market Valuation, and Size-Adjusted Evidence," *Journal of Finance,* 39, 3, July 1984, 727–743.

Fama, E., et al., "The Adjustment of Stock Prices to New Information," *International Economic Review,* 10, 1, February 1969, 1–21.

Fatemi, A. M., and Furtado, E. P. H., "An Empirical Investigation of the Wealth Effects of Foreign Acquisitions," *Recent Developments in International Banking and Finance* (Lexington, MA: Lexington Books, 1988).

Fieleke, N. S., "Exchange Rate Flexibility and the Efficiency of the Foreign Exchange Markets," *Journal of Financial and Quantitative Analysis,* 10, 3, September 1975, 409–428.

Hilliard, J. E., "The Relationship Between Equity Indices on World Exchanges," *Journal of Finance,* 34, 1, 1979, 103–114.

Ibbotson, R. G., Carr, R. C., and Robinson, A. W., "International Equity and Bond Returns," *Financial Analysts Journal,* 38, 4, July/August 1982, 61–83.

Jarrell, G. A., Brickley, J. A., and Netter, J. M., "The Market for Corporate Control: The Empirical Evidence Since 1980," *Journal of Economic Perspectives*, 2, 1, Winter 1988, 49–68.

Jensen, M. C., "Takeovers: Their Causes and Consequences," *Journal of Economic Perspectives*, 2, 1, Winter 1988, 21–48.

Jensen, M. C., and Ruback, R. S., "The Market for Corporate Control: The Scientific Evidence," *Journal of Financial Economics*, 11, 1, April 1983, 5–50.

Mathur, I., and Hanagan, K., "Are Multinational Corporations Superior Investment Vehicles for Achieving International Business Diversification?" *Journal of International Business Studies*, 14, 3, Winter 1983, 135–146.

Roll, R., "The Hubris Hypothesis of Corporate Takeovers," *Journal of Business*, 59, 2, 1986, 197–216.

Solnik, B. H., and Noetzlin, B., "Optimal International Asset Allocation," *Journal of Portfolio Management*, 9, 1, Fall 1982, 11–21.

Thaler, R. H., "The Winner's Curse," *Journal of Economic Perspectives*, 2, 1, Winter 1988, 191–202.

Chapter 18

Managing Technology in Developing Market Economies: Host Country Priorities and a Firm's Competitive Interests

Paul Steidlmeier

Abstract *Technology strategy is shaped by many variables which emanate from the external environment, an industry, and a particular firm. This chapter first explores the problem of goal conflicts between host country development priorities and a firm's strategic mission. Following this, alternative policy options are discussed.*

INTRODUCTION

In past years intellectual property has been the focus of considerable discussion. This is not surprising, for private property rights form the bedrock of a market economy. My concern is twofold: to determine, in a developing market economy, (1) what technology a firm sets out to accumulate and how, and (2) what strategy configurations are most conducive both to protecting the firm's technology endowment and exploiting its potential.

The regulation of intellectual property poses special problems for two reasons. First, intellectual property possesses economic characteristics not found in tangible commodity property: it is readily divisible and transportable and can be easily appropriated by many parties at once. Secondly, intellectual property plays such a pivotal role in the development prospects of many countries that they cannot afford to be excluded from access to it. These issues have been the focus of the Uruguay Round of GATT currently under way as well as of recent initiatives to forge international standards under the aegis of the World Intellectual Property Organization. There are numerous points of contrast between a company's strategic mission and the socio-economic priorities of developing countries. I first discuss the developing country position and then the strategy options of a corporation.

THE DEVELOPING COUNTRY POSITION

Developing countries tend to articulate a notably different set of rules for the governance of intellectual property rights than developed countries do. They attempt to fit the property rules to their development needs. Developing countries resist the preferred property rules of developed countries and aim for alternate forms of regulation for three reasons. First, they believe that the property rules of developed countries will lock them into a cycle of technological dependence. Secondly, they are convinced that meeting the basic needs of their own people takes priority over protecting the exclusive property rights of those who are already well off. Thirdly, local power groups (especially domestic firms) in developing countries put pressure on their governments to establish a set of property rights favorable to their own interests.

Developing countries are basically arguing that the right of people to development takes priority over individual property claims. In what follows I rely on the Government of India position paper for the Uruguay Round of the GATT negotiations as well as interviews at the Indian embassy in Washington, D.C. In essence, India and other developing countries argue that intellectual property is a form of common property.

Attention must be paid to the logic of the development position, which intends to set forth a comprehensive set of property rights for all peoples. Developing countries implicitly reject the "trickle-down theory" of development linked to individual property rights. They shift priorities and define property rights first of all in a social sense and only secondarily in an individual way. The argument contends that the right people have to development takes precedence over other claims upon which property rights are based. To this end the Government of India argues:

> It is relevant to note that the food, pharmaceutical and chemical sectors have been accorded a different treatment in the patent laws of developing countries because of the critical nature of these sectors to their socio-economic and public interests.

The statement goes on to link patent monopolies to predatory pricing in pharmaceutical and agro-chemical sectors and concludes:

> Every country should therefore be free to determine both the general categories as well as the specific products or sectors that it wishes to exclude from patentability. . . .

Regarding economic efficiency it is argued that the marginal productivity of new technologies when employed in the third world is far greater than in the first. This point suggests a utilitarian theme: that global redistribution of property rights would benefit the majority of people in the world, especially those who are poor.

Approaches to acquisition of property differ according to whether one defines technology in commercial or noncommercial terms. If technology is viewed in commercial terms the approach to its acquisition is a contractual agreement between the owner and acquirer. This may take the form of direct sales, licensing, or agreements to provide technical, engineering, or managerial assistance. The means to protect technology are straightforward enough and encompass economic sanctions against violators as well as legal action. The legitimacy of all this depends upon the validity of the argument presented in the preceding section. Clearly third world countries are more prone to viewing intellectual property as a quasi-free good. Even in cases in which they accept the validity of patents and copyrights they find the extensive monopoly protection of property rights to be fundamentally unjust.

THE STRUGGLE OVER PROPERTY RIGHTS: LEGAL, MARKET, POLITICAL

Business interests in the United States are frequently at odds with those of the developing countries. The developing countries cite their rights to a return on their investment and research efforts, and the positive role that strict protection of property rights plays in terms of incentives to innovate and promote market efficiency. To protect their interests they devise a host of political, economic, and legal strategies.

The regulation of intellectual property by developing countries therefore faces the challenge of safeguarding national development priorities in the face of stiff international threats. First, these countries must judge when such new rules would be compatible with their present stage of development and future plans. Secondly, given the dependence of their markets on the developed countries, they must evaluate their risks when facing trade pressures.

Legal Means

There is no such thing as international patent, copyright, and trademark protection. At present, business practices are governed by regional treaties and a number of international conventions.

If patents are to be the core of a firm's strategy, it is important at the outset to patent worldwide. This can be expensive—average costs are $10,000 in the United States and $50,000 for a world-wide patent; these figures are applicable if the patents do not have to be defended in legal challenges; otherwise, the figures are far higher. In addition to being expensive, the patent process is slow. In the United States biotechnology patents take anywhere from 2.5 to 4 years; in 1989 there was a backlog approaching 8000 petitions for the Patent and Trademark Office's 100 biotechnology patent examiners. Furthermore, both in government bureaus and in courts there is a distinct lack of qualified personnel. Foreign patent systems are frequently worse in terms of complexity and preconditions. For example, Japanese patent procedures average 5 to 7 years and that is only if they are uncontested. In a celebrated case Texas Instruments waited 29 years to attain a patent on its integrated circuit in Japan.

The legal approach is consistent with capitalist systems in which the protection of property has long been a major role of law and government. United States law, however, differs from that of most other countries in several respects. For example, the United States grants patents to those who are the first to invent, whereas Europe and other regions protect those who are the first to file. The United States has no laws that a patent be exploited, whereas many developing countries insist that it be fully "worked" within the region or else be subject to forfeiture. Whereas the United States grants exclusive intellectual property rights and bolsters them with a series of "unfair competition" laws, it also insists that U.S. firms obtain a foreign filing license. Developing countries generally do not favor such exclusive rights over such extended periods of time (17 years), insisting rather on the rapid diffusion of technology at manageable cost.

However, until recently even the United States did not possess a legal framework and set of institutions adequate to the task of protecting intellectual, non-tangible property even within its own set of laws. This has changed in the last decade, notably with The Semi-Conductor Chip Protection Act of 1984.

Patents generally protect processes and products, but not abstract ideas. Because patents are published with the description of the research, they eventually spread innovations around the globe. Within U.S. borders patent protection has been strengthened through the creation by Congress in 1982 of the Court of Appeals for the Federal Circuit in Washington, a court that specializes in patent cases. Since 1982 it has upheld patents 80% of the time as compared with 30% under the previous system. Its formation helped overcome the problems caused by contradictory verdicts by the 12 existing Courts of Appeal (which the Supreme Court seldom tackled) and a lack of technical competence on the bench.

Congress has also acted to define the law in areas of copyrights and trademarks. International copyright protection is afforded by the Berne Convention, which stems from 1885 and which the United States ratified in 1988 joining 77 others countries. However, enforcement by that organization is sporadic; more often disputes are pursued through the U.S. courts. To pursue such a path has its dangers, however; in a very able review of the U.S. law in question Stephen Englund has shown that copyright law in the area of computer programming is fraught with difficulties of precedent and interpretation. All in all, opting to litigate copyright infringements has its payoffs but it is a long and arduous process.

The major problem for U.S. companies arises when they see their property rights being violated and are unable to pursue the culprits through the U.S. legal system. Developed countries generally regard intellectual property as a legal right. Infringement occurs, but generally as a result of inadequate laws or inadequate enforcement. International legal options vary considerably from country to country. The best chances for litigating infringements are in Western

Europe, Canada, Australia, and New Zealand where the legal traditions are similar to those of the United States. Japan, however, has a markedly different legal/cultural tradition.

The governments of developing countries often do not want to offer strong protection of property rights in the first place because they place international intellectual property rights within the context of their own economic development policies. International organizations such as the International Court of Justice and the World Intellectual Property Organization are useful in providing a forum in which to air grievances but up to now they have not proved to be very effective.

Political Means

Increasingly, American companies are turning to the political framework to gain their objectives. This takes the forms of the U.S. government bringing pressure to bear upon other governments, on the one hand, and eliciting government support in underwriting research and development expenses, on the other. In diplomacy the main tools used have been the Uruguay Round of the current GATT talks and the application of The Omnibus Trade and Competitiveness Act of 1988.

In the current GATT discussions the U.S. government has been a leader in insisting on a new world order for intellectual property. The heart of the approach is to put in place a binding set of international regulations together with adequate institutions of appeal. The developing countries, led by Brazil and India, have vigorously resisted such an approach because they find it prejudicial to their development plans. This issue is not close to being resolved.

More pragmatically, companies are asking the U.S. Trade Representative to vigorously apply the Omnibus Trade and Competitiveness Bill in their favor. The Trade Office's most recent list of intellectual property offenders featured China, Brazil, and India. The approach is straightforward: countries that fail to adequately protect intellectual property will find U.S. markets increasingly closed to them. This approach has had some effect with Taiwan and South Korea who are heavily dependent upon U.S. markets. Brazil and India's trade with the United States, however, accounts for a much smaller portion of their total exports and so they are not as susceptible to such pressures.

The diplomatic approach carries some strategic risks for both the U.S. government and business interests. It invites negative reactions in trade—where countries will shift their imports to other suppliers—as well as in geopolitics, where the United States may find that its international policies lack support in key areas. Furthermore, countries with heavy external debt loads, such as Brazil and Mexico, link this issue to their economic productivity and debt repayment schedules. More and more, explicit attention is being paid to political risk management, with emphasis given to shaping the political environment itself and to adaptive restructuring of the firm.

In addition to diplomacy, the government is increasingly sought out as cooperative partner in a company's research and development strategy. The scope of such partnership focuses upon two points: funding and the regulatory environment. The National Science Foundation estimated that in 1988 United States research and development expenditures totaled $132.2 billion. Of this $62.7 billion came from the federal government and $64.0 billion from industry, with $3.7 billion from the academic sector and $1.8 billion from other nonprofit sources. Of this amount the federal government performed $14.7 billion worth of research, $95.3 billion went to industry, $18.5 billion to academe, and $3.7 billion to other sources.

In addition to government funding, corporate and industry representatives are very active via lobbying and Political Action Committees (PACs) in shaping their operating environment. The legislative history of the National Cooperative Research Act of 1984 provides a "Who's Who" of American high technology corporations.

Market Measures

Many companies choose simply to keep their product or process innovations secret. Even then, increasingly these trade secrets are targets of industrial espionage. Business enterprises usually meet this threat by taking measures to tighten up internal security and by placing restrictive clauses in the contracts of those who deal with sensitive proprietary information.

More and more, given the difficulty of legal and political measures, companies are turning to cooperative alliances and joint ventures. Up until recently U.S. antitrust law posed a formidable obstacle to such options. A major change in the operating environment took place when Congress passed the National Cooperative Research Act of 1984. In the past 5 years the fervor to reform antitrust law in this area has continued. The House Subcommittees on Monopolies and Commercial Law held hearings on this issue in 1987 as did the Senate Subcommittee on Antitrust, Monopolies and Business Rights. Growing out of four 100th Congress Bills and two 99th Congress Bills, the Intellectual Property Antitrust Protection Act of 1989 was proposed in 1989. Business has not been slow to take advantage of this new environment. Actions range from outright joint ventures and licensing to bartering technology or swapping R&D knowledge with another company.

A number of research efforts have been directed toward assessing the effectiveness of collective and competitive strategies for managing the intellectual property environment. Firms pursue collective/cooperative strategies at both inter-industry and intra-industry levels.

Strategic alliances take many different forms and are also focused upon different stages of the innovative process. Joint research and development is advantageous when protection of property is weak and a developing firm cannot monopolize the discoveries for a period sufficient to justify the research and development outlays. In addition to the costs, the rapid pace of technological change makes it difficult for any one firm to stay ahead and, therefore, makes strategic alliances necessary both in terms of a firm's long-term strategic plan as well as in terms of improving its competitive position. In short, the joint venture provides a pooling of resources, a sharing of risks, and a blending of expertise not otherwise available. Collaboration is most fruitful when the strategic goals of companies converge, and their competitive goals do not. Rather than being competitive surrender, healthy collaboration is competition in a different form. It is especially critical for firms with modest size and market power.

A recent McKinsey study revealed that the number of joint ventures in research & development increased sixfold from 1976 to 1987. Most of these were concentrated on high technology and took place in Common Market countries. In addition to motives of technology development and acquisition, these joint ventures were also driven by competitive commercialization factors; namely, to gain a foothold in markets and to satisfy host country pressures for technology and local research and development efforts. The "boundaries" of an innovative firm are an important strategic variable and may deprive it of any significant advantage from its innovation.

As Teece has pointed out, when legal intellectual property protection is weak (either because of the legal structure or the ease with which patents can be "invented around"), "co-specialized assets"—in areas of manufacturing, distribution and service—assume critical importance if a company is to reap rewards from its technology assets. It is important to become allied with those who control complementary assets. In terms of transaction costs, cooperative arrangements arise when both parties involved depend upon complementary assets. In such a scenario a firm seeks the fruits of specialized assets that it has difficulty either producing internally or obtaining from market exchange.

CONCLUSION

In the end a firm may simultaneously use a number of strategies to pursue its strategic objectives. The viability of market, political, or legal strategies varies considerably from place to place. Legal strategies in some ways offer the most security, but they are troublesome. First, an adequate international legal framework is far from being in place. Secondly, the legal process is both costly and slow. Political solutions, on the other hand, can proceed more quickly. Their drawback is that they invite retaliation by other governments and their companies. Further, they expose the company to risks from other powerful interest groups. Market solutions are risky in that they offer less protection. Cooperative ventures and alliances, however, can remedy part of that problem. The market, in the long run, leaves companies most free to maneuver and it also leaves the creative atmosphere necessary for further innovation less endangered.

REFERENCES

Ammer, Karen, "The Semi-Conductor Chip Protection Act of 1984," *Law and Policy in International Business,* 17(2): 395–420, 1985.

Astley, W., "Toward an Appreciation of Collective Strategy," *Academy of Management Review,* 9(4): 526–535, 1984.

Bergier, Jacques, *Secret Armies,* New York, Bobbs Merrill, 1975.

Bottom, Norman R. Jr., and Gallati, Robert R., *Industrial Espionage,* New York, Butterworth, 1984.

Benko, Robert, *Protecting Intellectual Property Rights,* Washington, D.C., American Institute for Public Policy Research, 1987.

Braga, Carlos Alberto P., "The Developing Country Case for and Against Intellectual Property Protection," in Wolfgang E. Siebeck, ed., *Strengthening Protection of Intellectual Property in Developing Countries: A Survey of the Literature,* World Bank Discussion Papers, No. 112, Washington, D.C., World Bank, pp., 69–88, 1990.

Bresser, R., "Matching Collective and Competitive Strategies," *Strategic Management Journal,* 9(6): 375–385, 1988.

Devlin, Godfrey, and Bleackley, Mark, "Strategic Alliances—Guidelines for Success," *Long Range Planning,* 21(5): 18–23, 1988.

Dobkin, James A., "Structuring and International Technology Joint Venture," *International Financial Law Review,* 7(9): 20–23, 1988.

Englund, Stephan, "Idea, Process or Protected Expression? Determining the Scope of Copyright Protection of the Structure of Computer Programs," *Michigan Law Review,* February, 1990, pp. 866–909.

Gadbaw, R., and Richards, T., *Intellectual Property Rights: Global Consensus, Global Conflict?* Boulder, CO, Westview Press, 1988.

Galen, Michele, "Is It Time to Reinvent the Patent System?" *Business Week,* December 2, 1991, pp. 110–113.

Globerman, Steve, "Addressing International Product Piracy," *Journal of International Business Studies,* 19(3): 497–504, 1988.

Government of India, "Paper Presented by India in Uruguay Round Multilateral Talks," Indian Embassy, Washington, D.C., 1989, pp. 7–8.

Hamel, Gary, Doz, Yves L., and Prahalad, C. K., "Collaborate With Your Competitors—and Win," *Harvard Business Review,* 67(1): 133–139, 1989.

Harrigan, K., "Joint Ventures and Competitive Strategy," *Strategic Management Journal,* 9(3): 141–158, 1988.

Hladik, Karen J., and Linden, Lawrence H., "Is an International Joint Venture in R&D for You?" *Research-Technology Management,* 42(4): 11–13, 1989.

Kennedy, Charles R. Jr., "Political Risk Management: A Portfolio Planning Model," *Business Horizons,* 31(6): 26–33, 1988.

Marshall, Patrick G., "Is the U.S. Patent System Out of Date?" *Editorial Research Reports,* vol. 1, no. 19, May 18, 1990. Congressional Quarterly, Washington, D.C.

Merrifield, Bruce, "Strategic Alliances in the Global Marketplace," *Research Technology Management,* 32(1): 15–20, 1989.

National Science Foundation, "Highlights," NSF-89-301, April 21, 1989.

Nielsen, R., "Cooperative Strategy," *Strategic Management Journal,* 9: 475–492, 1988.

Ouchi, William G., and Bolton, Michele Kremen, "The Logic of Joint Research and Development," *California Management Review,* 30(3): 9–33, 1988.

Shan, Wei Jian, *Technological Change and Strategic Cooperation: Evidence From Commercialization of Biotechnology,* Ph.D. dissertation, University of California, Berkeley, 1987.

Stalson, H., "Intellectual Property Rights and U.S. Competitiveness in Trade," Washington, D.C., National Planning Association, 1987.

Sullivan, Sharon, "Battling Pirates? Patents May Be the Best Defense," *The International Executive,* July-August, 1989, pp. 9–13.

Teece, David J., "Capturing Value from Technological Innovations: Integration, Strategic Partnering and Licensing Decisions," in Guile, Bruce, and Brooks, Harvey, eds., *Technology and Global Industry: Companies and Nations in the World Economy,* Washington, D.C., National Academy Press, 1987, pp. 65–95.

United Nations Industrial Development Organization, *Trends in Technology Transfer Flow* (preliminary version) ID/WG.454/5, November 20, 1985.

U.S. Department of Commerce, "Protecting Intellectual Property: An Introductory Guide for U.S. Businesses on Protecting Intellectual Property Abroad," *Business America,* July 1, 1991, pp. 2–7.

U.S. Congress, *National Cooperative Research Act of 1984,* Public Law 98–462, October 11, 1984.

U.S. Congress, House of Representatives, Subcommittee on Courts, Civil Liberties, and the Administration of Justice, *Copyright and New Technologies,* November 20, 1985, August 7, 1986.

U.S. Congress, Senate Bill 270, *Intellectual Property Antitrust Protection Act of 1989,* March 13, 1989.

U.S. International Trade Commission, *Foreign Protection of Intellectual Property Rights and the Effect on U.S. Industry and Trade,* USITC Publication 2065, Washington, D.C., 1988.

Chapter 19

Technology Strategies of Japanese Subsidiaries and Joint Ventures in the United States

Lois S. Peters

Abstract *Technology and R&D investment strategies of 100 Japanese subsidiaries in the U.S. are analyzed. The primary motivation of the parent in establishing foreign subsidiaries is market entry and development, but access to technological resources is increasingly important. For 50 subsidiaries conducting in-house research, the most important objective was to expand the present business by adapting current product lines to local needs. Affiliate R&D is an extension of parent company objectives and R&D activities at home. Subsidiary R&D technology strategies vary by industry.*

INTRODUCTION

This chapter examines the technology objectives and sources pursued by foreign subsidiaries in the United States and government options in developing a policy toward them. The discussion draws on a study of Japanese subsidiaries and joint ventures in the United States that inquires into their scope of activities, functions, and effectiveness for technology trade.

Previous literature answers general questions about the determinants and consequences of research and development (R&D) and foreign direct investment (FDI) at three levels. Some writers address the subject at the firm level (Cordell, 1971; Ronstadt, 1977; Pearce, 1989), others at the industry level (Lall, 1979; Mansfield and Romeo, 1980; Porter, 1990), and still others at the national or macro-economic level (Vernon, 1966; Swedenborg, 1982). There is also a substantial literature on the consequences of activity at each level (Coase, 1937; Vernon, 1966; Kindleberger, 1969; Gray, 1985; Dunning, 1988). Linking of the three levels has rarely been attempted except in the eclectic approach of Dunning (1988). Comparisons are usually made at the level of the firm. The behavioral and organizational aspects of foreign subsidiaries of multinational corporations (MNCs) are less understood and there has been little research on their technology strategies. Differences in technology strategies among firms from different industries and different nations have also been an infrequent subject of attention.

In recent years, establishment of Japanese subsidiaries in the United States has drawn considerable popular attention (Sease, 1985; Kolata, 1990). Japan's FDI in the United States increased from $19.3 billion in 1985 to $69.7 billion in 1989. During that same 5-year period, U.S. Department of Commerce data show that Japanese manufacturing investment in the United States increased by 84% from $2.8 billion to $17.3 billion. MITI predicts that until the year 2000 Japan's manufacturing investment in the United States is expected to grow at an annual rate of 14%.

Deals such as Matsushita's takeover of MCA and its relationship to Japanese interests in leading the way to high-definition TV standards, NEC's establishment of a basic research laboratory in Princeton, and growing recognition of Japanese effectiveness in commercializing products based on sources of R&D external to the firm (Mansfield, 1988), suggest that the characteristics of R&D and technology development in Japanese subsidiaries are an important starting point for analyzing the role of subsidiaries in globalization strategies.

Japanese subsidiaries based in the United States are therefore an important focus of study because: (1) their presence in the United States is increasing, (2) recent research suggests that the Japanese are particularly good at managing technology-business interfaces, and (3) there have been accusations that the Japanese are freely absorbing U.S. technical resources, a charge that also implies Japanese effectiveness in technology trade.

THE STUDY

During 1989, we surveyed general managers and technology directors at 435 Japanese manufacturing subsidiaries in the United States listed in the Japanese External Trade Organization's (JETRO) 1987 survey of Japanese manufacturing investment in the United States. We achieved a 25% response rate. The study covered industrial sectors ranging from food products, chemicals, and drugs, to scientific instruments and electronic components. Participant size ranged from less than $10 million to greater than $500 million in sales. Interviews held with 10 managers of Japanese subsidiaries conducting research in the United States and another 20 Japanese company representatives supplemented the survey results. This chapter presents our general findings on strategies and the conduct of research by Japanese subsidiaries in the United States and compares activities according to type of ownership (joint venture, wholly owned) and product line.

INTERVIEW RESULTS

Interviews with survey participants reveal multiple strategies and motivation for R&D investment in the United States. Responses relate in part to the technical base of the industry in which the firm participates.

Reasons to invest in the United States include: the need to be close to customers, market access, and access to centers of technological excellence, recruitment, and information collection and monitoring. Hitachi conducts research in the United States because of the technological sophistication of the U.S. market in electronics. Customers expect high performance and establish technical specifications based on frontier technologies primarily generated in the United States. To produce products in certain segments of their business lines, they must conduct research in the United States. NEC representatives on the other hand say that NEC set up a research unit near Bell Laboratories to repay the debt that NEC owes Bell and the United States. The structure here suggests that the important consideration is the desire to be part of an information network, which helps the firm learn about future technologies and markets.

Discussions with representatives of Japanese subsidiaries and the NEC Research Institute itself confirm that NEC's basic research activity in the United States is unique for a Japanese company. Indeed, Japanese firms carry out most of their research and development at home. This implies that they believe that there are technology ownership advantages that must be carefully controlled. One subsidiary representative referred directly to this need for central control, and a subsidiary manager discussed at length the difficulty he had in convincing the parent that the subsidiary needed to have its own technology-generation capacity in the United States.

In the pharmaceutical sector where European and American MNCs have long conducted research outside their borders, Japanese firms do not pursue research in the United States. They are, however, beginning to set up joint ventures to carry out clinical trials in the United States rather than licensing their drugs to U.S. pharmaceutical firms as they have done in the past. The smaller direct presence of Japanese firms in global pharmaceutical markets no doubt relates to the lack of research presence of Japanese pharmaceutical firms in the United States. This indicates that global performance and not just technology control plays a role in the decision making process. In the chemical industry, where Japanese companies do not match the global strength of German and American companies, there is almost no R&D conducted by Japanese companies in the United States. An exception is the R&D carried out by Reichold Chemicals, which was acquired by Dainippon Inc. in 1987. Companies do, however, have joint R&D efforts with American companies in Japan.

Japanese micro-electronics subsidiaries in the United States frequently locate near high-technology centers such as Palo Alto, San Jose, and Route 128, and biotechnology subsidiaries locate near Rockville, Maryland (because it is located close to the National Institutes of Health), and in California. Some subsidiaries set up research facilities directly on the premises of small U.S. firms to gain access to their innovative technology. Biotechnology firms follow such practices as well as negotiate joint research ventures with small firms to tap into their pioneering research. Companies in the electronics sector have used similar alliances with small firms to build U.S. presence. In developing its U.S. modem business, NEC started out by establishing joint development agreements with American companies. After developing a successful design but not a successful business, the company set up its own R&D Center in San Jose, brought Japanese engineers to the center, and hired 15 American engineers. This launched a successful business in 1985.

Technology flows are complex, not unidirectional, and dependent on business circumstances. NEC started manufacturing private branch exchanges (PBXs) in the United States in 1975 through acquisition of an American company. To develop the product fully, they used American engineers and brought Japanese engineers to the U.S. operation. This began NEC's first technology transfer to the United States. It involved production technology concepts for using integrated circuits (ICs) in PBXs. In their development of switches for the United States NEC transferred process engineers and technology to the United States. Thus the Japanese have contributed both product and process technologies to the United States.

Our discussions with Japanese subsidiary managers in all industries revealed their close contact with Japanese headquarters and central research facilities. For those industries where Japanese companies are already globally competitive, subsidiary representatives were more active in technology generation in the United States. These interviews largely verify the findings of our mailed survey, which is presented in the next section. The survey results confirm differences in R&D activities and strategies according to industry sector. However, they do not reveal the sharp differences that we infer from our interviews. The survey results underscore the importance of the parent as a source of technology.

SURVEY RESULTS

Subsidiary managers rank market access as the main reason for their Japanese parent company operating in the United States (table 1). Gaining access to basic research is a less important perceived reason for establishing U.S. subsidiaries. Subsidiary managers believe that their competitive edge derives from good quality control and efficient production processes (table 2).

R&D Activities

Among the 110 respondents, 45% conducted in-house R&D. On the average, however, each unit spent only 2% of its annual sales on R&D. Of the 50 firms conducting R&D, 20 were acquired subsidiaries and the rest were newly established plants or "green field" investments. Acquired firms are more likely to have in-house R&D than the "green field" plants. Eight out of 21 joint ventures had an R&D operation. More than 45% of the participating firms in the

Table 1

Subsidiary Managers' Perceived Reasons of Why Their
Japanese Parent Company Operates in the U.S.

Reasons	Weighted point average
Access to U.S. market	2.83
Better customer services	2.71
Yen's appreciation	1.50
Transportation costs	1.43
Overcome trade barrier	1.36
Access to technology	1.31
Access to design research	1.05
Access to R&D professionals	1.01
Access to basic research	0.92
Environmental regulations	0.65
Access to capital	0.64

3: very important, 2: important, 1: less important.

following industrial sectors had in-house R&D: chemicals, machinery, electronic instruments, food, and textiles.

The primary R&D objective of those subsidiary plants with in-house R&D was to expand and support present business (table 3). This is consistent with the plant managers' beliefs that technological support of production processes was a reason for their plant's competitive edge. Nevertheless, managers in the 50 subsidiary plants with in-house R&D said their major R&D task is new product development (table 4). Explanation of this apparent contradiction may be that the justification for existence is technological support, but the hope of the managers is to push on in new areas. Discussion with R&D managers suggests that once you establish an R&D unit there is almost an inevitable drive from the unit to do more than just support existing businesses. It is also true that the objective

Table 2

Subsidiary Managers' Perception of Their Competitive Edge

Reasons	Weighted point average
Better quality control	2.45
Efficient product process	2.09
Better overall technology	2.08
Better product design	2.03
Lower costs	1.83
Product differentiation	1.60

3: very important, 2: important, 1: less important.

Table 3
R&D Objectives of 50 Subsidiary Plants
with In-House R&D

Reasons	Weighted point average
Expand present business	2.76
Support present business	2.58
Provide base for new business	2.02
Meet environmental regulation	0.79

3: very important, 2: important, 1: less important.

of product expansion can be met by adaptation and modest improvement of existing products. Process R&D, which may be of greater general value to the United States and have more fundamental implications for new product lines, constitutes a less important task.

Of the 60 plants that conducted no R&D, 22% said they had access to R&D conducted at a facility located elsewhere in the United States and owned by their parent firm, 13% said they expected the parent to set up an R&D facility in the United States, and 35% said they expected that their plant would soon conduct R&D. Of the latter group, 16 were planning to have laboratories in place by 1991.

Channels of Technology Transfer

Technology transfer from the Japanese parent company is overwhelmingly regarded as the single most important technology source by a majority of participants. However, apart from the parent, U.S. sources were more important than Japanese sources (table 5).

Survey participants listed licensing as a less important channel of technology transfer (table 6), but 47 firms reported a total of 935 licenses from partners.

Table 4
Major R&D Tasks in 50 Subsidiary Plants
with In-House R&D

Reasons	Weighted point average
New product development	2.79
Product adaptation	2.10
Process improvement	1.90
New process development	1.70

3: very important, 2: important, 1: less important.

Table 5

Importance of Technology Sources for Subsidiary Plants

Reasons	Weighted point average
Japanese parent(s)	2.78
Other U.S. sources	1.28
Other Japanese sources	1.15
U.S. partners (if any)	1.14
Joint R&Ds	0.82

3: very important, 2: important, 1: less important.

The technology flow is primarily one way from Japan to the United States, if measured in terms of licensing. Only 12 subsidiaries reported 76 licenses to their Japanese parents. Among the technologies transferred from the parent companies, only 26% were recently developed and 40% were more than 5 years old.

About 40% of the participants had collaborative activities with U.S. universities, with research contracting, consultancies, and joint research centers being the most important types of linkage (table 7).

Differences According to Ownership and Industry Sector

Mean responses to questions did not vary significantly ($p < .05$) according to whether the site was acquired or newly established. Responses by representatives of plants conducting R&D placed more importance on access to U.S. technology, basic research, and design research as reasons for operating a Japanese manufacturing subsidiary in the United States. These respondents valued better product design and product differentiation for competing in the U.S. market as compared to those that did no R&D on site ($p < .05$).

Table 6

Perceived Importance of Technology Transfer Channels
Between the Subsidiaries and Their Japanese Parents

Reasons	Weighted point average
Technical assistance/consultancy	2.83
Provision of technical staff	2.07
Employee training	1.98
Licensing	1.57

3: very important, 2: important, 1: less important.

Table 7
Preferred Types of Interactions with Universities

Activities	Weighted point average
Research contracting	1.95
Consultancy	1.95
Joining research centers	1.92
Fellowships	1.63
Gifts	1.50
Grants	1.43

3: very important, 2: important, 1: less important.

Four industry categories—chemical and allied products ($n = 6$), industrial machinery and equipment ($n = 10$), electronic and electric equipment ($n = 19$), and instruments ($n = 11$)—were compared. The electronics sector valued U.S. partners as a source of technology more than the other sectors, but no firm credited its U.S. joint venture partner or other U.S. organizations as the most important sources of technology. All ranked the parent Japanese corporation as the most important source of technology. Representatives of the electronics sector also valued provisions of technical staff by the parent as a mechanism of technology transfer significantly more than representatives of the chemical industry.

DISCUSSION

Our 1989 survey appears to be representative of the Japanese R&D sites in the United States. A 1991 survey by the Science and Technology Agency (STA) of Japan reports that 104 Japanese companies now have R&D facilities in the United States and 56 have such facilities in western Europe. An additional 33 companies have R&D facilities in developing nations and the Asian NICs. Another 25 sites are in planning stages, of which two are expected to be established in the United States and 16 in Europe. This same STA survey shows that the majority of Japanese MNCs with foreign R&D activities employed 10 to 19 research personnel but that by 1996 this is expected to rise to 20 to 96.

According to the STA survey most overseas R&D facilities have been established to match product development to local needs. Of the firms surveyed, however, 25% affirmed that they made contributions and grants to foreign academic institutions in Fiscal Year 1990, mostly on the order of 10 to 100 million yen. These STA findings are also consistent with the results reported here. The U.S. public investment of R&D in universities and in certain industry sectors (e.g., aircraft) as well as its strong industrial research base has created a sophisticated technological market, and Japanese executives frequently refer to the importance of the U.S. technological leadership as a strength of the U.S. business environment.

Contrary to articles implying that extensive basic research is being conducted by American arms of Japanese companies (*New York Times*, November 11, 1990—"Japanese Labs in U.S. Luring America's Computer Experts"), our research suggests a more traditional approach by Japanese multinational firms with regard to conducting foreign R&D. Japanese R&D in the United States focuses on support of existing manufacturing operations; it is really applied technical support, not technological development. There is an association between the degree of internationalization (i.e., the existence of overseas manufacturing operations) and foreign R&D. This is the general pattern described in empirical studies of multinational firms undertaken in the late 1970s (Craemer, 1976; Behrmann and Fischer, 1980; Herschey and Caves, 1985). Our survey lends support to the views that technological advantage stemming from innovative R&D is a prerequisite for a firm's ability to establish manufacturing subsidiaries abroad; that technology is transferred in a unidirectional flow from the parent company; and that affiliate R&D is primarily concerned with an adaptation of the transferred technologies to the special needs of host markets (sometimes with additional innovation to serve these markets).

Although our study confirms that product development matched to local needs is the primary concern of these Japanese subsidiaries, our interviews also point to the potential for subsidiary managers' lobbying for greater roles in global technology strategy. The strong central R&D and technology control of Japanese firms may impede the speed with which this occurs. It is also our observation that Japanese R&D affiliates are effective listening posts for gathering information about U.S. frontier technology development and change. Since the technological strategies of Japanese subsidiaries in the United States appear to complement parent strategies, this should lead to their further success in innovation.

POLICY IMPLICATIONS FOR THE UNITED STATES

Japanese subsidiary R&D strategies exhibit elements of rational economic behavior and predisposition to internalize R&D. In addition, there is evidence of activities aimed at seeking to be a part of the U.S. information network. Significant R&D activity only occurs in a few industries, and much of that activity involves engineering design and development. Investment in subsidiary R&D in the United States is mainly to understand customer needs, but in a few industries gaining access to basic research is important. Most Japanese executives say they expect their companies to conduct more research in the United States in the future, and at the same time to increase their ties to U.S. research universities.

Although Japanese companies, like other foreign firms (Peters, 1991), use their subsidiary units for information gathering and transfer to Japan of American technological ideas, our survey also shows that the Japanese bring new technological capability to the United States through transfer of technology and engineers, and that they expect to increase this activity. In special cases, Japanese firms must conduct advanced R&D in the United States and introduce new products here first. Because the United States is a sophisticated technological environment, Japanese economic activity is drawn to it. Nevertheless, Japanese and European firms, by having ties to universities and U.S. firms and by hiring U.S. researchers in their U.S. subsidiaries, take advantage of the great U.S. public investment in R&D.

If the U.S. did not spend on R&D, companies based in Europe and Asia could go elsewhere. Some measures show similar (approximately 2.8% of GNP) Japanese, U.S., and German expenditures on R&D, but nearly half the U.S. expenditures are on military-related activities (NSF, 1991). It is not just total spending but also the balance among centers of technical excellence, distribution among manufacturing areas, and allocation between public and private activities that are important. The U.S. national R&D investment has been an important factor in building the components of the U.S. technical base and in facilitating reinforcement among its components (including industry, governmental, and academic centers). Part of the strength a company draws on in the United States is its broad-based technical infrastructure. This strength provides companies with more choices and options than are available elsewhere. Significant reduction in national technical spending or improper distribution would weaken our broad technical infrastructure, which is a necessary but not a sufficient condition to ensure U.S. competitiveness.

In an ideal system where technology flows are linear and systematic, policy options to deal with the situation of foreign use of U.S. technical resources is straightforward. Surcharges can be put on foreign transfer of technology. Given extensive U.S.-Japanese private sector technical alliances (Peters, 1987), the potential economic and R&D contribution of Japanese subsidiaries to the United States, and the reality that the innovation process itself is not compartmentalized or systematic, we have to live with the potential for free technological riders.

All this suggests plausible policy objectives for the United States. First, support of fundamental R&D of general interest to U.S. firms is essential and needs to be maintained in a variety of institutions. Second, the technology should provide special incentives for public/private technology transfer between U.S. public institutions and U.S. companies. Third, the policy climate should be such that it encourages U.S. firms to tie into Japanese subsidiary networks.

REFERENCES

Behrmann, J. N., and W. A. Fischer (1980). "Transnational Corporations: Market Orientations and R&D Abroad." *Columbia Journal of World Business,* Fall, pp. 55–60.
Bell, J. (1985). "The New Face of Japanese Science: A Crash Program to Reorient Research." *World Press Review* 32, 23–25.

Burns, T., and G. M. Stalker (1961). *The Management of Innovation.* London: Tavistock.

Coase, R. H. (1937). *The Firm, the Market and the Law.* Chicago: University of Chicago Press, pp. 33–55.

Cordell, A. J. (1971). *The Multinational Firm, Foreign Direct Investment and Canadian Science Policy,* Science Council of Canada, Special Study.

Craemer, D. (1976). *Overseas Research and Development by United States Multinationals 1966–1975,* New York: The Conference Board.

Dunning, J. H. (1988). *Multinational Technology and Competitiveness,* London: Unwin Hyman, p. 280.

Dunning, J. H. (1988). *Explaining International Production,* Unwin Hyman, London, p. 378.

Graham, E. M. (1991). "Foreign Direct Investment in the United States and U.S. Interests." *Science* 254: 1740–1745.

Gray, P. H. (1985). "Domestic Efficiency, International Efficiency and Gains from Trade." *Weltiver Tschaflliches Archive,* 121: 460–470.

Herschey, R. C., and Caves, R. E. (1985). "Research and Transfer of Technology by Multinational Enterprises." *Oxford Bulletin of Economies and Statistics,* 43: 115–130.

Kindelberger, C. P. (1969). *American Business Abroad: Six Essays on Direct Investment,* New Haven, CT: Yale University Press.

Kolata, Gina. (1990). "Japanese Labs in U.S. Luring America's Computer Experts." *New York Times,* Sunday, November 11.

Lall, S. (1979). "The International Allocation of Research Activity of U.S. Multinationals." *Oxford Bulletin of Economics and Statistics,* 41: 313–331.

Mansfield, E., and A. Romeo. (1980). "Technology Transfer and Overseas Subsidiaries of U.S.-Based Firms." *Quarterly Journal of Economics,* 95: 737–750.

Mansfield, Edwin. (1988). "Industrial R&D in Japan and in the United States: A comparative study." *American Economic Review* 78(2): 223–228.

NSF. (1991). *Science and Engineering Indicators,* tenth edition.

Pearce, R. D. (1989). *The Internationalization of Research and Development by Multinational Enterprise.* Macmillan Lin On.

Peters, L. S. (1987). "Technical Network Between U.S. and Japanese Industry." Center for Science and Technology Policy, Rensselaer Polytechnic Institute, Troy, N.Y.

Peters, L. S. (1991). "Management of Technology and MNC Globalization." *International Trade and Finance in the 1990s,* Vol. V, pp. 1635–1651.

Porter, M. E. (1990). *The Competitive Advantage of Nations.* New York: The Free Press, Macmillan Inc., p. 855.

Ronstadt, R. C. (1977). "International R&D: The Establishment and Evolution of Research and Development Abroad by Seven U.S. Multinationals." *Journal of International Business Studies,* 9: 7–24.

Sease, D. R. (1985). "Japanese Firms Set Up More Factories in U.S., Alarm Some Americans." *Wall Street Journal,* March 29.

Swedenborg, B. (1982). *The Multinational Operations of Swedish Firms,* Stockholm: Almarist and Wiksell, pp. 56–60.

Vernon, R. (1966). "International Investment and International Trade on the Product Cycle." *Quarterly Journal of Economics,* 80: 190–207.

Part Four
Country Studies

Chapter 20

Colombia's Experience with Import License Auctions

Kristin Hallberg and Wendy E. Takacs*

Abstract *Colombia used a system of import license auctions to measure tariff equivalents of existing licensing requirements as part of the 1990 trade liberalization program. The license auctions attracted relatively few bidders, except in a few categories, notably automobiles, consumer electronics, and edible oils. The low demand for licenses and low bids limited the usefulness of the auctions for raising revenue, but provided the government with useful information about the state of import demand. The Colombian experience indicates that import license auctions are feasible in developing countries and provides some lessons for the design and conduct of license auction systems.*

INTRODUCTION

When countries embark on trade liberalization programs, one of the first reforms is normally to dismantle quantitative trade restriction such as quotas or licensing systems. An immediate elimination of all such restrictions may strike policymakers as too drastic a measure, so they may seek ways to liberalize more gradually.[1] One option for gradual reform would be to eliminate the restrictions on a product-by-product basis, but which products should be liberalized first? Another option is to convert the quantitative restrictions to their tariff equivalents and then reduce and rationalize the tariff rates, but what tariff rate would be equivalent to a given quantitative restriction? Yet another option would be to increase the quantities allowed to be imported, but by how much should each category of product be increased?

Import license auctions are one mechanism that a government could use to

*The views expressed in this chapter are those of the authors and do not necessarily reflect the views of the World Bank.

obtain information to answer these questions. In its 1990 trade liberalization program, the government of Colombia used auctions of import licenses as a method of measuring tariff equivalents of existing licensing requirements for a wide variety of products.[2] The following sections explain the auction procedures, report on the results of the auctions, and, on the basis of the Colombian experience, evaluate the use of import license auctions as transitional measures in trade reform programs in developing countries.

THE COLOMBIAN LICENSE AUCTION PROCEDURES

The import license auctions allowed prospective importers to bid for licenses to import many products, mostly consumer goods, for which import licenses had previously been denied. A total of US $150 million worth of licenses was to be auctioned during the 1990 calendar year. The 745 tariff positions covered by the auctions were subdivided into 8 groups of products, with allocations equal to approximately 3% of domestic production in each group. The eight groups, the amount of foreign exchange allocated to each group in the first set of auctions, and the number of tariff positions in each group can be found in table 1.

In addition to the limit imposed by the amount of foreign exchange allocated per group, limits were imposed on the allocation to any single tariff position within the group, and to any single importer within a tariff position.[3]

Two thirds of the foreign exchange allocation for the year for importation of the auctioned products was made available in the first round of five auctions held during May and June of 1990. The limits by tariff position and the limits by importer were also set at two thirds of the annual limits. Each auction in this first round offered licenses for one or two of the eight groups into which the products had been divided. Each auction was announced at least 20 days in advance of the 3- to 5-day period during which bids could be submitted.

The auctions were administered by INCOMEX, the agency that had administered the import licensing system, with the cooperation of the Central Bank, which provided observers to witness the opening of the bids. Bids were submitted in sealed envelopes in special urns in INCOMEX offices in Bogotá, Pereira, Cali, Barranquilla, Cucuta, and Medellín.

Prospective bidders had to submit bids specifying the amount they wished to import, in U.S. dollars, and the extra *ad valorem* surcharge rate, over and above the existing tariff rate, that they were willing to pay to import the product. Each bid also specified the tariff position of the goods to be imported, the national identification number of the bidder, the unit value of imports, and the number of the import license request that each bidder had to submit simultaneously according to the standard procedure and on the standard forms.

Bidders were also required to submit a deposit equal to the full amount of the bid. For example, a bidder bidding 10% to import $100 worth of a product had to deposit the peso equivalent of $100. Deposits could be made in any branch of

Table 1

Results of Colombian Import License Auctions, 1990

	Number of tariff positions	Number without bids	Number of bidders	Quota limit ($1000s)	Total requested ($1000s)	Valid bids ($1000s)	Value approved ($1000s)	Extra tariff levied*	Average Tariff March 1990	Average Tariff November 1990
Food and drink	139	110	48	27,939	4477	4249	3143	6.84	46.5	45.4
Textiles	93	66	41	12,462	2629	2067	2067	3.26	47.4	46.1
Garments	78	61	18	14,941	470	363	363	3.32	50.0	50.0
Construction materials	57	49	13	6566	314	227	227	1.51	36.4	36.3
Automotive goods	32	15	194	7236	18,393	12,621	7011	10.50	45.9	47.8
Household goods	114	62	57	8040	1857	1720	1686	3.80	42.1	46.4
Jewelry and consumer electronics	72	40	68	1139	1944†	1760	786	10.57	31.1	41.1
Miscellaneous	160	119	57	22,177	1224	977	977	3.10	40.0	41.1
Total first round	745	522	496	100,500	31,307	23,983	16,260	7.45	42.7	43.1
Total second round	552	332	784	133,700	57,917	51,691	36,398	7.05	42.7	43.1

*Weighted average for group, using value of approved licenses as weights.

†The total value of license requests exceeded the total available even though no single limit by tariff position was reached because the sum of the limits by tariff position exceeded the total foreign exchange allocated to the group and the bids were fairly widely dispersed among the tariff positions making up the group.

one of three public banks: Banco Cafetero, Banco del Estado, or Banco Popular. A receipt for the deposit had to be included with the bid.

INCOMEX officials reviewed each bid to verify that the forms had been correctly filled out, the correct amount of deposit had been made, and the simultaneous import license request form had been submitted properly. If the forms were not properly filled out or the deposit was insufficient, the bids were rejected. In the automotive sector each model to be imported also required the approval of the National Transportation Institute to ensure that it met the specifications for Colombian roads. In the food sector, prior authorization was required from the Ministry of Health. Many bids in the automotive sector were rejected because the models were not yet approved.

The bids were then ranked from the highest to the lowest, and were accepted beginning with the highest until all of the foreign exchange allocated to each group was exhausted or until the tariff position limitations were reached. All successful bidders were required to pay the lowest bid accepted.[4]

RESULTS OF THE FIRST SET OF AUCTIONS

Table 1 reports the results of the first round of bidding. The most striking feature of the first set of auctions was the low demand for import licenses. No bids were submitted for 522 of the 745 tariff positions. Only US $31.2 million worth of requests were received, well below the US $100 million maximum to be allocated. More than half (by value) of the bids received were for licenses to import motor vehicles. License requests exceeded available allocations in only two of the eight groups: the motor vehicle group and the consumer electronics, watches, and jewelry group. In the motor vehicle group bids submitted totaled $1.9 million, compared with the allocation of $1.1 million. In the other groups the amount bid for fell far below the limits imposed for the group. The total value of bids received exceeded the limits imposed by tariff position in only 8 of the 745 tariff positions: 5 in the automotive sector, 2 types of edible oils, and birdseed.

The surcharges resulting from the auction process were also relatively low. The highest surcharge paid in any tariff position was 25%, which was levied on a few categories where there were only one or two bidders at that rate. The practice of setting the surcharge equal to the lowest accepted bid implied that if there was only one bidder, that bidder paid the amount bid. The eighth column of table 1 reports the weighted average extra charge in each group. The average reached a high of about 10.5% in the automotive and consumer electronics groups, but was low (3% to 7%) for most other groups, and very low (1.5%) for construction materials.

THE SECOND ROUND AND SUBSEQUENT LIBERALIZATION

Acting on the outcome of the first set of auctions, the government decided in July of 1990 in effect to allow free importation of 247 of the tariff positions that had been auctioned in the spring. Of these, 169 positions had received no bids and showed less than $20,000 of imports in 1981 when most had been free of licensing restrictions. The government also decided to auction licenses for an additional 54 tariff positions that had been on the prohibited list.

A second round was held in late September to auction the $133.7 million of import licenses left unallocated after the first round. The tariff positions remaining from the first round, plus those that had been transferred from the prohibited list were all combined into one group containing 552 tariff positions. The limits by tariff position and by importer were retained.

Before the results of the September auction were announced, the auction system was overtaken by events. The new administration, which had taken office in August of 1990, decided to accelerate the liberalization by removing all products from licensing requirements in October of 1990, with the exception of certain agricultural products and imports restricted for health and safety purposes.

Despite the discontinuation of the auctions in the middle of the second round, the bids in that round still provide some interesting information. It had been announced that the second auction would be the last, but bidders had no way of knowing that licensing requirements would be dropped completely before licenses were allocated for the second round. Therefore, bidders presumably bid as they would have if licenses had in fact been allocated according to the auction procedures.

The results of the second auction, also reported in table 1, were similar to the first in that the quota limits by tariff position were reached only in the edible oils (soybean and sunflower oils) and in five of the motor vehicle categories. The limit by importer constrained the beer category, where one bidder bid for the maximum amount allowed any single importer.

The second auction elicited more response from bidders than the first. License requests increased from a total of just over $31 million in the first round to almost $58 million in the second. The number of bids submitted increased from 1172 to 2085; the number of bidders increased from 496 to 784. In the motor vehicle sector the number of bids more than tripled in four categories, and more than doubled in another. Despite the increased number of bidders, the winning bids were on average about 3 percentage points lower than in the first set of auctions. Only in some passenger vehicle categories were the bids noticeably higher.

The lower average bids, despite increased competitiveness due to more bidders, probably reflect increased sophistication among bidders. In the second round bidders had the additional information that there had been few bidders in the first auction, and that bids had been relatively low. Also, in the first auction many bidders paid positive surcharges even when the total bids submitted fell short of the limits for the categories; this was due to the rule that the lowest accepted bid would be the surcharge for that category. In the second auction bidders changed their bidding strategies and submitted zero bids along with positive bids. This tactic was relatively costless because no deposit was required with a zero bid, and it ensured that if the limit for the category was not reached the surcharge would be zero.

Information from the auctions contributed to decisions on some tariff adjustments at the time licensing requirements were removed. Many of the products in the auctioned categories had been subject to tariff rates of 40%. The liberalization measures in October simplified the tariff structure to a limited number of rates, which included 30% and 50%, but not 40%. Items for which bids were high in the auctions were put in the 50% category; items with no or low bids were transferred to the 30% category. The tariff on four-wheel drive vehicles also doubled from 50% to 100%, and the tariff on luxury vehicles was set at 300%. The last two columns of table 1 report the average tariff rates for products in each group before the auctions and after the tariff adjustments following the abolition of licensing requirements. Overall, the average tariff was marginally higher than before the auctions and subsequent liberalization.

INTERPRETATION OF THE AUCTION RESULTS

The apparently low demand for import licenses in the auctioned categories surprised government officials and interested observers. The limited participation and low demand may have been due in part to the novelty of the process, coupled with a low incentive to learn the mechanics of the new system given its temporary nature. The auctions did receive widespread publicity, including meetings between government officials and prospective participants to explain the procedures, and front-page newspaper articles explaining the procedures and reporting the results. Nonetheless, the publicity may not have reached all prospective bidders, particularly those outside Bogotá, where the vast majority of all bids were submitted.

Another factor may have been the lack of established commercial channels for many of the products auctioned. Licenses for most of these products had previously been denied, so potential importers had no established commercial relations with suppliers abroad. More bids did appear to be forthcoming in those sectors where importers already had contacts abroad because they had been allowed to import similar products. For example, automobile distributors had been allowed to import vehicles for diplomats, and imports of some types of alcoholic beverages had been allowed, but not others. In these sectors it was relatively easy for importers to obtain information from suppliers on products and prices, which may have contributed to the relatively high demand for licenses.

The costs for submitting bids may also have deterred prospective bidders. These costs included not only the usual administrative cost of filling out license applications and bid forms, but also the cost of depositing the amount bid for a period of about 45 days without knowing whether the bid would be successful. In an inflationary, high-interest rate environment, interest-free deposits can involve a substantial cost. At the prevailing interest rate in Colombia of about 33% per annum, the opportunity cost of submitting a 45-day deposit on a bid of 50% for a $20,000 automobile would be about $406, or a tariff equivalent of 2%, without any guarantee that the bid would in fact be successful.

Another plausible explanation of the lack of bids is simply lack of demand to import products in these categories. Import demand in general was moderate because of Colombia's realistic exchange rate policy. The government had continued to devalue the peso in real terms throughout 1990, in anticipation of the impact of the trade liberalization. The fact that importation of most of the goods in the auctioned categories had been prohibited led to the presumption that demand had become pent up. However, there simply may not have been much demand to import the products in question, or smuggling may have satisfied whatever demand did exist.[5]

IMPORT LICENSE AUCTIONS AS A TOOL IN TRADE LIBERALIZATION

What can be learned from Colombia's brief experiment with import license auctions? First, the auction procedures are feasible for a developing country with a longstanding licensing system. Despite a few administrative problems during the first round,[6] the procedures appeared to operate smoothly.

Second, import license auctions provided a mechanism for allocating import licenses in controlled categories on a basis other than administrative discretion. Licenses had been allocated on an historical basis to importers of record in previous years. For most of the products in the auctioned categories there was no history to go by, because requests for import licenses for these products in the past generally had been denied. Auctions provide a market-oriented answer to the question of who should receive the available licenses.

Third, the Colombian experience suggests that auctions can provide policymakers with useful information about import demand. Importation of the products for which licenses were auctioned had been virtually prohibited, so there was no information on the magnitude of potential import demand. Policymakers had expressed concern that liberalization would prompt a flood of imports, threaten domestic industries, and result in a balance-of-payments crisis. The low demand for imports in most of the product categories that was revealed by the auctions provided useful information. The government used this information in its decision to drop licensing requirements for products that received no or low bids in the first auction. One interpretation of this decision is that the absence of bids indicated an absence of import demand, in which case those categories could be liberalized without a drastic increase in imports or without being a blow to competing domestic industries. The size of the bids also provided guidance in adjusting tariff rates in categories that attracted high bids.

A word of caution is in order regarding the use of license auctions to adjust tariff rates. A mechanism that arbitrarily sets upper limits on the value of imports by product category, then sets tariffs equal to the bids that clear the license market, in fact sets tariffs that preserve the arbitrary pattern of imports. The conversion to tariffs would liberalize trade in the sense that tariffs would replace licensing requirements, but further downward adjustment of tariff levels would be required to open the economy to increased import competition. The tariff pattern that results should only be a first step in a tariff reform that reduces tariff dispersion and levels. Similarly, a system that removes quantitative restrictions at the prevailing tariff rates for products with no bids essentially maintains a pattern of prohibitive tariffs. One danger of using an import license auction system as a basis for tariff reform is that the tariffs that emerge from the auction process might be interpreted as some type of "optimal" tariff or "scientifically determined" tariff rate, when in truth they depend importantly on the initial quota limits.

Some features of the Colombian experiment could be altered if in the future other countries decide to use import license auctions as a transitional tool. If one goal of license auctions is to obtain estimates of tariff equivalents of quantitative restrictions, the system should be designed in a way that encourages bidders to reveal their true estimates of the value of the license. The Colombian practice of setting the price that all successful bidders pay equal to the lowest accepted bid is superior to requiring each bidder to pay the full amount bid. If the surcharge were set at the amount bid, bidders have an incentive to submit bids below their estimates of the true value.[7] An even better arrangement would be to set the surcharge equal to the highest rejected bid and impose no surcharge if requests for licenses fall short of the limits imposed for each category or group.

If other countries use license auctions to obtain information on import demand, more sets of auctions over a longer period of time may be preferable to the relatively brief Colombian experiment. The second round of auctions in Colombia attracted more bidders, and bids appeared to be adjusting downward in most categories as bidders became more sophisticated in their bidding strategies and incorporated information from the first round. In other categories an influx of additional bidders increased the market-clearing bids. It is reasonable to conclude that a few rounds of auctions would have been needed before bidders became familiar with the system and bids stabilized.

NOTES

1. For a detailed discussion of options for gradual liberalization see Takacs (1990).

2. The Colombian import license auctions were referred to as "encuestas arancelarias," literally translated as "tariff surveys." The name was chosen to avoid the Spanish equivalent of the word auction, "subasta," which engenders the image of a lottery. When license auctions were first publicly discussed, the government was criticized in the press for "gambling with the nation's foreign trade." The intention to use the auction results as a guide to revising tariffs when licensing requirements were removed was

stated explicitly in the decree creating the auction procedure. See Departamento Nacional de Planeacion (1990) for a description of the entire reform programs.

3. The limitations, in millions of dollars, by tariff position, were intended to protect domestic producers from large, sudden increases in import competition. The limit in each tariff position was determined by first taking a simple average of (1) the amount that would correspond to 20% of domestic production at the 2-digit (tariff chapter) level, equally divided among the tariff positions in the encuesta belonging to that chapter, and (2) an equal division of the foreign exchange available for the group across all tariff positions included in the group. Discretionary adjustments took place where the resulting limits seemed unreasonable. The limitation by bidder was intended to avoid monopolization of the import market for any single product. No single bidder would be allocated more than 20% of the limit by tariff position. The limits by tariff position and by bidder were public knowledge before the auction.

4. Once the winning bidders and surcharge for each tariff position were determined, the banks were directed to transfer the appropriate proportion of each deposit to the customs authorities; INCOMEX sent letters to all bidders, which allowed them to reclaim from the banks the proportion of their deposit in excess of the amount due, or reclaim their entire deposit if their bid was unsuccessful or rejected for technical reasons. The deposits were to be refunded within 45 days of the auction.

5. See Gomez (1990) for a discussion of license auctions in the presence of smuggling.

6. In their first auction some bidders were not able to submit their bids by the deadline because of delays in processing the standard forms to request import licenses. Problems also arose in the automotive sector because of the requirement that the vehicle to be imported had to be approved by the National Transportation Institute. In one truck category 33 of the 38 bids submitted were rejected because the models to be imported had not been approved by the Institute. Some bids were also invalidated because the forms were not properly filled out or the deposit was less than the required amount.

7. The literature on the theory of auctions and bidding uses a game theoretic approach to bid formulation to derive optimal bidding strategies. Explanations of bidding strategies that result in bids below the bidders' true valuations when they must pay what they bid can be found in Vickrey (1961), Harris and Raviv (1981), Weber (1983), McAfee and McMillan (1987), and Milgrom (1989).

REFERENCES

Departamento Nacional de Planeacion (1990) "Programa de Modernizacion de la Economia Colombian," *Revista de Planeacion y Desarrollo* 22: 1–313.

Gomez, Hernando Jose (1990) "Apertura y Sustitucion de Instrumentos de Proteccion—Notas acerca de la Determinacion del Arancel Equivalente via Subastas en Presencia de Contrabando (Opening and Substitution of Instruments of Protection—Notes on the Determination of the Equivalent Tariff in the Presence of Smuggling)," Banco de la Republica, mimeo, April.

Harris, Milton, and Arthur Raviv (1981) "Allocation Mechanisms and the Design of Auctions," *Econometrica* 49: 1477–1499.

McAfee, R. Preston, and John McMillan (1987) "Auctions and Bidding," *Journal of Economic Literature* 25: 699–738.

Milgrom, Paul (1989) "Auctions and Bidding: A Primer," *Journal of Economic Perspectives* 3: 3–22.

Takacs, Wendy (1990) "Options for Dismantling Quota Systems in Developing Countries," *World Bank Research Observer* 5: 25–46.

Vickrey, William (1961) "Counterspeculation, Auctions, and Competitive Sealed Tenders," *Journal of Finance* 16: 8–37.

Weber, Robert J. (1983) "Multiple Object Auctions," In Engelbrecht-Wiggans, Richard, Martin Shubik, and Robert M. Stark, eds., *Auctions, Bidding, and Contracting: Uses and Theory*, New York: New York University Press.

Chapter 21

A Pooled Time-Series Cross-Sectional Analysis of Exports: An Application to Turkey

Burhan F. Yavas

Abstract *This study examines the role of major variables in determining the demand for Turkish exports. Using pooled time-series (1963–87), cross-sectional (ten countries) regression analysis and various tests of homogeneity of the relationships, the study finds a significant direct relationship between exports on the one hand, and gross domestic product and exchange rate of the importing countries on the other. The results also hold for two subsets of countries examined.*

INTRODUCTION

This chapter studies the determinants of Turkish exports. The analysis has been carried out by using pooled cross-sectional (10 countries) and time-series (25 years) data. Utilizing multiple regression methodology, the study makes use of two different versions of the basic model to determine the sensitivity of the estimates to the various assumptions made. Several different data arrangements have also been tested for appropriateness of pooling cross-section with time-series data.

Exports are one of the most important sources of income for an economy. Export income is even more critical for countries that experience large foreign trade deficits. Since the import substitution growth strategies of the 1960s largely failed to live up to expectations, interest in export promotion strategies has been growing. Especially after the remarkable success stories of such countries as Japan, South Korea, Taiwan, and Singapore many governments have started to take aggressive action aimed at improving their export performance.

In the case of Turkey these policies mainly took the form of tax and income subsidies, assistance in identifying potential markets, help in forming export trading companies, and so forth. Largely as a result of these incentives, Turkish exports recorded substantial gains in the 1980s, reaching an impressive 24.5%

in 1984, 11.5% in 1985, and 20.5% in 1987. It is important to note that these accomplishments came at a time when both developing and less developed countries (LDCs) were experiencing declines in exports in real terms. Based on this performance many international observers made comparisons between Turkey and South Korea, and expected Turkey to follow the same pattern. Indeed, Turkey has been used as an example of how a developing country riddled with bureaucracy and exchange controls only a decade ago can become a success story.

Despite the significance of the topic, research on the determinants of export demand has not been very extensive. The most comprehensive study, undertaken by Tansel and Togan (1987), deals with price and income elasticities in Turkish foreign trade. In a similar vein, Ersel and Temel (1984) concentrated on evaluating Turkey's export performance. Altay (1987) calculated both short-term and long-term income elasticities of imports. Other studies, although not empirical, have nevertheless isolated several factors as major forces responsible for the expansion of Turkish exports. These are (1) the Turkish lira was allowed to float freely instead of being grossly overvalued as in the 1960s and 1970s; (2) major customers of Turkish exports experienced sustained economic growth in the 1980s, which translated into increased demand for imports; (3) petroleum prices, which in the 1970s caused many countries to run balance of payment deficits, stabilized in the 1980s, thereby allowing expansion of trade in general; and (4) major customers of Turkey improved their trade balances in the 1980s.

Yet very little empirical analysis has been conducted to investigate the validity of the above hypotheses. In addition, even when statistical tests were performed, methodologies on which they were based were less than satisfactory. This chapter is an attempt to overcome both these problems. Its main purpose is to discuss some hypotheses so as to test empirically the effect of previously identified factors.

In the initial stages of the study, six different hypotheses were considered for testing. These involved the relationship between exports (EXP) on the one hand; and bilateral exchange rate (EXCH), petroleum prices (PETR), balance of trade of the importing country (BOT), gross national product of the importing country (GNP), GNP growth (DGNP), and lagged exports to the pth country, on the other hand. Among these variables, petroleum prices proved to be insignificant based on t tests. BOT, EXCH, DGNP, and GNP were found to be highly correlated. In an aggregate study such as the present one, a certain level of correlation among the independent variables is expected. However, because of problems associated with severe multicollinearity, only two independent variables, GNP and EXCH, are retained for further analysis.

HYPOTHESES

H1. There exists a positive relationship between demand for EXP from Turkey in the year t and GNP of the importing country in year t-k. The expectation is that demand for foreign-made products increases as the country in question experiences economic growth measured by its GNP.

H2. There exists a positive relationship between the demand for EXP from Turkey in the year *t* and the EXCH between the Turkish lira and the currency of the importing country in year *t-k*.

This hypothesis states a simple demand relationship: the lower the price of an exported good, the higher will be the quantity demanded of that good.

These hypotheses are tested using multiple regression analysis over time (25 years) and across countries (10 countries). The 10 countries, listed in table 1, accounted for 64% of the Turkish foreign trade earnings, and perhaps more importantly, about 70% of all exports in 1988. This percentage is considered sufficiently high to allow inferences concerning the whole population.

DATA

Data on Turkish exports were obtained from the Turkish Prime Ministry, Treasury, and Foreign Trade Undersecretary. Data on GNP and EXCH were obtained from the International Financial Statistics of the International Monetary Fund. The GNP values were indexed values of the United States dollar amounts. The EXCH was calculated by converting the EXCH in currency per Turkish lira. The resultant rates were multiplied by the ratio of the consumer price index (CPI) of the importing country to the Turkish CPI, so as to obtain bilateral real exchange rates. The numbers used are period averages.

Model

Given *p* countries, and *m* observations on the variables in each country, the basic model is as follows:

$$\text{LogEXP}_t = \beta_0 + \beta_1 \text{LogGNP}_{i,t-k} + \beta_2 \text{LogEXCH}_{i,t-k} + \epsilon_{it}$$

$$(i = 1, 2, \ldots, P; \text{ and } t = 1, 2, \ldots, M)$$

$$\text{with } p = 10 \text{ countries and } m = 25 \text{ years.}$$

where the β_i is the regression parameter, ϵ_{it} is the error term, and the variables are as defined above. The independent variables are all lagged *k* years. In this study, the model is estimated for *k = 0* and *k = 1*. In both cases, F tests are conducted in order to test the overall significance of the regression equation given above. In addition, *t*-tests are carried out for individual regression coefficients. All *t*-tests are one-tail tests with the null hypotheses of $\beta_i = 0$ for all i = 1,2; and the alternative of $\beta_i > 0$.

Table 1
Regression Analysis: Individual Countries (k = 0)

Country	β_0	β_1	β_2	R^{2a}	F
Germany	−.46	2.9[†]	.31[†]	.95	458
Italy	1.2	2.4[†]	.48[†]	.91	123
Iran	−2.2	3.5[†]	.95[†]	.80	50
Iraq	−4.8[†]	4.6[†]	.44	.85	69
U.S.A.	2.7[†]	1.0*	.32[†]	.85	72
S. Arabia	−1.8[†]	2.6[†]	.95[†]	.97	677
U.K.	−.47	2.4[†]	.38[†]	.86	79
France	.24	2.3[†]	.29[†]	.97	363
Netherlands	−.99*	2.8[†]	.28[†]	.98	564
Belgium-Luxembourg	1.6	1.6[†]	.35[†]	.88	95

*Indicates significance at the 5% level.
[†]Indicates significance at the 1% level.

Pooling Cross-Section and Time-Series Data

As indicated above this study uses pooled time-series cross-sectional data. The most important advantage of such an approach is the enlargement of the sample size. The sample is considerably larger than if only time-series or cross-sectional data were employed. As a result, a single pooled regression has the advantage of containing greater precision than several different regressions. On the other hand, inappropriate pooling may increase the possibility of violating some of the main regression assumptions, thereby resulting in inaccurate estimates (Yavas and Vardiabasis, 1987). In this study, several tests are conducted to assess the appropriateness of pooling.

First, covariance analysis was used to test the differences in the complete relationship between countries. Second, covariance analysis was used again to tests differences in intercepts (slopes assumed constant for all countries). This is usually referred to as the test of intercept homogeneity (Johnston, 1972, p. 199). Finally, differences in slopes between countries were tested (test of slope homogeneity, Johnston, 1972).

The results of these tests were used to assess the appropriateness of certain methods of pooling (Yavas, 1989). In addition to formal statistical tests of homogeneity, this study uses two different versions of the basic model to estimate regression coefficients. The purpose here is to determine the sensitivity of the parameter estimates to the various assumptions on which the models are based. Specifically, the two versions of the basic model are the following: (1) the ordinary least squares (OLS) model and (2) the covariance (COV) model.

The OLS and COV models have the same assumptions concerning the stochastic disturbance, homoskedasticity, cross-sectional independence, and timewise nonautoregression. The COV model differs from the OLS model for its treatment of the intercept. The COV model utilizes p-1 dummy variables for the p countries pooled, in order to estimate better the effect arising from country differences. Therefore the intercept is no longer constrained to β_0 for all countries, as it is in OLS, but is allowed to vary so as to take into account country-specific effects.

RESEARCH FINDINGS

Each country in the sample was initially evaluated individually. This was necessitated by the homogeneity tests performed for assessing the appropriateness of pooling. The results for $k = 0$ are reported in table 2. This model is judged to be better than the 1-year lagged model both in terms of the plausibility of parameter estimates and tests of homogeneity. Note that all of the individual regressions have high adjusted R^2 and significant F values. The estimated coefficients are comparable in their magnitudes and exhibited signs that are in agreement with expectations on theoretical grounds. All variables are expressed in logarithmic forms because this model resulted in a better fit. The coefficient of GNP indicates that one unit increase in log GNP would increase log EXP by 2.9 for Germany while keeping the other variable (EXCH) constant. Similarly, a 0.31 unit increase in log EXP is expected as a result of a unit increase in log EXCH.

In the next stage, data from different countries were pooled. The first pooling arrangement brings together all 10 countries. The COV model is more appropriate than the OLS model because the tests of homogeneity resulted in the rejection of the hypotheses for both slope and overall homogeneity. The computed F values for the tests are 6.38 and 18.21 respectively. Critical F values are $F_c(18,220) = 2.03$, and $F_c(27,220) = 1.79$ at the 1% significance

Table 2
Regression Results: Different Pooling Arrangements ($k = 0$)

Pooled units	β_0	β_1	β_2	R^2	F
OLS Model					
All countries	$-4.1^\dagger$	$4.6^\dagger$	$.105^\dagger$	.72	321
Euro seven	-2.4^*	$3.8^\dagger$	$.04^\dagger$	.62	140
Euro five	$-3.4^\dagger$	$4.4^\dagger$	$-.02$	.62	103
COV Model					
All countries		$3.8^\dagger$	$.33^\dagger$	.86	144
Euro seven		$2.2^\dagger$	$.33^\dagger$	.93	306
Euro five		$2.5^\dagger$	$.34^\dagger$	.95	432

*Indicates significance at the 5% level.
†Indicates significance at the 1% level.

level. Notice that both OLS and COV models indicate that GNP and EXCH are significant variables.

Two other pooling arrangements have been tried, as indicated by Euro seven and Euro five. In the case of Euro seven, which included all of the European countries in the sample, we find again the COV model to be more appropriate on the basis of the homogeneity tests as well as the plausibility of the results. The COV model finds both GNP and EXCH to be significant at the 1% level, whereas only GNP was found to be significant in the OLS model. Also, if R^2 values are compared, one finds a significant improvement going from the OLS to the COV model (62%–93%).

The last pooling arrangement brings together five European countries (Euro five) out of the seven included in our sample. Cattin and Wittink (1976) argue for combining cross-sectional units that have the same overall relationships. An examination of the results revealed that Germany, Italy, the United Kingdom, France, and the Netherlands can be combined for this purpose. When the test for common slopes is carried out, it is found that computed F value of 2.28 fell in the acceptance region because $F_c(8,110) = 2.69$ at the 1% level. Accordingly, the hypothesis of common slopes is accepted, which indicates appropriateness of pooling. Next, a test for intercept homogeneity was conducted. The computed F values of 234.1 was well within the rejection region since $F_c(4,118)$ turned out to be 3.51 at the 1% level. This result strengthens the view that the COV model is a better model. Note again that the rejection of common intercept implies inappropriate pooling as far as the OLS model is concerned. Given that the slope homogeneity is accepted, there is no problem with pooling for the COV model.

Briefly, the results of the COV model indicate that both GNP and EXCH are significant determinants of export demand. In addition, three of the five country dummies turned out to be significant, negative for the United Kingdom and France but positive for Italy. This result may suggest that not all the relevant variables have been included in the model, and that certain features of these countries have resulted in the reduced (increased) import activity in the United Kingdom and France (Italy).

CONCLUSION

Using multiple regression methodology, this study finds a significant direct relationship between Turkish exports on the one hand, and GNP and the bilateral real exchange rate of importing countries on the other. The results confirm expectations regarding determinants of export demand. The results also provide further evidence of, and support for, the usefulness of pricing policy. The exchange rate can be used as a policy tool to increase and improve the trade balance by increasing the demand for exports.

Furthermore, pooling of countries permits the policy maker to differentiate among the countries within the group. For example, exchange rate policies in a group of countries can result in increase in exports to all. Simultaneously, the intercountry differences indicate that responses to exchange rate policies will differ among countries.

REFERENCES

Altay, S. "Terms of Trade and Income Elasticity of Imports," *Central Bank Staff Paper,* Number 8803, 1987.

Bond, M. "An Econometric Study of Primary Commodity Exports from Developing Country Regions to the World," *IMF Staff Papers,* 34:2, 1987.

Cattin, P., and Wittink, D. "Industry Differences in the Relationship Between Advertising and Profitability," *Industrial Organization Review,* 4: 156–164, 1976.

Ersel, H., and Temel, A. "Evaluating the Performance of Turkish Exports," *Toplum ve Bilim,* 27: 107–133 (in Turkish).

International Monetary Fund. *International Financial Statistics—1970–1989.*

Johnston, J. *Econometric Methods,* Tokyo: McGraw-Hill, 1972.

Kmenta, J. *Elements of Econometrics,* New York: Macmillan, 1986.

Neter, J., and Wasserman, W. *Applied Linear Statistical Models,* Homewood, Ill.: R. D. Irwin, 1974.

Republic of Turkey, Prime Ministry, Undersecretary of Treasury and Foreign Trade. *Foreign Trade Statistics,* 1980–1989.

Tansel, T., and Togan, S. "Price and Income Effects in Turkish Foreign Trade," *Weltwirtschafhiches Archiv,* 23: 3, 1987.

Yavas, B. F., and Vardiabasis, D. "Restaurant Franchising in the Western United States," *Journal of Applied Business Research,* 3(3): 129–136, 1987.

Yavas, B. F. "The Role of Economic-Demographic Factors in U.S. International Restaurant Franchising: An Empirical Investigation," *Journal of Global Marketing,* 2(1): 56–72, 1989.

Chapter 22

Islamic Economy and Economic Growth: The Case of Iran

Masoud Kavoossi

Abstract   *The general resurgence of fundamental Islamic values in many parts of the world has its economic component, with a number of countries attempting to transform their economic system to accord more closely with the tradition of Islam. The more far reaching attempts have taken place in the Islamic Republic of Iran, although this phenomenon occurs, to varying degrees, in most Islamic countries. This chapter describes the functioning of an economy that adheres strictly to Islamic law.*

INTRODUCTION

The fundamental problem facing an Islamic republic is how to reconcile foreign debt and investment for developmental purposes with some of Islam's basic tenets, such as doctrines against usury and direct foreign investment. As long as profound questions concerning foreign borrowing remain unresolved, the prospects for a sustained progress toward development, which requires Western assistance, remains unclear. These are the issues with which this chapter is concerned.

Specifically, the paper consists of four sections. First, the economy in Iran from 1980 to 1988 and from 1988 to the present is reviewed. Second, the conceptual and ideological aspects of an Islamic economy are discussed. Third, the significance and implications of Islamic banking are analyzed for our understanding of an Islamic economy in general and of the Iranian economy in particular. Finally, it will be shown that standard economic concepts and methods can be fruitfully employed to analyze issues in Islamic economics.

IRAN'S ECONOMY, 1980–1988

The events that took place in Iran in the 1980s brought profound institutional and structural changes to the economy. As a result of the migration of many business and property owners and skilled workers, and a decision to bring strategic industries and activities under state control, the bulk of the country's manufacturing, services, and oil sectors shifted to government ownership. Moreover, the Iran-Iraq war prompted the government to extend its regulation and control of the economy in such areas as prices, distribution, and the external sector. As a result, the scope and activities of the private sector were greatly reduced (IMF survey, 1990).

These developments were reflected, in turn, in marked changes in the composition of government expenditures and in the composition and direction of foreign trade. In an atmosphere of war and insecurity, faced with an acute shortage of foreign exchange, the government was compelled to reorient the economy both toward domestic production and toward meeting its war needs by exercising greater control over the exchange and trade system.

Despite the dislocation and disruption to the economy, the country experienced relatively high, albeit uneven, real output growth in the first half of the 1980s. Between fiscal years 1982 and 1986, real GDP growth averaged about 8% annually.

From 1987 to 1988, however, the economy contracted by 10% as the intensification of hostilities and economic sanctions resulted in a sharp compression of imports. The fall in imports, a shortage of spare parts, and other factors inhibiting new investment also contributed to the economic contraction.

The industrial sector, heavily dependent on imports, was the most severely affected, with output contracting by 5% to 6% in fiscal years 1987 and 1988 as capacity utilization fell below 40%. The large services sector also contracted during this period, reflecting in large part damage to the infrastructure, particularly transport and communications, leading to balance of payments disequilibrium. This was caused partly by the nationalization of industry, which removed any incentives to be efficient and competitive.

The stresses and strains on the real sector of the economy during the 1980s were also reflected in the emergence of large domestic and external imbalances. During the same period the government cut budget expenditures in real terms by about half, with the deepest cuts occurring in the capital budget (First Five-Year Plan, 1989).

Despite the many pressures on the economy from fiscal year 1983 to the end of the decade, the budget deficit was maintained within a range of about 4% to 8% of GDP by deep cuts in expenditure (OPEC Bulletin, 1990).

In the 1980s bank credit to the government constituted the primary source of broad money growth, which ranged from 15% to 20% during most of the past decade (IMF Survey, 1990). During this time, monetary policy, which was conducted within the context of major institutional changes, was aimed increasingly at checking inflationary pressures and channeling resources to priority sectors (Iran Times, 1990). To generate further revenues the government has recently embarked on tax reform, including simplification of the income tax system and evaluation of the possible introduction of both a value-added tax and a general sales tax.

Meanwhile, the institutional Islamization of the economy continued as banks and other financial entities were nationalized and reorganized. More than 150 previously private commercial banks were merged into 9 state-run banks. Their practices and policies were reformed so as to conform to Islamic doctrine and principles. For instance, in February 1981 the central bank began to phase interest rates out of bank operations; instead banks were authorized to levy service charges on borrowers and to pay depositors a profit. In August 1983 the Majlis (parliament) enacted legislation requiring banks to bring the terms of their deposit liabilities into line with Islamic principles within 1 year, and similarly to align the terms for all other bank operations within 3 years (Shirazi, 1988).

By 1985 the government was attempting to neutralize and reduce the inflationary effects of excess liquidity by implementing credit ceilings and minimum reserve requirements. Credit ceilings differed among the various sectors according to official priorities. The reserve requirements currently stand at about 20% for commercial banks. Through these instruments the authorities have sharply curtailed bank credit to the private sector in recent years.

The balance of payments was also under pressure during the 1980s. Developments in the current account were dominated by fluctuations in oil earnings. Oil receipts are estimated at $11.5 billion in fiscal year 1980, and about $12 billion in 1991. In the intervening period, receipts swung from a peak of $21 billion in fiscal year 1984 to as little as $6 billion in 1987 (OPEC Bulletin, 1990).

However, the current account deficit ranged between $2 billion and $5 billion in most years, and the capital account exhibited large swings. These variations were associated in part with the freezing of Iranian assets abroad in fiscal year 1981 and the partial release of those assets in later years. Fluctuations in the capital account also reflected the amortization of virtually all the country's medium- and long-term foreign debt during the period.

THE CHALLENGES AND OPPORTUNITIES FOR THE 1990s

Since the suspension of hostilities with Iraq in August 1988, Iran's economy has displayed an encouraging degree of resilience. After 2 years of recession, real output expanded by almost 2% in fiscal year 1989, by over 4% in fiscal year 1990, and is estimated to have risen by 12% in 1991. Much of the impetus for the recovery came from a resurgence of oil revenues and from services (Iran Times, 1990). Total crude oil production capacity has been restored to about 3.14 million barrels per day (m b/d) and is to be expanded to 4.5 m b/d over the next 5 years.

There has also been progress in restoring domestic refining capacity. With continued progress and the completion of new refineries, total refining capacity is expected to rise to about 1.5 m b/d by mid-1994 (OPEC Bulletin, 1990).

In addition, the government plans substantial capital investment in petrochemicals, and steps are being taken to exploit the country's enormous natural gas resources, which are estimated at more than 17 trillion cubic meters, about 12% of proven world gas reserves. Increased gas-refining capacity should open the way for exports of natural gas in the near future (Middle East Economic Digest, 1990).

Such new directions in policy have been foreshadowed in a 5-year plan for the period through March 1994. The plan, recently approved by the parliament, envisages a significant acceleration of growth to an average of 8% annually.

To implement this plan, the government is considering a number of major policy reforms. It plans to privatize a number of industries and firms that are now wholly or partially government owned and, more generally, to strengthen the climate and incentives for a rebirth of the private sector.

The government recognizes that its large domestic borrowing requirements in past years and the rigorous credit ceilings that were applied to mitigate their potential inflationary effects have constrained the growth of the banking system. In the future, as envisaged in the plan, the steady reduction in the government's financing needs is expected to eliminate excess liquidity, facilitating a progressive increase in the share of total credit to the private sector. At the same time, the government is confident that the prospective economic recovery will increase returns to investors, thus justifying the payment by banks of higher returns to depositors.

The government expects to follow up the recently changed exchange and trade policies with far-reaching liberalization of both current restrictions and multiple currency practices, in order to boost incentives and strengthen the balance of payments. Furthermore, external financing for the development program is anticipated. In fact, Iran now enjoys a low external debt, less than $1 billion.

A total of about $30 billion in foreign financing is projected through fiscal year 1994, a portion of which will carry an official guarantee. This total comprises approximately $12 billion, largely for industrial development based on buy-back contracts (borrowers repay the creditors in the form of the output produced), $3 billion in long-term credits for financing dams and power stations, $3 billion for the development of offshore gas revenues, $9 billion for special project financing, with service payments met from the earnings of the projects, and $3 billion for a petrochemical complex, under a buy-back agreement.

The borrowing strategy requires two phases. Phase 1 includes reducing the budget deficit and releasing resources for use by the private sector. Phase 2 involves raising funds through international bond markets, domestic banking guarantee programs, international financial institutions, and investment funds attracted for developmental purposes.

THE ISLAMIC PERSPECTIVE

Although Iran, Pakistan, and Sudan adhere strictly to Islamic banking regulations, other Islamic countries in the Middle East, such as Egypt, Bahrain, Kuwait, Libya, Iraq, and Syria, apply a dual system that includes both conventional banking practices as well as Islamic ones. There are banks that avoid usury and others that do not. Under the interest-free banking system, the interest rate is replaced by other factor remunerations, such as profits.

In the case of Iran, an analysis of that country's debt and development requires a clarification of the Islamic perspective on international debt, foreign investment, and banking. Development in an Islamic setting involves certain axioms. For instance, an Islamic society is defined as one in which Islamic laws and institutions prevail, and the majority of whose individuals believe in Islamic ideology and practice its way of life. An Islamic society changes the pattern of income distribution through taxation and prohibition of usury, in order to bring about a greater degree of equality in distribution of wealth and income. Therefore, usury in an Islamic society is prohibited by law. Because any interest rate is considered usury, the rate of interest on debt should always be zero. There is no discrimination as far as the prohibition of interest is concerned between creditor and debtor.

Acquisition of any collateral in addition to the taking of the subject property itself may be considered against the *Sharia* (Islamic legal code) principles. Investment must concentrate on the basic necessities of life, which have relatively inelastic demand as compared to the demand for comforts and luxuries.

The Present Banking System: Credit

Usury is prohibited by the Quran. The theme of usury is dealt with in the Quran in four suras: *Sura Rum*, verse 39; *Sura Bagara*, verses 275, 276, 298, and 279; *Sura Aal-i-imran*, verse 130; and *Sura Nissa*, verse 161.

Coordination of the credit policies of interest-free banks with the economic policies of the government in various spheres has been strengthened. Bank investment in productive and developmental projects must be submitted in the country's budget bill for the approval of the Majlis. Once approved, the central bank notifies commercial banks of the planned project (e.g., construction of low-price housing units), and instructs them to carry out the financing aspects. Interest is replaced by profit rate.

Regulations for the fixing of the expected profit or rate of return emanating from credit granted by banks, and the minimum and maximum expected profits or rates of return, are formulated by the central bank and then promulgated to the banks; these regulations must be strictly obeyed and implemented.

Grant of bank credits to the private sector for the purpose of imports has been prohibited. This means that importers cannot get credit from government-owned banks. Banks must use a part of their resources in the form of loans to small businesses and low-income individuals (Shirazi, 1988).

Similarly, the following are requisite characteristics for credit transactions. The applicant must be trustworthy and dependable; the bank must certify that the applicant enjoys a good reputation for meeting commitments; the bank also must determine the applicant's prospects for continuing economic activities and his technical capability for proper and maximum utilization of resources. Islamic banking requires that financial institutions investigate the position and financial standing of the applicant. Facilities should be made available only on the basis of real need and in proportion to the applicant's financial capacity; this is to ensure the return of the bank's resources.

Throughout much of the Islamic world interest-based securities are being replaced by various profit-sharing interest-free instruments. An interest-free Islamic bank plays the roles of partner, investor, and trader, always cognizant of the interest-free modes of operation designed by Islamic financial institutions, and obeys the dictum: "God permits trading and forbids *riba*" (interest) (Sura, Bagara).

Because Islam enjoins against the taking and giving of interest, Islamic banks have organized their operations on the basis of profit/loss sharing, which is permitted in Islam. For example, Islamic banks accept demand deposits and time deposits. Demand deposits are fully repayable on demand and do not get any return. Holders of time deposits are given a share in the profits earned by the bank according to a profit-sharing ratio made known in advance.

Interest-free institutions offer a wide range of services, of which "mudaraba," "musharaka," "murabaha," and "gard-al-hassanah" are prominent. Under "mudaraba" one party deposits capital that the borrower uses for trade or investment. If the project is profitable the profits are shared between both parties in the ratios agreed on at the beginning of the project. Clients receive funds from the bank and manage their operations independently. The contract defines what the client must or may do with the money, what he may deduct as expenses, and what percentage of the profits he receives.

"Musharaka" is an active partnership under which the Islamic bank provides funds that are combined with the funds of owners of a business enterprise. All providers of capital are entitled to participate in management but are not necessarily required to do so. Profits are distributed among the partners at ratios that have been previously agreed upon, and loss is borne by each partner, strictly in proportion to their respective capital contributions.

"Murabaha" is a cost-plus contract. The client wishing to purchase equipment or goods requests the Islamic bank to purchase the items and sell them to him at cost plus a declared profit.

"Gard-al-hassanah" is a loan transaction. The client obtains money from the bank to be returned at a stipulated future date, free of charge. Some banks may levy a modest service charge to administer the loan; therefore loans are considered interest free.

Among the foregoing schemes, "mudaraba" has the most prominent role in interest-free Islamic banking; it was designed to assist small businesses. After that "musharaka" enjoys the most popularity.

One problem in defining Islamic banking is the nature of certificates of deposit. If foreign investment, for example, is in the form of a certificate of deposit, the "Sharia" requires certain procedures to be followed; these will be discussed briefly.

An accepted definition of a deposit is as follows: an agreement between two legal entities, whereby one submits to the other things of value and the second agrees to return them on request. This definition has been adopted in the legal codes of many Islamic countries, including Lebanon, Iran, Egypt, and Syria. A certificate of deposit need not be cash, but whatever the form of deposit, the Quran and religious jurisprudence agree on the sanctity of those deposits— deposits must be well protected and returned to their owner immediately upon request.

The following rules apply to deposits generally (and to certificate of deposits in particular) and their recipients. The depositor is under no religious obligation to place his wealth with anyone; if he believes that he cannot responsibly protect his wealth, he is obligated to deposit it with someone who can. The recipient of the deposit must be reasonably certain that he can protect the wealth or else he is not to receive it, unless the depositor is fully aware of the risk. In the event that the recipient knows with certainty that he cannot protect a deposit, it is illegal for him to retain the depositor's wealth and money.

The Present Banking System: Foreign Investment

As far as portfolio investment is concerned, foreign entities must form a local corporation (legal entity) that in turn can purchase securities, stocks, etc. This brings the foreign entrepreneur under the control of local legal authorities.

Direct foreign investment must also go through locally chartered corporations, and in such a way that foreign investors cannot obtain a controlling percentage of the investment. In any event the following rules apply to a direct investment. There can be no investment in the production of luxury consumer products. To qualify for direct investment, the amount of capital may not be less than 40% of the total capital needed. In the event that local banks are involved in the form of loans (joint ventures), it would be the bank's responsibility to examine carefully the investment on technical, financial, and economic grounds. It is only when the investigation justifies the commitment of a bank's financial resources that the bank may be so involved. All foreign direct investment must be reported to the central bank, which notifies government agencies, which in turn submit the information as part of the annual budget. When local banks are involved, once the project is completed, they can withdraw by selling their share of the investment to the public. Banks are also required to audit on an annual basis all companies involved in direct investment. This auditing should be done through an independent agency with the approval of the ministry of economic affairs. However, the central bank may choose to have its own auditors to review the process.

CONCLUSION

Although the number of studies on Islamic economics and Islamic banking has grown enormously in recent years, there is still a dearth of analytical work on the subject. In many ways the lack of understanding and confusion that exists about Islamic economics can be attributed to the virtual absence of formal descriptions of the theory underlying the proposed system. In this chapter an attempt is made to offer an analysis that explicitly incorporates the constraints imposed by religion on the conduct of financial transactions. Such an analysis can provide a reasonable portrayal of the types of Islamic banking and economic system that have been put into practice in Iran and can demonstrate that standard economic concepts can be employed to analyze issues in Islamic economics.

REFERENCES

The First Five Year Economic, Social and Cultural Development Plan of the Islamic Republic of Iran (1989-1993), Tehran: Bank Markazi Jomhouri Islami Iran, 1989.

"Iran," *Middle East Economic Digest*, Sept. 7, 1990, p. 10.

"Iran's Oil Industry," *OPEC Bulletin*, 21(17): 18–30, 1990.

"Minister of Economy and Finance," *Iran Times*, Sept. 7, 1990, p. 2.

"Office of Budget and Planning," *Iran Times*, Sept. 7, 1990, p. 4.

"Quota Problem will be resolved by 1992," *OPEC Bulletin*, 21(17): 14–16, Aug. 1990.

"Rise in Oil Production Aids Iran's Recovery," *IMF Survey*, 19(15): 225–229, July 30, 1990.

Shirazi, Habib (ed.). *Islamic Banking: Contracts*, Tehran: Central Bank of the Islamic Republic of Iran; No. 6, 1988.

Shirazi, Habib, "Qard-Al-Hassanah Grant," in *Islamic Banking: Contracts*, Tehran: Central Bank of the Islamic Republic of Iran; No. 6, 1988.

Chapter 23

The Supply-Side Economics of German Unification

Anton P. Mueller

Abstract *This chapter is an analysis of the political economy of German unification. First, the process of economic transformation of East Germany from socialist planning to a market economy is examined. Second, an assessment is made of the costs of unification and of the resulting budget deficit. Third, the effects of current German policies on international trade and capital markets, and in particular their impact on the European Community and the other major trading partners of Germany, are analyzed. Finally, the chapter describes recent developments and offers an outlook on the international consequences of the German economic policy.*

A THREEFOLD EXPERIMENT

Supply-side economics has a long tradition in Germany. It is called "Ordnungspolitik" and guided the reconstruction of West Germany after World War II. In contrast to modern supply-side economics, however, "Ordnungspolitik" is a more comprehensive concept. It sets guidelines not only for economic policy but for labor and social policy as well. Its major economic principles are stable money, a balanced budget, and open markets. In addition, "Ordnungspolitik" includes the idea that a modern industrial society needs a well-knit social net, which should be provided with a minimum of interference with the market mechanism. The economic policy of German unification is taking place within this framework.

With the so-called Unification Treaty, East and West Germany became one country. On July 1, 1990, the East German currency—the mark—was abolished, and the West German deutsche mark became the legal tender in East Germany. On October 3, political and economic unification was completed with East Germany becoming a part of the Federal Republic of Germany. With the stroke of a pen, the legal framework of a market economy replaced the socialist system. East and west Germany are now governed by the same laws and the same political system. However, united Germany's economy remains deeply divided. It is characterized by extreme disparities between east and west. Germany now has two economies: one that is booming in the west, and another that is in a deep structural crisis in the east. The buoyant optimism of the time when the Berlin wall came down has vanished and is replaced by skepticism. United Germany faces tremendous challenges: Will the reconstruction of eastern Germany succeed and lead to a boom in Europe, or will united Germany become overburdened? How quickly can eastern Germany transform into a market economy and become independent of massive capital inflow from west Germany? Will united Germany be the new center of boom in Europe and become the locomotive of economic recovery in Europe, or will the depression in eastern Europe spill over into western Europe?

With economic and monetary unification between west and east Germany, the Federal Republic has begun a threefold economic experiment. The first one tests the question of how a country that has had a socialist economy for more than 40 years can transform itself into a market economy. The second experiment tests the feasibility of a monetary union between two economies at very different levels of development and structure. Third, the German experiment is about to test the effects of a combination of tight monetary and expansive fiscal policy on growth, trade, exchange rates, and international financial flows. The outcome of these experiments will have profound effects on Germany's trading partners and on international capital markets. Given the speed and intensity of German monetary, economic, and social unification, the transformation of east Germany reveals the problems that occur when a planned economy is replaced by a market economy. East Germany is somewhat of a pioneer in the transformation process and *mutatis mutandis* lessons can be learned from the German experience for the transition towards market economies in eastern Europe.

ONE COUNTRY—TWO ECONOMIES

Statistics available in 1989 and 1990 did not suggest that the integration of East Germany's economy would be a severe problem.[1] With 16.5 million people, East Germany represented one fourth of the population and one tenth of the gross national product of West Germany. For decades, the German Democratic Republic (GDR) had enjoyed the highest standard of living among the socialist countries. Official statistics of the GDR suggested that the growth rate of its net material product (NMP) was an annual 5.9% in the period from 1950 to 1988, and almost 1% higher than the growth rate of West Germany's gross national product. In 1988, official statistics showed that the GDR had a trade surplus of about 1% of its net material product, that total gross fixed investment grew by 2%, and machinery and equipment by 5%. At 7.1% household savings (out of disposable income), East Germany had an impressive savings rate and although the households owned fewer durable consumer goods than in the west, East Germans seemed to be relatively well off compared to their eastern neighbors. Although they lacked many modern goods and services, East German planners took pride in having stable prices, full employment, and stable economic growth. In addition, socialist planning made sure that essential goods would be low priced and affordable to everyone. A comparison of the macro-economic data of East and West Germany on the eve of unification may even have suggested the existence of a dynamic and relatively prosperous economy in East Germany. It did not seem out of place to fear that the merger of the two most efficient economies in western and eastern Europe respectively would result in a new supereconomy in Europe.

But since monetary unification massive problems have appeared in east Germany. With a productivity rate that is one fifth of the west German standard, unresolved property rights, lack of competent manpower, and huge environmental damage, east Germany is not yet attractive to private investors. Since unification, production has plummeted and unemployment has risen sharply.

The recent development in east Germany stands in sharp contrast to the economic performance of west Germany where domestic demand is booming. The additional demand from east Germany is accelerating the pace of growth that west Germany has been experiencing for the past 9 years, compensating for the lack of demand caused by the recessionary tendencies in west Germany's major export markets.

THE LEGACY OF SOCIALISM

Although it was well known that statistics from centrally planned economies were highly unreliable and even intentionally manipulated, the true extent of the economic inefficiencies in east Germany came as a surprise. During the months following monetary union, widespread allocative distortions emerged and revealed that with very few exceptions east Germany's former state companies were not sufficiently competitive by western standards. The very symbol of east Germany's standard of manufacturing know-how—the Trabant automobile— would have been a better indicator of the true level of industrial capability than the available statistics. In fact, in durable consumer goods and housing, the gap between east and west Germany may be about 30 years. Given the discrepancy in price and quality between east German products and the world standard, it is no surprise that east Germans have demanded almost exclusively western products.

The decline of production and rising unemployment have caused a lack of funds in the new five federal states (Länder) in east Germany, making it very difficult to improve the material infrastructure, which is needed to attract investors. There is also an educational gap resulting in the lack of competent administrative and legal staff, which leads to backlog of unresolved legal disputes, particularly about property rights. The squeeze in tax revenue and competent manpower limits the ability of the new federal states to initiate the reconstruction of east Germany; the country is confronted with the risk of the vicious cycle of underdevelopment—the declining incomes limit tax revenues, and insufficient tax revenues limit the capability of the government to provide infrastructure and education. Financially, east Germany has become dependent on the transfer of funds and competent manpower from west Germany.

Over 50 years of dictatorship—more than 40 years of planned economy and 12 years of fascism—have left deep marks on east Germany. The decayed material infrastructure is only the most obvious legacy. Doing away with misallocations that have built up during 40 years of a planned economy will be much more difficult than assumed, and no one knows how quickly the entrepreneurial spirit, efficiency, the capitalist work ethic, and the simple understanding of how market economies function will return. East Germany needs an infusion of the entrepreneurial spirit but it continues to suffer from the drain of manpower that has been going on for decades and came to a new peak of 130,000 persons per month when the iron curtain fell (OECD 1990, p. 66). Given the desolate state of the east German economy, it came as no surprise that monetary union could not stop migration to west Germany. Although migration has slowed down in the past months it does continue at a considerable rate.

To stop this trend, east Germany needs attractive income opportunities. This, in turn, requires a swift increase of productivity and thus major capital investment. Before massive private investment can occur, the government must provide material infrastructure and competent administrative, legal, and technical manpower. With insufficient funds of her own, the recovery of east Germany depends on the transfer of funds from west Germany.

THE PROCESS OF TRANSFORMATION

The sharp economic downturn in east Germany is largely due to monetary union. With the introduction of the deutsche mark, east German companies lost the protection that an inconvertible currency had given them. Now they must compete with the most efficient businesses from the industrialized countries on the same playing field. East Germany's productivity, which was already low by western standards, has dropped further after the introduction of a market economy because many products are noncompetitive in the new environment. Unemployment has risen sharply because the shutting down of old factories happens at a much faster pace than the erection of new ones. But it would be wrong to attribute the economic decline to the introduction of capitalism. Market forces first fulfill a function of information; and when capitalism replaces a planned economy, markets first present a diagnosis of the extent of misallocations in the form of the breakdown of enterprises and of unemployment before the incentives of the price system start to work. Thus monetary and economic union has not brought about a viable market economy but rather the final breakdown of the socialist economic system. The central question confronting Germany now is how the process of "creative destruction" can be accomplished as quickly as possible so that a way may be opened for recovery.

With the introduction of the deutsche mark in east Germany on July 1, 1990, the first step towards economic transformation was made. In order to fulfill its function as a means of information and incentive, the price system needs a stable monetary framework. Stable monetary conditions cannot be introduced step by step. In order to do away with misallocations, correct information on demand and supply conditions is necessary. A stable currency is thus the major precondition for starting the transformation process. But in east Germany a stable currency was introduced in the form of monetary union with west Germany, and the introduction of the deutsche mark in east Germany had the additional effect of abruptly cutting the ties with its Comecon trading partners. East Germany was confronted with a major reallocation of its productive factors. The specialization that its economy had acquired over the decades of integration into the Communist trading bloc became suddenly obsolete. In one step east Germany's economy was removed from this old environment and placed into the world economy. Monetary integration exposed east Germany's companies to west German competitors and—given the openness of the Federal Republic—to the world markets. In relation to their western trading partners, east Germany's companies lost the protection of an exchange rate that compensated for their lack of competitiveness. In this respect, the replacement of the old currency had the same result as that of a massive appreciation of its currency. While black market rates were at a peak of around 20 east German marks for 1 deutsche mark in November 1989, monetary unification established an exchange rate of 1 to 1 for wages, salaries, and rents, and (within certain limits) for savings, and of 2 to 1 for other domestic financial assets and liabilities. This was a political concession whose economic consequences were severely felt in the months to come. With the introduction of the deutsche mark eastern Germany also lost its customer in the former centrally planned economies as these did not have convertible currencies in sufficient amounts to pay for their imports. Monetary unification thus exposed the east German economy to a double shock. East German companies had to begin competing with the west while they were losing most of their trade in the east. While east German companies could not yet compete successfully with the west due to their low productivity, they had lost their customers in the east who could not pay in hard currency (table 1).

In addition to the introduction of a stable monetary system, the change from central planning to a decentralized market economy requires the introduction of individual property rights. But in contrast to establishing a new monetary framework, the introduction of private property is much more time consuming. There were around 8000 former state companies (Volkseigene Betriebe) and combines (Kombinate) with approximately 40,000 factories in East Germany (SVR 1990-1991, p. 229). For their privatization they were placed under the authority of a trust fund (Treuhandanstalt)—a form of holding company. Taking into consideration that East Germany was the fifteenth largest economy in the world, the Treuhandanstalt may in fact now be the largest "corporation" in the world. Its major task is the selling and consolidation of individual companies.

Table 1
Exports: East Germany 1985–1990*

	1985	1986	1987	1988	1989	Q 3 1990[†]
Total hereof to:	148.2	133.1	133.5	135.3	141.1	−73.7%
Industrialized countries	71.3	59.6	59.0	62.5	68.4	−93.9%
Comecon	60.6	58.8	60.5	61.0	60.9	−46.2%
Developing countries	12.5	10.8	10.1	7.4	7.4	−76.5%

*In billions Valuta-Mark; third quarter 1990 in deutsche mark.
[†]Percentage change; third quarter to year before.
Source: Sachverständigenrat, Jahresgutachten 1990–1991, p. 265 and author's calculations.

This is a job of tremendous proportions, and as it turned out, much harder to accomplish than foreseen. The sale of the east German companies has been slow for several reasons. First, it is extremely difficult to assess the value of companies that have had no western standard of accounting and that have had activity confined to fulfilling central plans. Second, the ownership of a large part of the property is unclear.[2] Third, there is the risk of hidden environmental damage. In addition, the overall investment climate is not yet very attractive: besides low productivity and the lack of competent manpower, there is the risk of social unrest as a result of the unemployment and psychological stress that come with adapting to a new socio-economic and political environment. This contributes to the need to accomplish a turnaround in east Germany as quickly as possible.

FINANCING UNIFICATION

The constitution (Grundgesetz) of the Federal Republic demands an active policy in order to achieve equal standards of living (gleiche Lebensverhältnisse) throughout Germany. Traditionally, there have been active regional policy and extensive subsidies for disadvantaged areas. Unified Germany will have to continue this regional policy albeit on an even larger scale.

In the fourth quarter of 1990 the federal government provided funds for east Germany that amounted to 35 billion deutsche marks. It is estimated that for the next 10 years up to 50 billion deutsche marks will have to be provided annually (SVR 1991–1992, p. 183). In 1990 the transfer was largely financed by credit markets. The public sector borrowing requirements (federal and state) for the fourth quarter of 1990 increased steeply to 30 billion deutsche marks, as compared with 9 billion in the last quarter of 1989 (Bundesbank 1991–1992, p. 21). Within little more than a year, German interest rates (Umlaufsrenditen) of government bonds rose from 6.1% in 1988 to 9.1% in January 1991 (Bundesbank

1991–1992, p. 57). However, it seems that credit markets may have overreacted. There is considerable room for deficit spending in the budget, as West Germany had successfully conducted a policy of reducing deficits in the past years when the ratio of deficit to GNP was brought down from an average of 2% to 0% (OECD 1990, p. 74). The German Council of Economic Advisors (Sachverständigenrat) estimated that in 1992 the public sector deficit would recede to 4.3% of gross national product after a peak of 4.8% in 1991, and then would continue to drop to 1.3% by 1995 (SVR 1991–1992, p. 188).

In one scenario the International Monetary Fund estimates that 1100 billion deutsche marks of net investment are needed in the next 10 years in order to bring east Germany's productivity level up to 80% of west Germany's (Lipschitz and McDonald 1990, p. 85). Assuming that a minimum of three quarters of these investments is provided by the private sector and assuming continued economic growth of 2% to 3% annually, the German governments (federal and state) would be capable of providing sufficient funds without raising the ratio of the deficit to GNP to excessive levels, that is, to more than 4% or 5%. Nevertheless, this credit demand would be sufficient to keep interest rates high in Germany. In turn, high interest rates will cause the deutsche mark to appreciate, thus providing the macro-economic framework for increased imports. A part of east Germany's reconstruction will then be financed by the reduction of Germany's trade surplus, a process that is already under way (table 2).

Rising interest rates in Germany have put a severe strain on most European economies, particularly on those that participate in the exchange rate mechanism of the European momentary system or that link their currency directly to the deutsche mark. But increased German imports compensate for the restrictive effects of rising interest rates. There is ample room to finance the increase

Table 2
West Germany's External Trade

	Exports	Imports
European Community	−0.8	18.6
France	−2.0	10.2
UK	−9.4	13.4
Italy	−3.4	20.1
Other European industrialized countries	−0.2	15.5
Non-European industrialized countries	−6.1	−4.0
USA	−7.1	−9.6
Japan	14.7	2.7
State trading countries	−13.4	24.3

Percentage changes; fourth quarter of 1989 to year before.
Source: Deutsche Bundesbank, Monatsbericht Februar 1991, p. 40.

in import demand because Germany has been a major exporter of capital in the past (table 3).

For the reconstruction of east Germany, however, funds will be needed for many years to come. In order to attract the inflow of foreign capital, Germany would have to continue offering high interest rates. Given the extent of east Germany's funding needs, Germany's overall foreign assets—which amount to roughly $300 billion U.S. dollars—would vanish within a couple of years. With the continuing high debt burden of the developing countries, the substantial foreign debt of the United States, and the possible reduction of Japan's trade surplus, the world would be confronted with a major shortage of capital.

In February 1991, however, the German government initiated a steep tax increase and announced plans to cut government expenditures, particularly of subsidies to the west German economy. The government thus pursues a strategy of financing the recovery of east Germany using four sources of funds: the domestic credit market, increase of government revenue through taxation, cut in domestic subsidies, and reduction of German foreign assets through higher imports.

RECENT DEVELOPMENTS AND OUTLOOK

Throughout 1991 east Germany's structural economic crisis continued. Nevertheless, the steep fall in production leveled off, and in the second quarter of 1991 the first signs of a turnaround appeared. Some sectors of eastern Germany's economy, particularly services and construction, even showed signs of the beginning of a boom. To a large extent, however, the effective demand of east Germany's consumers is still based on financial transfers from western Germany. In addition, many of the fundamental issues remain unresolved. First, legal disputes over property rights and the lack of competence of eastern Germany's administrative staff continue to complicate public and private investment despite a new regulation that gives new investment the priority over property rights. Second, the brain drain has not stopped, resulting in a serious shortage of effective managers and qualified manpower in east Germany. Third, the equalization of wage rates between east and west Germany is proceeding at

Table 3
West Germany's Balance of Payments*

	1985	1986	1987	1988	1989	1990
Current account surplus	48.3	85.8	82.1	88.3	104.1	71.9
Net capital exports	54.6	82.6	38.9	127.1	128.2	90.1

*In billions deutsche marks.

Source: Deutsche Bundesbank, Monatsbericht Februar 1991, Statistical appendix, p. 75.

a fast pace despite the gap in productivity. But given the ample resources of west Germany, it is possible that an economic recovery in east Germany can be accomplished without overburdening German consumers and taxpayers.

Since unification, Germany's economic policy has been characterized by a clash between monetary and fiscal policies. During 1991 it became obvious that the German central bank takes a tough stand towards expansion in money supply. The Bundesbank made it clear that it is ready to fight inflation even at the cost of a potential recession. In the face of an increase in the inflation rate to around 4% in the second half of 1991, the German Bundesbank increased the Lombard rate to 9.75% and the discount rate to 8%.

The strategy of Germany's economic policy follows the principle that even in the face of the tremendous challenge of unification, no deviation from budgetary discipline and price stability should be allowed. Temporary strains on economic performance have to be accepted in order to obtain long-term benefits. Germany wants to accomplish economic unification within an environment of relatively moderate budget deficits and stable prices. This implies a relatively stable real effective exchange rate of the deutsche mark and only moderate pressure on international capital markets. In the transition period, Germany's major trading partners, particularly within the European Community, can profit substantially from German import demand. In fact, this is already happening.

With unification, Germany has replaced the United States as the economic locomotive at a time when U.S. recession was about to spill over into Europe. The European Monetary System has remained intact even in the face of high German interest rates. With the expected slowdown of economic activity in Germany, prices were predicted to stabilize and interest rates to fall in the course of 1992. This in turn should have provided the framework for solid growth of the world economy when dampened economic growth in Germany would be accompanied by the end of the recession in the United States.

Editor's Note: Some of the points made in the last section of this chapter have been overtaken by the events of September 1992. The financial turmoil in Europe, engendered by high German interest rates, forced the U.K. and Italy to withdraw from the exchange rate mechanism of the EMS, while Spain and Portugal had to devalue and impose capital controls.

NOTES

1. Data are compiled from Statistisches Bundesamt, Statistisches Jahrbuch der Bundesrepublik Deutscheland, 1989; Staatliche Zentralverwaltung für Statistik der DDR, Statistisches Jahrbuch der DDR, 1989; Deutsche Bundesbank, Monatsberichte; The World Bank; Bank for International Settlement, 60th Annual Report, Basle, 1990; Leslie Lipschitz and Donogh McDonald (eds.), German Unification. Economic Issues. IMF Occasional Paper 75, Washington, D.C., 1990.

2. Before the socialization and collectivization of private property by the German socialist government, there were expropriations conducted by the Soviet military government. In addition, there are still unresolved claims of persons who were persecuted by the Nazis, and—as East Germany abolished the former federal structure—there are claims by the individual states that were re-established with unification.

REFERENCES

Bundesbank (1991/1) - Deutsche Bundesbank, *Monatsbericht Februar 1991*.

——— (1991/2) - Deutsche Bundesbank, *Monatsbericht January 1991*.

Lipschitz, Leslie, and Donogh McDonald (eds.), *German Unification-Economic Issues*, IMF Occasional Paper *75*, Washington, D.C., 1990.

Organization for Economic Cooperation and Development, *Wirtschaftsbericht Deutschland*, Paris, 1990.

SVR (1990/91) - Sachverständigenrat zur Begutachtung der gesamtwirtschaftlichen Entwicklung. *Auf dem Weg zur wirtschaftlichen Einheit Deutschlands*, Jahresgutachten 1990–91, Stuttgart: Metzler-Poeschel, 1990.

——— (1991/92) - Sachverständigenrat zur Begutachtung der gesamtwirtschaftlichen Entwicklung, *Jahresgutachten 1991/92* Bundestagsdrucksache 12/1618, Bonn, 1991.

Index